LEE UNIVERSITY

LEE UNIVERSITY

The Path from Church of God Bible Training School to Modern University

John D. Coats

The University of Tennessee / Knoxville

Copyright © 2025 by The University of Tennessee Press / Knoxville.
All Rights Reserved.
First Edition.

Library of Congress Cataloging-in-Publication Data

Names: Coats, John R. author
Title: Lee University : the path from the Church of God Bible Training School to modern university / John Coats.
Description: Knoxville : The University of Tennessee Press, [2025] | Includes bibliographical references and index. | Summary: "In 1918, the Church of God established a Bible training school in Cleveland, Tennessee. Originally construed as the Christian training arm of the Church of God, Bible Training School (its early official name) began to outgrow its mandate: a division for high school was added during the Great Depression, a defunct Methodist college was purchased post-WWII, and the namesake college was born in honor of BTS's second president, Rev. F. J. Lee. In contemporary times, Lee University has broadened its outreach beyond the Church of God to a larger evangelical Christian base, and its enrollment has grown to more than five thousand students, one of the largest enrollments among the Appalachian Colleges Association, of which Lee University is a member. Coats argues that the beginnings, stalled rise, and modern iteration of Lee University is directly linked to larger trends within the Church of God denomination. Coats also argues the church's Holiness-Pentecostal tradition is linked with the university's operation in Appalachia, and the region and its religion played an extensive role in both the university's growth and its reputation"— Provided by publisher.
Identifiers: LCCN 2025015710 (print) | LCCN 2025015711 (ebook) | ISBN 9798895270554 cloth | ISBN 9798895270578 adobe pdf | ISBN 9798895270561 kindle edition
Subjects: LCSH: Lee University (Cleveland, Tenn.) | Christian universities and colleges—Tennessee—History
Classification: LCC LD2956.5 .C63 2025 (print) | LCC LD2956.5 (ebook)
LC record available at https://lccn.loc.gov/2025015710
LC ebook record available at https://lccn.loc.gov/2025015711

To my wife, Leigh Ann

Contents

Preface	ix
Introduction	1
Chapter 1. Origin Stories, 1918–1924	9
Chapter 2. The Bible Training School, 1924–1947	29
Chapter 3. Years of Promise and Crisis: Lee College, 1947–1960	55
Chapter 4. Rebirth and Consolidation: Presidents Ray Hughes and James Cross	81
Chapter 5. Accreditation and Desegregation	99
Chapter 6. President Charles Conn and the 1970s	117
Chapter 7. An Era of Limits, 1978–1986	135
Chapter 8. Expect Something Great: President Paul Conn	151
Chapter 9. The Lee Experience: The University Enters the Twenty-First Century	175
Chapter 10. Transitions	199
Appendix A. The Church of God Declaration of Faith	213
Appendix B. Lee University Community Covenant	215
Appendix C. BTS/Lee College/Lee University Presidents with Service in Church of God Leadership, 1909–2020	217
Appendix D. Enrollment, 1930–2020	219
Notes	221
Bibliography	255
Index	263

Illustrations

Images

General Assembly House	10
Ambrose Jessup Tomlinson	15
Church of God Publishing House	18
Church of God Elders Council	19
Bible Training School's First Class	20
Flavius Josephus Lee	26
Bible Training School, 1920-21	27
Bible Training School Female Quartet, 1935	35
Bible Training School at Sevierville	38
Zeno C. Tharp	39
Bible Training School Students	48
Old Main	56
Lee College Neon Sign	58
J. Stewart Brinsfield	67
Ray Hughes	82
Lee 1964 Neon Sign	88
Delton Alford	91
Lee Singers, 1965	92
Delta Zeta Tau Sorority	94
Lee Basketball	95
First Desegregation Students	112
First African American Graduates	115
Charles W. Conn & Evaline Echols	121
1970s Students	123
Charles Paul Conn	152
Ellis Hall Fire	166
Lee Day	176
Operation Christmas Child	178
Chapel	180
Global Perspectives Program	185
Paul and Darlia Conn	189
Paul Conn at Celebration	200

Tables

Table 1. Faculty Credentials	71
Table 2. Core Enrollment at Lee College, 1948-1960	74
Table 3. Leadership Cadre Service, 1950-86	84
Table 4. Segregation Status, 1963	109
Table 5. Budget and Income Sources	127

Preface

Writing institutional history has many of the same opportunities, twists, peculiarities, and pitfalls of writing the biography of a person with a long and storied life. Institutions have their own stories, myths, and traditions that shift and evolve over time as people remember, reinvent, transform, memorialize, and romanticize the past. Institutions promote their successes and hide their failures; have gaps in their records and memory; follow moral and immoral paths; are influenced by both the broader culture and powerful personalities; have crises, defeats, and victories.

In spite of ourselves, those of us who write such histories ultimately make a decision to embrace or distance ourselves from our subjects. Hagiography or outright vilification might be rare, but it is increasingly commonplace in our highly politicized society to choose sides. In writing the history of Lee University, I recognize that my worldview, life inside the institution, and outsider status affect my narrative. As a Christian, I am supportive of Lee's mission to offer a university education from an intentionally Christian worldview. As a member of the Lee faculty for nineteen years, I have had a firsthand view of the school's most recent history. For the historian, such knowledge can be a double-edged sword that can provide both insight and prejudice. At the same time, any Lee insider would not hesitate to affirm my outsider status. I am not a member of Lee's sponsoring denomination, the Church of God, or any of its Pentecostal cousins. Of equal importance, neither myself, my wife, nor my parents attended Lee (although my two children are both graduates). And finally, I have not spent my entire career at Lee—a common characteristic of almost all Lee administrators and senior faculty. On balance, then, I hope that my status helps me write Lee's history with an insider's sympathy and an outsider's sense of perspective—not as a court historian, but as one who wishes to fairly represent the women and men who give the school life.

Writing a book is never a path walked alone. I would like to thank Lee University and the Church of God for their assistance and cooperation in my efforts. Lee granted me research funding and a sabbatical that allowed me to complete the manuscript. The university also invited me to present my research in a number of venues, including our faculty seminar and the university's centennial celebration. The staff of the Pentecostal Research Center and Squires Library have been consistent and patient in their support of this project, and my special thanks goes to the director of the center, David Roebuck, and archivist Gene Mills. Not only did they guide me through the church and university archives, but they made available uncatalogued material and helped me make sense of Church of God's history and culture. Likewise, I appreciate the participation of the Lee community in providing oral histories to support my work, both as individual narrators and in sharing their own interview materials (thank you Jeff Salyer and Eric Moyen).

I would also like to acknowledge my colleagues, students, and family who have listened, motivated, prompted, and corrected me as I worked through Lee's history. I especially thank my readers, Daniel Brantley, Terry Cross, David Roebuck, and Jared Wielfaert for their input, wisdom, and editorial suggestions. Finally, I express my deepest gratitude to my wife, Leigh Ann, for consistently encouraging, critically reading, patiently listening, and always believing in me.

INTRODUCTION

D. C. Barnes straightened his jacket and prepared to defend himself before the Supreme Council of the Church of God. The thin, spectacled young teacher was popular with his students at Lee College, but the support of eighteen-year-olds meant little when facing the Council, which consisted of the church's most senior and powerful leaders. The church fathers had warned Barnes, repeatedly, to rethink his doctrinal position, but he stubbornly maintained that a common Church of God teaching was in error. Namely, he contested the teaching that Christians, through the sanctifying power of the Holy Spirit, could put away sin and live a holy, even sinless, life. Instead, Barnes argued that believers were not instantly made holy but were gradually conformed to the will of God and image of Christ through the work of the Holy Spirit. Now, like Martin Luther some four centuries earlier, Barnes had been summoned to answer for his teaching.[1]

The question was not as cut and dried as it might first appear. In 1949 the teaching of total sanctification might have been both common and popular within the Church of God, but the young Pentecostal denomination had no clear doctrinal position on the matter. In fact, the church rejected creeds and confessions as man-made instruments that could undermine the plain teaching of Scripture. The absence of a clear confessional statement gave Barnes some theological room to maneuver. His position at Lee College, however, turned his dissent into a lightning rod for those holding to the teaching of total sanctification. The college operated as a division of the Church of God, was a jewel in the denomination's institutional crown, and was tightly controlled by the church. Barnes might take his theological stand in the pulpit of some sympathetic congregation, but it would not be tolerated behind a classroom podium.

In truth, when the church fathers first told him to stop teaching his controversial beliefs in class, Barnes acquiesced. To do otherwise meant he would lose his job. Yet, while the young professor had stayed true to his agreement, he lived by the letter—not the spirit—of the agreement. At his hearing, Barnes asserted that he honored the restrictions in his contract, even to the point of avoiding the chapter in the textbook that spoke to the issue. The Council knew this to be true, for they had sent a Council member to question Barnes's students. Those interviews revealed that Barnes allowed students to write on the topic and engaged in conversations with students outside of the classroom. When questioned, Barnes readily admitted to talking with students after class, saying, "It has been difficult to push off two hundred students." Rather than argue his theological position, he simply disagreed with those who claimed that "if you modify a belief it is to destroy it." The Council ultimately approved a resolution recommending the college administration keep Barnes on the faculty. Despite this endorsement, he did not return to Lee for the fall 1949 semester.[2]

Barnes's story represents the key to understanding Lee University's history—you cannot separate the history of the school from that of the Church of God. From the earliest days, when the church and Bible Training School (BTS) shared facilities and personnel, to the years of Lee College, which operated as a division of the church, to the most recent university era, where the school created some separation from the denomination, the histories are deeply intertwined. And despite the recent loosening of ties between school and denomination, Lee remains one of the Church of God's most prized institutions. As such, the school has often been at the center of ongoing generational debates between the church's traditionalist and progressive wings. The conservative traditionalists embraced the church's Pentecostal holiness traditions, which set them apart from the broader American culture. Progressives sought to loosen some of the more severe strictures governing everyday life. They were holiness people themselves and could only have been called liberal within a denominational context—an outsider would have a difficult time distinguishing between the groups. The tension between the two is a constant in Lee's history, although the positions of each group changed over time as the denomination slowly conformed to the broader culture. In other words, 1950's progressives often became 1980's traditionalists. Both sides used Lee as a measuring stick for continuity and change in the denomination, so the school tended to be both progressive and conservative simultaneously. The church establishment, typically dominated by traditionalists, worried that Lee was not upholding holiness standards. At the same time, each generation of incoming students chafed against rules that were often stricter than those set by their families. Administrators typically kept church traditions alive, but students represented the next generation of progressives in the church.

While the two wings of the church sparred, the long-held Pentecostal belief in the direct experience of God's presence through the work of the Holy Spirit consistently underpinned university culture. Pentecostals believe that God is not distant or removed from everyday life but is immediately present and accessible to believers. Their daily interaction with the Spirit leads to transformative experiences which they share with others. These personal narratives, known as witnesses or testimonies, are essential to the Church of God's culture—and therefore to the school's culture. One can hear stories of repentance, conversion, transformation, sanctification, healing, provision, and blessing in any Christian community, but in the Church of God these testimonies of God's direct intervention are second only to the Bible as the foundation on which the church rests. In the modern Lee context, testimony plays a central role in most faith-based gatherings. Each semester starts with a chapel at which faculty gather to hear colleagues explain how they came to work at Lee. Each semester ends with a commissioning service the night before commencement. There, five students tell their "Lee story," which usually includes the work of God in their lives. And in almost any community gathering one will hear faculty, staff, or students explaining their experience with the divine.

The belief in the transformative power of the Spirit led to a number of school practices, including a commitment to welcome students (and eventually faculty and staff) from outside the Church of God. The school and denomination have always hoped that all students confess the Christian faith, but never required their ideal, Spirit-filled, Pentecostal conversion. So, from the early years of the Bible Training School, Lee admitted non-Church of God, non-Pentecostal students, only asking that they respect the church's traditions and culture. Those students were joined by the occasional faculty member from other Christian traditions and, over time, both non-Pentecostal students and faculty became more common. Students were bound by a community covenant and faculty by contractual restrictions that privilege Church of God theology and practice. Today, around half of the university community does not have Pentecostal roots, and while all full-time faculty are professing and practicing Christians, not all students share the Christian faith.

The school did not require theological conversion, but its leaders and faculty believed that education could change the lives of students. The first generations of BTS students often included students with marginal educational backgrounds who believed they were called by God to ministry. As Pentecostals they believed that God would use their educational experience to transform them into more effective preachers, teachers, missionaries, and Sunday school workers. BTS students and faculty drew few lines between religious and practical education, leading to a school culture where God was seen working in classrooms and dorm rooms as well as chapel and prayers services. School leaders also knew that even modest admission standards would have excluded the denomination's rank and file. Additionally, the tuition-driven institution needed students to survive and was rarely positioned to turn away even the most unprepared student. By the turn of the twenty-first century, the school had become a university and was in the middle of an extended period of growth. The administration was in a position to raise entrance standards and better the reputation of the school, but instead welcomed ill-prepared students. Institutionally, the university remained committed to what it called "second-chance students," promising them the opportunity to put behind them past failures and create a new academic life.

For the Church of God, evidence of personal transformation is often judged by students' external appearance and behavior. Secular persons might find the church's standards to be out of touch with mainstream culture, but the church's call to holiness (to be set apart from the common culture) is central to a life lived in response to the Spirit's direction. The first generations of students lived under strict holiness codes that governed most of their waking hours. They attended regular prayer and worship meetings, were largely segregated from the opposite sex, obeyed carefully defined dress codes, and abstained from tobacco products and alcohol. School administrators expected students to shun movie houses, dance halls, sporting events, and other activities that the church considered worldly amusements. Those early codes softened over time, but Church of God traditionalists continued to scrutinize the dress and deportment of Lee students as a measure of the school's holiness. Modern students still are expected to abide by conservative Christian rules. Today, Lee has no coed dorms, forbids the use of alcohol, condemns premarital sex, does not affirm homosexuality, and requires chapel attendance. Whether in 1930 or in 2020, Lee purposefully set itself apart from other universities with boundaries on personal behavior.

The Church of God's emphasis on the experiential included traditions that prioritized the immediate needs of the church and students.

The church rejects the creeds and confessions that form the foundation of many Christian traditions, believing them to be man-made obstacles to the leading of the Holy Spirit. The church also teaches the certainty of the imminent, physical return of Jesus Christ. Together, these teachings caused it to live in the present with an eye toward the immediate future and, concurrently, to deemphasize careful exploration of institutional identity and long-term planning. To meet the needs of church and student constituencies, Lee developed an entrepreneurial habit that encouraged experimentation in a broad range of extra-curricular activities and academic programs. The Bible Training School began with a narrowly defined course of biblical training, but almost immediately expanded its offerings by adding a correspondence course. Over the next thirty years, BTS added a high school, secretarial school, music school, and liberal arts junior college. It then opened a four-year Bible college, followed by a liberal arts counterpart. Accrediting agencies insisted that the school, by then called Lee College, prune back its diverse offerings to a traditional liberal arts model. More recently, Lee University returned to the earlier entrepreneurial model, broadening its offerings to include graduate programs, a school of nursing, and a host of new majors and online degrees.

The school's experiential emphasis created enormous energy for missions, short-term projects, and initiatives with immediate impact. Unfortunately, this same focus left little space for archives, memoirs, or reflection. Lee, which operated as a department of the Church of God for seventy years, made little effort to formally mark the institutional boundaries of its faith and practice. In the mind of school administrators, that was a denominational concern. Similarly, Lee had little sense of its history. When Lee began to chart a more independent, evangelical course, it did so without a clearly defined notion of what it meant to be a Christian institution.

As a whole, then, Lee's history is best understood in relation to the history of the Church of God, a Pentecostal denomination that has moved from its holiness roots to a more general charismatic identity. That evolution has been contested, with traditionalists and progressives wrestling for control of a denomination that saw each generation challenge the holiness standards and teachings of their parents. After a long period of tight denominational control, Lee tempered its Pentecostal identity and adopted an evangelical one that embraced a more inclusive definition and understanding of the Christian faith.

Placing Lee in the historical landscape of other church-related colleges and universities in the United States can lead to the conclusion that it will move steadily and irresistibly away from any religious foundation and toward a more secular identity. Many institutions have retreated (or advanced, depending on one's worldview) so far from their founders' beliefs that they are now somewhat embarrassed by their religious roots. The two most prominent historical studies of church-related schools, George Marsden's *Soul of the American University* and James Burtchaell's *Dying of the Light*, conclude that accommodation to culture causes a move toward secularity. This trend was further reinforced when Marsden and Bradley Longfield published a collection of case studies that found a general decline in religious tradition in a variety of church-sponsored schools. Philip Gleason discovered a similar pattern of missional decline among Catholic schools.[3]

This movement usually took decades, could accelerate suddenly after years of stability, and varied based on local conditions. While each had unique twists and turns, school after school walked the same path. Many, like Lee University, began as unaccredited training schools for a denomination's pastors and leaders. These sectarian schools had a narrow focus, internal audience, and founders who often sought to create a school offering a degree of protection from outside, secular influences. They drew students, leadership, faculty, funding, accountability, and credibility from their sponsoring denomination. Some schools hold to this founding paradigm, but they typically remain small and often are isolated from the broader academic world.

Most often, Protestant denominational start-ups evolved into broadly evangelical institutions. Within the world of Christian higher education, this new identity might be called intentionally Christian. Although still identified with the sponsoring denomination, the school began welcoming Christians from a wider range of traditions. The move to open the school to new constituencies might have a number of causes. Sagging enrollment may have led to financial crises that caused schools to bolster enrollment with students from outside the sponsoring denomination, if not outside the faith. Sometimes accrediting agencies caused schools to take a more open stance, especially in recruiting faculty and implementing procedures to create a more diverse campus. And, usually in combination with financial and accrediting considerations, forward-thinking leaders (often representing a new denominational generation) found new benchmarks to judge their school's success. Rather than looking back to their elders' values and goals, they measured success against standards set by other institutions. Whereas denominational purity once set a school against outside influences, those same counter-cultural stances came to be seen as obstacles to growth and institutional respectability.

In time, the intentionally Christian school further distanced itself from its origins. In doing so, the school justified its faith-based status by employing the language of "critical mass"—it is Christian enough, a notably variable measure. At this point, a sufficient number of students, faculty, board members, and staff accepted the school mission and practiced the Christian faith (usually a key consideration for intentionally Christian schools) to satisfy more traditionally minded constituencies. At the same time, admissions and business office staff often argued for the inclusion of more students from outside the faith to add diversity and bolster the balance sheet. Likewise, talented faculty sympathetic to the mission, if not the faith, improved the school's academic reputation. Throughout, a sufficient critical mass of faith practitioners remained, but the balance shifted from mostly Christian to a majority to some. In time, the overwhelming majority of the school's constituents had no connection to the sponsoring denomination or its faith. They wondered why the school clung to outdated language and traditions and moved the institution to a final stage on the spectrum: a secular school that acknowledged, although often with some embarrassment, its religious roots.[4]

Researchers use many variables to measure the shifting nature of a school's religious environment: hiring standards, denominational control, curricular requirements, student body make-up, behavioral standards, and campus religious life. While there is some debate about the usefulness of such measures, their presence or absence does help place schools on a continuum from traditionally religious schools to secular institutions, or perhaps from conservative to liberal/progressive within church-related schools. Changes in these characteristics, like the telltale marks of aging, suggest deeper shifts in a school's identity. In most cases, liberalization of standards in these areas equates to a slow drift from the school's distinctly Christian mission and toward an accommodation with the broader culture. No single adjustment of a measure indicates a school is losing its Christian identity, yet in combination, those changes move a school toward making its Christian or church-relatedness a cultural identity and not a religious one. At some point such institutions become post-Christian schools that remember, more or less fondly, their denominational roots. Faculty and administrators who are committed to intentionally Christian higher education might be left to wonder if there is any room for change that does not compromise mission. Although the path may become increasingly difficult as the United States moves into a postmodern, post-Christian era, there will be increasing opportunities for faith-based schools to define themselves against an indifferent, and perhaps hostile, dominant culture.

Lee University, one such intentionally Christian school, measures quite well on most of the aforementioned measures. Founded in 1918 as the Bible Training School, the modern university is located in Cleveland, Tennessee. As of this writing, Lee is the academic home of around 3,200 students and 140 full-time faculty. Lee has enjoyed three decades of growth, expanding the number of students, faculty, programs, facilities, and—of course—administrators. Lee's six colleges (Arts and Sciences, Theology and Ministry, Education, Nursing, Business, and Music) compete for resources in an enrollment-driven budget, operating on a model that keeps tuition low. This model demands full classes, heavy teaching loads, and maximum resource utilization. Lee openly identifies as a Christian campus, maintains close ties with its sponsoring denomination, and requires faculty and administrators be practicing Christians. It monitors chapel attendance, requires twelve hours of Bible and theology, and maintains generally conservative expectations regarding the lifestyle of faculty and students.[5]

But, of course, that is a snapshot of Lee today, using modern measurements and judging Lee's Christian environment against its peers. If Lee's founders weighed its merits, the university might score very poorly. Lee does not require daily chapel or limit faculty to Church of God members. Its president is no longer a former denominational leader (known as the general overseer), and the university offers a wide variety of degrees that do not directly lead to ministry. Students are not limited to chaperoned, on-campus dates, and the white lines that once kept male students a safe distance from female dorms were removed long ago. Those stringent standards belonged to a more modest, narrowly focused, holiness Pentecostal school from a century ago. The school has evolved over time to meet the needs of its denomination, whose leadership and representatives approved its growth from the tiny, sectarian Bible Training School to a comprehensive, intentionally Christian university that celebrates its Pentecostal traditions while serving a more broadly evangelical Christian audience. At the same time, the very changes that have driven Lee's growth suggest that the university may have loosened the lines, but not set the school adrift, from its Church of God moorings.

Chapter 1

ORIGIN STORIES, 1918–1924

The Church of God, with its Appalachian, Pentecostal origins, might seem an unlikely starting place for a history focused on higher education. The devout men and women who started the church came from a marginalized population in an isolated corner of the nation. They believed in a simple, commonsense reading of the Bible and mistrusted seminary-trained theologians who preached in the cities. Meeting in log cabins, the church's first adherents fervently searched Scripture, worshiped with emotional abandon, and intentionally set themselves apart from a nation that, at the turn of the twentieth century, was rushing toward a modern, urban, industrial future. The practices of those early worshipers established traditions that shaped Lee University's character and development. While that founding generation had little use for colleges and universities, they valued education—which made the decision to build a school for training denominational leaders a perfectly sensible one.[1]

The Church of God is a young denomination with origins in the holiness movements of the late nineteenth century. Founded by Richard Spurling in 1886 on the western border of North Carolina as the Christian Union and nurtured under the leadership of A. J. (Ambrose Jessup) Tomlinson from his church in Cleveland, Tennessee, the Church of God grew out of a small cluster of holiness congregations in rural Georgia, North Carolina, and Tennessee. Geographically and culturally isolated, the first churches met in tiny mountain communities, such as Camp Creek, Drygo, and Union Grove. Led by lay pastors, the tiny congregations rarely had more than thirty in attendance and possessed few resources beyond their members' faith and fervor. Only Tomlinson's church was based in the more substantial town of Cleveland, which in 1900 had a population of almost four thousand. In January 1906, twenty-one men

W. F. Bryant and R. G. Spurling outside the home that hosted the first Church of God General Assembly in 1906 at Camp Creek, North Carolina. (Courtesy of the Dixon Pentecostal Research Center, hereafter, PRC.)

and women met in Camp Creek, North Carolina, to establish an organization through which the associated holiness churches could come to a common understanding of theological questions, recommend guides for daily living, and share resources. The following year they chose the name Church of God, renounced any denominational aspirations, and then set about creating an embryonic organization that could make recommendations to, but could not command, member congregations in matters of practice and polity.[2]

The founders sought to restore the heart of first century New Testament Christianity, and in doing so, they worked within broader evangelical and fundamentalist contexts. Evangelicalism is a conservative movement within the Christian Protestant church that has its American roots in the religious revival known as the Second Great Awakening. British scholar David Bebbington aptly summarizes the theological core of evangelicalism as having four parts. First, evangelicals believe that the teachings of the Bible are the highest authority on matters of faith, life, and practice (biblicism). Second, they hold a traditional belief that Christ's death on the cross was an essential act of sacrifice necessary for the forgiveness of the sins of humanity (crucicentrism). In addition, they believe in Christ's literal bodily resurrection. Third, almost all believe that there is a life-transforming moment in which a person is saved, or converted, by accepting Christ as their savior (conversionism). Finally, evangelicals are committed to spreading their beliefs, the gospel, or good news, to others. This evangelism is a responsibility of all believers, not simply the pastorate or missionaries (activism). Evangelical activism often engages culture through a broad and changing set of initiatives and institutions, including educational ones. In the Church of God, this activism was evident from the founding days of the denomination, during which church members emphasized personal evangelism, missionary work, and revivalism. In these four areas, at least, the Church of God rested firmly within the evangelical mainstream.[3]

The church's relationship with the fundamentalist movement of the first half of the twentieth century is more complicated. Theologically, areas of agreement and divergence clearly stand out. The Church of God would agree with the five fundamentals: 1) biblical authority, 2) the virgin birth, 3) substitutionary atonement, 4) Christ's bodily resurrection, and 5) the authenticity of miracles.[4] Like many fundamentalists, the church embraced a premillennial eschatology that envisioned a time of tribulation followed by the return of Christ to establish a literal thousand-year reign from Jerusalem. The Church of God also aligned with the fundamentalist belief that modernist, liberal theology threatened to destroy the church, which helps explain their restorationist (or primitivist) call to return to the teachings and practices of the first century church. This restorationist view caused them to embrace a distinct, anti-creedal tradition, which argued that written confessions and doctrines limited immediate revelations through the Holy Spirit and distorted the Bible's simple, commonsense truths.

A pair of central denominational beliefs—an uncompromising commitment to a holiness lifestyle and the Pentecostal belief in the baptism of the Holy Spirit—moved the church to the margins of evangelicalism and outside fundamentalist circles. The Church of God's embrace of total sanctification and holiness living set its people apart. Here the church grew out of an older and broader tradition that had its clearest origins in John Wesley's call for Christian perfection. Wesley, the founder of the American Methodist church, believed that God would forgive sins, resulting in regeneration or new birth. He also believed in a second act of grace that would transform sinners into saints, the process of sanctification. According to Wesley, this sanctification is instantaneous, removing a person's sinful nature (original sin) and empowering them to live a life free from sin, in complete obedience to God. This belief in total (or entire) sanctification was a clear departure from most Christian traditions, which view sanctification as an ongoing process through which believers are progressively transformed to Christ's example, but never perfected in this life. While never a dominant tenet of American Methodism, holiness beliefs took root in a number of small, often short-lived denominations and local independent churches, including those that came together in the Church of God.

Those who held perfectionist beliefs most commonly were known by their holiness lifestyle, marked by strict codes of behavior and dress that set them apart from the dominant culture. The Church of God undertook a lifestyle guided by what the church would later call its "Practical Commitments," but which, in the first years of the church, were defined more simply as abstinence from alcohol, tobacco, drugs, certain "meats and drinks," and connections to lodges or secret orders.[5] To join the Church of God required commitment to a new way of thinking about daily life and habits. Members dressed simply, did not wear jewelry (even wedding rings), eschewed the use, or even handling, of alcohol and tobacco, and avoided the broader culture's fascination with popular music, sports, film, and other forms of entertainment. They attended church services and prayer meetings on Sunday, but also set aside time for midweek services, Bible studies, and revivals that regularly lasted deep into the night.

The church also came to embrace the Pentecostal belief in baptism by the Holy Spirit. In addition to traditional Christian water baptisms, Pentecostals believe in a second baptism of the Holy Spirit after conversion. This experience is evidenced by glossolalia, or speaking in tongues—a practice the Bible records as taking place on the day of Pentecost. There, according to Acts 2:4, early followers "were all filled with the Holy Spirit and began to speak in other tongues as the Spirit gave them utterance."[6] In the Church of God this supernatural practice usually took the form of ecstatic speech in an unknown language, and the denomination made speaking in tongues the initial evidence of the baptism of the Holy Spirit. Therefore, from the earliest days, glossolalia formed a central tenet of their faith.

The American Pentecostal movement, which has roots in the late nineteenth century, first attracted attention in 1903, when Charles Fox Parham began a revival tour which took the message of Pentecost from Topeka, Kansas, to the South and Southwest. However, it gained real traction when William J. Seymour, an African American inspired by Parham's teachings, began the Apostolic Faith Mission on Azusa Street in Los Angeles, California, in 1906. Azusa Street's nightly services drew multi-racial audiences from around the nation and were characterized by emotional and charismatic worship, tongues, singing, miraculous healings, and speakers who took the floor when they felt so led by the Holy Spirit.[7] As converts took the Pentecostal message across the nation, they brought their vision of reform and revival to their home churches, as opposed to starting new ones. In some cases it was welcomed. More often, however, established denominations rejected the message—frequently expelling the Pentecostals from their congregations.

The doctrine of Holy Spirit baptism entered the Church of God following a June 1907 meeting in Birmingham, Alabama. On stage at the meeting was North Carolinian G. B. Cashwell, who was later known as the "Apostle of Pentecost to the South." Cashwell had only recently embraced Pentecostalism after receiving Spirit baptism and the gift of tongues during a visit to Azusa Street in 1906. In his 1907 tour of southern states, Cashwell preached faith healing, the imminent return of Christ, and speaking in tongues as evidence of the baptism of the Holy Spirit. During that Alabama revival, Tomlinson invited Cashwell to preach in Cleveland. Cashwell's January 1908 sermon in Cleveland led Tomlinson to experience the second baptism and the gift of tongues, which in turn brought the small, but growing, group of Church of God congregations into the Pentecostal movement. It also provided those churches with a clear, distinctive identity that complemented their commitment to holiness and charismatic worship.[8] In the minutes of their January 1912 General Assembly meeting, the church, despite their misgivings about creeds, published their official teachings. These included traditional evangelical, fundamentalist, and Pentecostal teachings, alongside references to holiness, divine healing, washing of the saints' feet, and premillennialism.[9] Even as the church organized, its people knew the heart of their religion was a call to "be saved, sanctified, and filled with the Holy Ghost."[10]

This collection of deeply held beliefs caused the first generation of the Church of God to create a distinct culture that would have a profound impact on its evolution and educational enterprises. The most obvious of these was an emphasis on holiness living, which came to be defined by an extensive set of formal and informal rules and standards. Some of these, such as abstinence from alcohol and tobacco, were not unusual—although the latter was somewhat controversial in a tobacco-growing region. Others, such as a prohibition on membership in lodges, labor unions, and secret societies (such as the Masons), spoke to the church's concern about allegiances other than those to Christ and biblical teaching. By 1914, the General Assembly had added prohibitions against swearing, opium and morphine use, and the wearing of gold for ornament or decoration."[11] Pastor Sam Perry passionately argued that sanctified believers must not "conform to the pride and fashion of the world about us or enter into it's [sic] ambition for money-making or pleasure-seeking, or even for selfish ease and luxury . . . [or] those who seek pleasure at resorts, and places of amusement, and deck themselves out in the latest styles . . . which is shown by the wearing of jewelry, rings, feathers, and artificial flowers, powdering and painting the face, wearing of garments [and] footwear that is so out of harmony with the designs of nature, and so far from the simplicity of the gospel."[12]

Over time, the church established a sizable list of prohibited activities. A member in good standing avoided carnivals, sporting events, movies, dances, mixed bathing (swimming with the opposite sex), and secret societies. Experimenting with any such activities meant that one had "backslidden," and, without public repentance, would be expelled from the church. One church leader described how a young person might fall from grace: late-night parties led to late-night beach parties, which in turn led to improper dress and all-night dances. Dancing caused improper physical contact, which led to sexual immorality, shame, disgrace, expulsion from the church, and ruin.[13]

The men and women who first adopted this lifestyle often came from marginalized places in American society. Most lived in small, rural communities in east Tennessee and western North Carolina. As described in the church newsletter, the *Evangel*, "Our people are all merely common livers and hard workers," but hard labor on a subsistence farm or in a textile mill meant a scarcity of hard currency and few creature comforts.[14] The economic standing and geographic isolation of the earliest congregations established an outsider status that was reinforced by the demands of separatist holiness living. In the small, poor churches nestled in the hills of east Tennessee and north Georgia, it was easy to find identity among people committed to a simple, fervent way of life that turned its back on the corrupt trinkets of a rapidly modernizing nation.

While the Church of God derived from congregations located in southern Appalachia, the church was not bound by that geographic region or narrowly defined by its culture. R. G. Spurling's Christian Union might have been steeped in North Carolina's mountain culture, but A. J. Tomlinson, an Indiana native, had a larger vision. He saw a Pentecostal movement that would spread across regional lines and national borders. Therefore, he based the denomination and its fledgling school not in the mountains, but in Cleveland, Tennessee. The city's resources, manufacturers, and critical rail connections provided practical aids to the Spirit's

Ambrose Jessup Tomlinson, the first general overseer of the Church of God and the first head of the Bible Training School. (Courtesy of the PRC.)

work proclaiming the message of Pentecost. By 1921, the Church of God had spread south to Florida, north to Illinois, and across the south to a total of twenty-three states. Its 18,500 members worshipped in 242 Appalachian churches, but 220 more congregations were outside the region and another twenty-five were outside the United States. In a single generation, the church had spread well beyond its Appalachian roots. By 1940, it had tripled in size to 63,000 members in almost seventeen hundred congregations in the United States; two thirds of those congregations were outside Appalachia. In the space of only forty years, the Church of God had taken its message of Pentecost from a cluster of mountain congregations to forty-two states and a dozen nations.[15]

The Church of God, like all early Pentecostals, viewed its congregations as part of a movement to restore authentic Christian worship, not the creation of a new denomination. Nonetheless, it quickly took on denominational authority and responsibility by creating a centralized governance structure of pastors and subordinated local congregations to that authority. In 1909, the annual assembly chose the popular, charismatic, and forward-thinking Tomlinson as their first general moderator (this title was later changed to general overseer). By 1911 the denomination had grown to fifty-eight churches and some eighteen hundred members. This growth led to the creation of an office to manage regional affairs: the state overseer. By 1917 the basic church structure was in place. Tomlinson, made general overseer for life in 1914, headed the church. By his side was the Council of Twelve—a body of pastors formed in 1916—and the state overseers. Nominally, these parties proposed and recommended policy for the approval of the annual General Assembly, however Tomlinson's control over the denomination grew over time.[16]

In its early years, the Church of God created two institutions in Cleveland that helped form the identity of the rapidly growing denomination. The first was the Church of God Publishing House, which resold religious literature and published a variety of original pieces. Most importantly for the church and later historians, the publishing house produced the *Evening Light and Evangel*. Serving as the official newsletter and organ of the church, the *Evangel* released its first edition in 1910. The *Evangel* included feature articles by its editor, A. J. Tomlinson, as well as sermons, testimonials, letters, and announcements of camp meetings and revivals. In 1913, the church built a new six-hundred-square-foot building, from which it published General Assembly minutes, Tomlinson's books, Sunday School literature, and scores of evangelical tracts, such as "Be Ye Holy," "Speaking in Tongues," and "The Latter Rain."[17]

The second institution that shaped the church was its Bible training school. From the start, the Church of God's general assemblies had a strong educational emphasis. Pastors and evangelists met to study and interpret Scripture, and as early as 1911, church leaders endorsed the need for "an institution of learning, for the training of workers who need a few months training to make them more efficient workers, and a general school or college work."[18] Little came from this impulse or from a similar proposal in 1914, when the church not only explored the possibility of a training school, but a primary, high school, and college as well. "Grandma Collier" of Calhoun, Georgia was so enthusiastic that she offered quilts for the beds of a proposed dormitory.[19] One can imagine the heated energy of those early general assemblies, with their fire-baptized services, inspirational messages, altar calls, and reports of new and growing congregations. In those moments, that founding generation found themselves swept up by the sure knowledge of the Holy Spirit working a new Pentecostal revival. This confidence inspired expansive dreams about the future, despite not having the immediate means to realize them.

In 1917, following six years of discussion, enthusiasm, and false starts, the General Assembly again agreed to create the Church of God Bible Training School. Tomlinson, who had become the dominant voice in church leadership, took the lead in promoting the new endeavor. While acknowledging that the church would, at least for the time being, need to rely on public schools for "common education," he warned the General Assembly that some of their young people had gone to other schools and, "if not lost to the Church of God entirely, they have lost their fiery zeal" in classrooms where instructors were indifferent, and sometimes hostile, to the message of Pentecost. Tomlinson called for a school in which the church's young people could take a six-month or year-long course of Bible and missionary training or prepare themselves for leading Sunday school classes.[20] The assembly responded by approving a school that would meet in Cleveland under the supervision of General Overseer Tomlinson. They also appointed a seven-member committee to oversee the school's organization. M. S. Lemons, head of the committee, made it clear that the school would use the Bible as its "principal textbook," but would also use "such literary work and music as is necessary."[21]

The creation of a Bible school fit squarely into the mainstream of the evangelical and holiness movements of the time. Higher education boomed in the last decades of the nineteenth century. In 1910, 355,000 students attended American colleges and universities, an increase of nearly 600 percent from the 52,000 enrolled in 1870.[22] Like Tomlinson's proposed Bible Training School, many of the nation's colleges were originally founded to train ministers. Most had moved far from those roots. By 1918, many offered courses of study that placed them in the center of the growing fundamentalist-modernist controversy by promoting the techniques of higher criticism to understand historical contexts and to reconcile scripture with science. The most liberal modernists came to view the Bible as a collection of stories and myths that suggested how God wanted people to live—with Jesus as the best example of that life.

Conservative Christians maintained traditional beliefs about the Bible's supernatural origins and narrative, including the virgin birth, resurrection of Christ, and other miracles. The Bible Training School set itself apart from the modernist threat to orthodoxy. Its aim was to provide a short, pragmatic course of study that prepared students for evangelism, the foreign mission field, or the pulpit. It focused on the study of the Bible and the application of its lessons, while also touching on the academic subjects of geography, languages, history, and music, which best supported those tasks. The church believed in Christ's imminent return

The Church of God's publishing house, 1919. Here, Nora Chambers taught the first BTS class in the upper room of the building. (Courtesy of the PRC.)

and that its people needed basic training for evangelism, not a four-year liberal arts program.

On January 1, 1918, Bible Training School held its first classes in an upper-floor room above the Church of God Publishing House. (The two institutions remained closely connected in the school's first decades, sharing administrators, staff, facilities, and sometimes funding.) The curriculum that first term centered on the Bible, but also included spelling, English, geography, music, and lessons from *Hurlbut's Teacher-training Lessons for the Sunday School*.[23] The use of that one named text reveals something about the first three-month course of study. *Hurlbut's* was not Pentecostal in any specific measure, but had grown from lessons for Sunday school teachers developed in the Methodist Chautauqua movement. It included lessons on the structure of the Bible, literary types, history, and geography, as well as a significant emphasis on child behavior and development.[24] Given the economically disadvantaged roots of many Church of God members, education at BTS started with a strong dose of grammar, penmanship, and spelling in the first term before moving on to more advanced topics in the last two terms.[25] So, while the school made the Bible the centerpiece of study, the students' education was somewhat broader. For some, it seemed that "they have just gotten to the place where they found out they know nothing."[26] However, by the time they reached the closing exercises on April 5, Pastor J. B. Ellis could report that the students gave sample lectures to the audience, each "with pointer in hand . . . on the rostrum with background lined with maps and outlines of the history of the world with its countries, mountains, rivers, lakes and peoples with the events connected with them."[27] As one student, Bertha Hilbun, told it, "I learned something about the Bible that I never knew before. Every reader of the sacred Book needs [also] to have a general understanding."[28] In short, the students understood what many Christian educators argue today, that students should be more broadly educated if they are to be effective witnesses of the good news.

The teacher of this inaugural class was Nora Chambers. Licensed in 1910 by the Church of God as an evangelist, Chambers was surprised that Tomlinson approached her for the job.[29] She "insisted that a man should be chosen for that position, but finally consented when all my suggestions met opposition."[30] In truth, Chambers was likely the most educated, experienced, and qualified person Tomlinson could find for the job in the entire denomination.[31] She was a graduate of Holmes College of the Bible in Altamont, South Carolina. Given that the school had identified itself in 1909 as Pentecostal, her education was above reproach. Chambers taught two years at Holmes, then had a successful stint as an evangelist before she and her husband moved to Cleveland to work under Tomlinson as a

The Church of God Elders Council meets in publishing house. This same room housed the first classes of the Bible Training School. (Courtesy of the PRC.)

The first BTS class, 1918. Back from left: Bertha Hilbun, Nannie Hagewood, Lillie Mae Wilcox, and Nora Chambers. Front from left: Jesse Danehower, Earl Hamilton, and Avery Jenkins. (Courtesy of the PRC.)

proofreader for the Church of God's press. As she saw it, the "object of the Bible school is to train young men and women for Christian service; and to understand the plan of salvation as revealed in Scriptures."[32] She said of her first day of class, "I didn't think I could carry it, but as the students prepared their lessons, I prayed. Soon I felt the presence of an unseen guest. He assured me that He would be with us and help us, and He did!"[33]

Chambers greatest challenge in the first term was not teaching in her 250-square-foot classroom but keeping her students at the school.[34] Five men and seven women from four states began the 1918 term. Four left in the first week: Arthur White, about whom little is known, left after only four days. Three employees of the Church of God Publishing House followed him two days later: Willie Mae Barrett (age 17), Stella Champion (20), and Maud Ellis (22). Later in the semester, two more students withdrew. Nannie Hagewood (23) of Southside, Tennessee, returned home and Horace Payne (25) of Sparta, Tennessee, was drafted to fight in the First World War. It was an inauspicious start for the fledgling school, with only six students remaining. The six almost became five when Bertha Hilbun (21) of Haynes, Arkansas, decided to return home. She packed her trunk and sent it on to the train station, but was convinced by her friends and Mary Jane, A. J. Tomlinson's wife, to persevere. Jessie Capshaw, the daughter of a church leader in North Carolina, was only 14 when she arrived at the training school to "study the Bible and music that I can be a greater help to papa in his work."[35] Avery Denver Evans (19) aspired to be a missionary to China but instead married A. J. Tomlinson's daughter, Iris, and remained in the States. Roy Earl Hamilton (19) from Sobel, Tennessee, was accompanied by his wife, Nora. The last two students to persist through the closing ceremonies on April 5 were Jessie Danehower (20) of Kentwood, Louisiana, and Lillie Mae Wilcox (18) of Savannah, Georgia.[36]

Bible Training School students and staff faced serious challenges in the school's first two years, including a pair of global tragedies. The first was the First World War, which began in July 1914. Church of God leadership, and Tomlinson in particular, spoke out forcibly against all wars, warning, "The awful war devil is still slaying his millions. His greed and thirst for blood is never satisfied." He argued, "As members of the Church of God we owe our first and best to God. Our first duty is to the church.... The War demon may try to persuade you that your first duty is to the stars and stripes, but this is a delusion."[37] When the United States entered the conflict in April 1917 and ordered men to register for the draft, Tomlinson told those who were called to service to register as conscientious objectors or to request non-combat assignments.[38] It is not clear the degree to which the church rank and file agreed with Tomlinson. The November 1917 General Assembly passed a resolution against members going to war, and a few church leaders were arrested for their pacifist stance. Most men registered; some won exemption from service or combat duties while other members served in France, including Tomlinson's son Homer.[39] At BTS, the draft syphoned students from the school, and Tomlinson called for women of the church to take the place of those called to fight.[40]

In 1918, women's role in the church, like many core issues in a young denomination, was unsettled. At Los Angeles' Azusa Street, men and women, African Americans and Hispanics, young and old led worship, spoke in tongues, and prophesied. The South had very different mores concerning the proper place of women and racial minorities, however women in the Church of God enjoyed, at least initially, remarkable freedom. Unlike the mainstream churches, which cited 1 Corinthians 14:34, "Let your women keep silence in the churches," the new denomination preferred to cite Joel 2:28, "Your daughters shall prophecy" to argue that Spirit-filled women should evangelize the unsaved.[41] With this springboard, women served as evangelists and missionaries, spoke in tongues, taught in the Bible school, ran orphanages, wrote for church publications, and regularly preached in the Church of God. As the church regulated itself, it limited the official standing of women to the office of deaconess (the wife of a deacon) and evangelist. Some women, like Nora Chambers, received certificates confirming their role as an evangelist. This certificate gave these women the authority to baptize and lead communion, although there is no evidence they exercised that power. In 1914 these two clergy-specific duties were removed from certificates granted to women.[42] Given the generally open environment to women in ministry (if not leadership), Tomlinson's oversight of the school, and Nora Chamber's teaching, it was not surprising that the school was strongly co-educational.

While it empowered women, the school and church were not as open-minded toward African Americans. California's Azusa Street movement was interracial, but that openness did not translate to the southeastern states, where the legacy of slavery and the reality of Jim Crow segregation dominated race relations. The Church of God openly faced down the draft, but it did not muster resistance to racism and its accompanying social and legal structures. Segregation satisfied the church's white members and—to some degree—its black members, who preferred some autonomy in the church to the direct control of white administrators. The first black Church of God congregations appeared in Florida in 1909, and by 1915 the state had seven African American congregations with 111 members between them. That same year, the church appointed Edmond Barr, a black Bahamian who had been instrumental in the growth of the Florida churches, as the overseer of African American congregations in the state.[43] The early black converts to the church were not, however, welcome at the Bible Training School. Records that would shed light on the school's teaching on race and the decision to exclude African American students no longer exist, but no person of color appears to have been enrolled in the school's first years. This segregation was supported by a 1901 Tennessee law forbidding integrated learning in higher education, although BTS may or may not have come under the law's jurisdiction.

A decade later, the church approved the separation of white and black churches. As part of the separation, African American minister Thomas F. Richardson was appointed the "Colored Overseer" of the black church.[44] By 1927, segregation was complete. For the next four decades the Church of God maintained a separate conference, administrative office, orphanage, and publication, known as the *Church of God Gospel Herald*, for black members.[45] Paralleling the broader geography of race relations, the church allowed black members to opt out of the colored church and work under the authority of the white regional overseer in nonsegregated states (as determined by the integrated or segregated nature of public schools). At the denomination's annual General Assembly, black attendees had voting rights and led Saturday night worship, but were separated from the white attendees by a rope stretching the length of the room—all the way to the altar and effectively to BTS campus.[46]

The third broader context that affected BTS's early days was the global influenza pandemic. First appearing in the US Army at Fort Riley, Kansas in spring 1918, the H1N1 virus infected over five hundred million people—fully a third of the world's population—and killed at least fifty million worldwide and around 675,000 in the United States.[47] Often called the Spanish flu, the disease was especially deadly for those aged twenty to forty years. The medical profession in 1918 had no vaccine to protect against the virus or antibiotics to treat secondary infections. Even if such treatments were available, church members may have adhered to Tomlinson's belief that "It is unreasonable for people to trust the Lord for the salvation of their souls and when they are sick resort to physicians and remedies."[48] By September the virus reached Tennessee, where it eventually took 7,721 lives. On December 23, it took the life of Bible Training School student Bennie Terrell, one of twelve church members cared for by the Tomlinsons in their home. The influenza threat was so great that the Church of God canceled its General Assembly in 1918, and the *Evangel*'s pages filled with memorials to those lost to the disease.[49]

As might be expected in a denomination that placed a high value on the miraculous power of the Holy Spirit, some church members questioned the need for formal training. If a person was called by God to preach the gospel, what more was needed than the Spirit to guide their words and actions? Though the official church minutes and newsletters did not publish such objections, they document the church's response to the criticism. R. E. Stockholm explained that "Some uneducated people are inclined to disparage learning . . . . There is a tendency among some of our people to say or think that all we need is power, love and fearless assertion of the truth."[50] A. D. Evans reported, "Many times people are embarrassed because they do not have the knowledge that is necessary for a minister of the gospel to possess . . . and very soon they have the true gospel so butchered that the people become so perplexed that they do not know which is the right way."[51] J. B. Ellis expressed a similar concern about the effectiveness of Church of God evangelists, given the "crude and unskilled methods" employed by some of its lay preachers. The solution was obvious: the Bible Training School must provide "trained, skilled and efficient laborers."⁵² Proponents of the school cited Scripture to support study and training. They pointed to Paul's weeks of study before beginning his ministry, Christ's teaching of the Apostles, and Paul's instruction of Timothy.⁵³ And in the era of progressive education reform, pastor F. J. Lee wrote, "I am convinced more and more that our ministers need to be up to date. We are living in an enlightened age. It has been said of some that they could be used to a good advantage in a 'back woods' place, having reference perhaps to people that are illiterate. Now I want to say, the time is coming and perhaps is at the door when there will be no back woods illiteracy for school buildings are being placed in reach of every child and the compulsory school law is being enforced. Can we not plainly see that the illiterate preacher will soon be no longer in demand?"⁵⁴ Without access to the church's press, critics continued to snipe from the wings of the denomination, but church leadership clearly held the high ground in supporting education.

Despite the support of the church, in its first years the Bible Training School grew slowly and rarely met its enrollment goals. When the second term began on November 11, 1918, seven students were enrolled. Only four remained when the term closed on December 26. Iris Tomlinson reported that in the spring of 1919, many students came to school, only to leave after a short time. She does not note why the students left, but the *Evangel*'s pages suggest that even the modest one-dollar-a-week tuition was beyond the reach of many church members.⁵⁵ In April 1919, five students appear to have completed the full spring term, and the school awarded its first two diplomas to Avery D. Evans and Earl Hamilton. BTS opened the September 1919 and January 1920 terms with pastor M. S. Lemons leading a two-week series of lessons on church doctrine, tithing, apologetics, and nightly evangelistic services before regular classes began. Twenty-two students from ten states attended Lemons' September sessions, but enrollment for the full term was likely under ten.⁵⁶

Low enrollment limited available resources, but rather than cripple the tiny school, shared hardship caused students and staff to create tight bonds that they recalled fondly in years to come. Most students boarded with the Tomlinsons, the teachers sometimes forewent their salaries, and at times even food for the table was in short supply (despite the occasional barrel of sweet potatoes, citrus, or meat donated by church members).⁵⁷ Yet, those who experienced those lean first terms remembered the community that formed and the work of God they saw in their midst. Jesse Danehower recalled that "we students and Sister Chambers spent many precious and happy hours reading, studying, praying and shouting the high praise of God. These were some of the happiest hours of our lives."[58] Testimonials from students and those who supported the school regularly appeared in the *Evangel*. I. J. Byrd wrote, "I thank God for the grand old Bible Training School, for its teachers and superintendent. Oh! How I do love my lessons, they have been such wonderful help and strength."[59] J. C. Lentz added, "Beloved, we need the Bible Training School.... If we take the instruction of the Training School, we will not bring any reproach on the cause."[60] The students saw the training as part of a spiritual journey, answering Tomlinson's call to ministry: "My Dear Friend: Are you planning to do more for Jesus? How little you have done for Him who has done so much for you! No doubt you have longed for some way of getting better prepared for the work which you feel the Lord would have you do. It may be preaching, missionary work, in the Sunday School, personal work—whatever it may be—the Church of God Bible School will help you, yes, wonderfully."[61] His appeal may have had an effect, as over thirty students attended the school in the fall of 1921.[62]

As the church entered the 1920s, it faced challenges that would split the denomination and threaten the Bible Training School. By 1920, Tomlinson had accumulated considerable power. On top of his lifetime appointment as general overseer, Tomlinson edited the *Evangel*, was superintendent of the school, authored a denominational constitution, and consolidated church finances into a single general headquarters treasury from which he paid pastors' salaries. He also led the church to take on debt to finance an auditorium and a printing press, just as the economy entered a sharp deflationary recession. In 1921 and 1922, over Tomlinson's objections, the church created new administrative positions for both the publishing house and school—both of which limited Tomlinson's power. Then in 1923, the church's judicial committee levied fifteen charges against Tomlinson, including misappropriating almost $14,000. Two charges related to the school: copyrighting parts of the correspondence course and making conflicting reports on the status of BTS. These complaints led the church to remove Tomlinson from office in July, but he refused to recognize their actions. Instead, he founded a new denomination which was, after lengthy litigation, known as the Tomlinson Church of God, and later yet as the Church of God of Prophecy.[63]

During the Tomlinson controversy, both the Church of God and BTS gained new leadership. Flavius Josephus Lee served for a term as head of the school before being elected as Tomlinson's successor as general overseer. Lee, a former Baptist minister, joined the church in 1908 after a conversion experience at a tent revival. He soon rose into leadership po-

Flavius Josephus Lee, the second general overseer and the namesake of the university. (Courtesy of the PRC.)

sitions, helping found the *Evangel* in 1910, pastoring, and serving as overseer of Tennessee from 1916 to 1918 and then of Florida from 1918 to 1922. Remembered for his even temperament, simple lifestyle, and holiness living, Lee guided the Church of God through the turbulent, financially troubled times following the schism and would, in place of Tomlinson, become the denomination's most-revered early leader.[64]

The financial crisis and church split directly threatened the school, which the new leadership decided to close. J. B. Ellis, a former Methodist preacher and public school teacher who joined BTS faculty in 1920 and led the school for the 1923–1924 term, recalled, "There were times when it seemed the school was almost ready to go on the rocks. Finances were low and there was little food, but the Lord supplied our needs in a marvelous way." Nora Chambers remembered, "It was a dark day when Brother Lee said the school would have to close. But we went to prayer and got our heads together to help answer our own prayers. Sister Lee gave her canned goods and bought no clothes that year. Sister Garner, the matron, did the cooking for no pay."[65] Their sacrifices made it possible to keep the school open, even though it meant delaying the start of the 1923-1924 term until November 12, when forty students arrived.

Only three years later, the BTS class of 1921 had tripled in size. (Courtesy of PRC.)

After a rocky five years, the Bible Training School had managed to survive its infancy. With two teachers, a handful of students, makeshift facilities, and an operating deficit, an outside observer would have been unimpressed with the church's educational experiment. The view from within the church was much different. Inspired by a deep faith that the Church of God represented the truest form of Christianity reborn in the last days before Christ returned, the *Evangel* could proclaim, "The Bible School is a great beginning. How grand the work it is doing for students! Let's get more squarely behind it. . . . Jesus said he was coming back, but He also said to occupy [engage in business] till He comes."[66] The path would not be an easy one, but slowly BTS would find a measure of stability.

Chapter 2

THE BIBLE TRAINING SCHOOL, 1924–1947

In the period 1924–1938, the Bible Training School remained small (under one hundred students), shared facilities with other Church of God departments, upheld strict holiness standards, and followed a narrowly defined mission. Committed to training men and women for the ministry, the school promised parents and congregations that students "would be protected from temptations to worldliness, and not only will they be thus protected, but they will be thrown among the best and most spiritual class of young people in the land."[1] The school intended to "prepare workers to think straight, [and] live straight" so as to gain "a better knowledge of the WORD which strengthens against the evils of these last days."[2] Most importantly, BTS wanted its students to experience "Regeneration, Sanctification, the Baptism of the Holy Ghost . . . and a Spirit-filled life."[3]

Sadly, the Bible Training School did not preserve or archive its records; as a result, little remains from the school's first three decades. Given the church's expectation that they were living in the last days before Christ's return, it makes sense that they did not think historically. Church publications printed numerous columns on Bible prophecy and its relation to current events. The excesses of the Roaring Twenties, rise of Soviet communism, depths of the Great Depression, the innovations of the New Deal, and buildup to World War II provided pastors with clear signs that the end was near. The rise of dictatorships was carefully followed: Stalin's attack on Christianity, Mussolini's restoration of the Roman Empire, Hitler's persecution of the Jewish people, and Zionist efforts in Palestine all pointed to the imminent rapture of the Church and the Great Tribulation—key elements of premillennial eschatology. Even Franklin Roosevelt's New Deal sparked concern, although church leaders reassured their people that the National Recovery Act's blue eagle was not the mark of the antichrist. With time growing short and countless souls to be saved, the church planned for the future with a caveat, "If the Lord tarries."[4]

Fortunately, a careful reading of the *Evangel*, which includes excerpts from the school newspapers, provides good insight into the daily lives of BTS students during the period from 1925 to 1937. Taken as a whole, the advertisements, columns, editorials, and letters speak of a school atmosphere that was closer to an intense religious retreat than the more traditional colleges of the day. Students arrived on campus for the start of the term in October, then stayed for about six months, ending the term in April. Breaks from study were brief (a week or less for Christmas), and the school program was religiously intense, emotionally engaging, and, for the many students who arrived with poor lower-school training, academically challenging.

Newly arrived students usually traveled to Cleveland and BTS by way of the Southern Railroad, which had regular service to the city. Most students were just over twenty years old, and about two thirds of the students were men and a third women. Some came with the full support of their families or local churches, but others arrived without the resources to pay the one-dollar-a-week tuition. The school did not have a campus to speak of, so students made the nine-block walk from the train station to a cluster of Church of God buildings near the corner of Montgomery and Twenty-fourth Street that the school occupied in whole or part. At times, these would include parts of the Publishing House, a church converted into classrooms and dormitory space (1922), the church's auditorium (first constructed to host the annual assembly, but outgrown by 1934), a church-turned-men's dormitory, and in 1937, a purpose-built, forty-seven-room dormitory. Students often shared a room with three others; the tight quarters sometimes caused grumbling, but at the discounted rate of four-and-a-half dollars a week, the spartan quarters matched the advertised price.[5]

For students, life soon took on a familiar routine revolving around a strict schedule of prayer (up to eight times a day), classes, communal dining, study, and worship. The day started at six thirty with a breakfast that included meals such as hotcakes and syrup one morning and grits and gravy another. Tea and coffee, once forbidden, made their way onto the menu by 1936. In the early years, the entire school would gather in BTS's single classroom, where they would pray and sing before settling in for their lessons, which were divided into four broad categories taught by two or three instructors: Bible study, literary studies (especially spelling and grammar), supporting disciplines (geography and history), and training for the evangelistic field (elocution, sermon outlining, Sunday

School training, and music lessons). Each class began with prayer, which regularly extended into a full Pentecostal experience. During these moments, students said that the power of the Spirit fell and the room seemed "like an antechamber to heaven."[6] Student Maggie Free described that "the great Messiah would send great waves of glory sweeping through the room, and it would seem that someone had turned on the electric current from the great power house above. We would shout and weep and pray, and sometimes it looked like we would not have any recitations, but we did not care as long as the Lord was working."[7] J. B. Cole agreed. "Oh how many times we were visited with the presence and power of God!" he said. "So many times the Holy Ghost took charge and we shouted, praised the Lord and talked in tongues for more than an hour. I remember several occasions almost every student was on the floor dancing or shouting while others sat in their seats crying or praising God. Yes, many times we missed two recitations but we didn't care because the Holy Ghost has control of this school."[8]

When classes proceeded without interruption, the teachers followed a curriculum that evolved over time. What started with Nora Chamber's Bible study and lessons from *Hurlbut's Teacher-training Lessons* slowly expanded into a course of study made up of three six-month terms. By 1929, that course of study looked like this:

First Term: Bible, Hurlbut's Teacher Training Course, Grammar, Orthography (Spelling), Penmanship, Vocal Music, and Instrumental Music (as an elective)
Second Term: Bible, Bible Atlas, Grammar (Advanced), Sermon Outlining, Ancient History, and Public Speaking
Third Term: Bible, Prophecy, Encyclopedia, Church History, Missionary Work, and Church of God Doctrine[9]

The first term's classes suggest a student body in need of remedial work, an idea confirmed by some of the students. W. Jackson was overjoyed to be admitted to BTS, given that "I only reached about the fifth grade in Grammar School."[10] One of Jackson's classmates encouraged other poorly prepared students to apply, stating, "You may think you are too ignorant to attend. If you can read and write English I boldly write, you are not. You will find others there who know as little as you do. . . . You may think you are too backward. Take courage, you are not. The School is not for developed and learned scholars."[11] Fortunately, no entrance exams were required, and BTS would "invite all to come . . . regardless of your former schooling."[12]

After lunch, classes continued until around three thirty, after which students mixed music lessons with study hall. Dinner was served promptly at five. In the leaner years students ate a diet of corn bread and clay peas (chickpeas). In slightly better times they added wheat bread, biscuits, and beans, and as the school stabilized they enjoyed meals like a "German" menu of mashed potatoes, cornbread, wieners, and sauerkraut. After a quick break to tidy themselves, the students were back in study hall from six to eight, with lights out by nine thirty.

On Fridays the schedule shifted, with a normal class schedule in the morning, followed by a pair of religious meetings in the auditorium at which the student body gathered to hear aspiring students give ten-minute sermons. Often a nerve-wracking experience for the young preachers, the sessions might have been more of a marathon for the audience. Five or six short experimental sermons, interspersed with prayer, hymns, and special music by soloists and quartets, would take most of the afternoon. After a closing altar call, the students gathered for dinner before meeting again for evening services. These started as gatherings for prayer, but in 1929 transitioned into the church's new youth program called the Young People's Endeavor. These meetings, often extended by Pentecostal outpourings of tongues and dancing, lasted well into the night, but not beyond the ten o'clock call for lights out.

BTS administrators enforced a number of rules in an effort to ensure a holiness culture amongst the students—not all of whom were from Pentecostal or Church of God backgrounds. School rules in the 1920s included:

> "You will not be expected to loiter around town at any time . . .
>
> Any demonstration of love making will not be tolerated by the faculty. If you can't refrain from this, please stay away.
>
> You will be expected to attend Sunday night, and Friday night services.
>
> No bad language or unbecoming conduct will be allowed anywhere.
>
> No smoking, or chewing, or using tobacco in any form will be allowed.
>
> You will be required to retire before 9:30 P.M. and be ready for breakfast at 6:30 A.M."[13]

and

> "Students of the opposite sex must refrain from walking and talking with one another at length, either in the buildings or elsewhere during the school term."[14]

It should come as no surprise that the school did not advertise the frequency with which students broke the rules, or the consequences that followed, but given the reputation of T. S. Payne (the school superintendent from 1924 to 1930) as a "real disciplinarian," the rules were undoubtedly enforced.[15]

Weekends offered little in the way of free time. Students had an extra thirty minutes of sleep before a seven o'clock breakfast, which was followed by a morning of cleaning and chores before lunch. The afternoon afforded a period "of relaxation, . . . playing ball, shopping, and aimless walking."[16] The nearby Woolworth's store was a favorite destination, but students had to receive permission from staff before they made their way into town. While some students found needed down time, others engaged in street preaching, evangelized at the local jail, and led worship services on the courthouse lawn. On Sundays, the day started with morning church services, which were followed by a special meal. After lunch was a mandatory prayer meeting in the auditorium, followed by a bit of free time before dinner and a six thirty evening worship service. All told, the weekends might have offered a student four or five hours of free time before they headed back to their twelve-hour school days. BTS appears to have taken seriously the idea that idle hands were the devil's workshop.

The administrators charged with upholding holiness standards were, unsurprisingly, drawn exclusively from the church's most influential leaders. In the period 1918–1937, four BTS superintendents served as general overseer and two on the church's top leadership committee. The superintendents were responsible, ultimately, to the church's leadership councils and the General Assembly, but between assembly meetings the superintendents were part of an evolving governance structure. Starting in 1923, the superintendent joined the general overseer and Publishing House editor in making up the Executive Committee. The superintendent, then, served both as a member of the top governing body of the church and as head of the school. In 1926 the assembly voted to create a five-person board of education, which reported to the church's leadership councils. Ultimately, as indicated by the church's 1921 constitution, all major decisions (and an unusual number of mundane ones) were considered by the church leadership, presented to the general membership, and voted on by the General Assembly.[17]

All school superintendents also spent time in the classroom teaching Bible classes, although that role began transitioning from a full-time teaching position to an administrative one in the 1930s. For most of this period, the school employed fewer than five faculty members in addition to the superintendent. Several teachers in BTS's early years were women. Nora Chambers served from 1918 to 1924, and E. L. Moore taught grammar and geography for five terms between 1925 and 1933. Often, these two women were the only full-time instructors other than the superintendent. Henrietta Ayre [Green] taught commercial classes from 1931 to 1947. Mildred Blackwell (1932–1937) and Vina Siler (1934–1947) were fixtures, but none outdid the tireless Avis Swiger (1935–1972), who was at BTS and Lee College for thirty-seven years.[18]

One developing theme in the school's history was the Church of God's entrepreneurial approach to education, a distinctive that persists into the twenty-first century. In June 1919, BTS added a correspondence course to its offerings. Advertised heavily in church publications, the school promised that the mail order course provided the same instruction as the on-site school. Open to anyone who could read and write, the course promised many of the same benefits as modern online classes: "study at home," "no time lost from work," "no books to buy," "training and experience combined," "complete in every respect," "the cost is slight," "instruction private," "only spare time required," "you are a class by yourself," and "you study when convenient."[19] The course was a resounding success. Tomlinson reported 208 enrolled when the courses opened in September and some 788 enrolled by the end of October. With a tuition of forty dollars that was payable in installments and an estimated delivery cost of thirty dollars, the extension department promised to generate income, but not for BTS. Instead, the publishing house owned the correspondence course until 1930.[20]

More than any other person, J. H. Walker expanded the school's offerings. The thirty-year-old Walker graduated from BTS as valedictorian in 1927 and joined BTS faculty that same year, while simultaneously preaching in Etowah, Tennessee and acting as the school's treasurer. On his appointment as superintendent in 1930, Walker immediately asked the general assembly to establish an endowment for needy students. Walker added three departments to the school, each headed by an important personality. Otis McCoy led the music department, Henrietta Ayre started the commercial department, and R. R. Walker was named the high school's first principal in 1934. Administratively, the 1936 Assembly passed a recommendation from the Executive Council for a three-person BTS Board of Directors. Appointed by the church, the directors were to "aid and concur with the Superintendent in determining the entire faculty, salaries, courses of studies, and to establish rules of Conduct." The

The BTS Female Quartet, one of many musical ensembles at the school, 1935.

changes also increased the workload of the superintendent of education to include oversight of the various state and regional Bible schools.[21]

From its earliest days, the school recognized the importance of music to ministry and taught a variety of vocal, instrumental, and music education classes. B. C. Robinson taught music lessons as early as 1925, but the start of a music department under Otis McCoy in 1930 marked an important point in the school's development. McCoy, a graduate of the James Vaughn Conservatory of Music in Lawrenceburg, Tennessee, did more than teach classes, he built a sound program with what was called a "determined-to-win" attitude.[22] One student wrote of McCoy that "when he incites action in some new branch of music expansion—and he's always doing that—he has fired such an upheaval of enthusiasm that it just won't subside."[23] McCoy would shape the music program at BTS for nine years, then became the editor of music publications for the church. There he helped publish the 1951 *Church Hymnal*, better known by many in the church as the beloved "Red-back Hymnal."

For the church, music was seen as an important element of evangelism, and the music program soon became one of BTS's (and later Lee's) most popular and visible calling cards. The faculty not only taught the discipline, but soon formed ensembles that would represent the school at church events. From informal groups like the Band Boys to the elite BTS Quartet, a variety of singing groups (with names ranging from the simple Quartet 1 to the more creative Gleeful Five) became staples at General

Assembly, state conventions, and camp revival meetings. Music also served an important "town-and-gown" role by providing evening music lessons to area residents. An impressive sixty-eight individuals attended such lessons in 1932 alone.[24] By 1939 the music department sponsored three string-and-reed ensembles, a string trio, a reed quartet, four vocal quartets, three trios, two duos, and a student body choir.[25]

Walker also opened a commercial department in 1930, which offered courses in shorthand and bookkeeping. Henrietta Ayre, the teacher for the classes, was splitting time between bookkeeping for the Cherokee Hotel and teaching private business classes when Walker approached her. No doubt, when she agreed to add classes at BTS, she had no idea that it would be the start of a sixteen-year career at the school. At first, Ayre joined her students in carrying typewriters to and from her downtown school to the third floor of the auditorium building. Over time, however, her commercial department became a fixture at the school.[26]

Notably, Ayre was not a member of the Church of God, although the school catalog assured readers that "she is a well-wisher, and comes to us highly recommended for noble Christian character and active church work."[27] A second non-church member and the first to hold a bachelor's degree, Katherine Lowery grew up across the street from BTS and began teaching Greek classes there in 1932. The church took a pragmatic approach to education, preferring Church of God people to other Pentecostals, and other Pentecostals to Christians who did not have the baptism of the Holy Ghost. Here, though, they drew a line. Only followers of Christ could teach at the school, and if saved, sanctified, and filled with the Holy Ghost, all the better.

In 1932 Superintendent Walker began a high school, which operated as a department of BTS and not a separate institution. He feared the "appalling conditions of the High Schools throughout the country as they grow more godless every day. So many of our good conscientious Holy Ghost filled girls and boys have been swept off their feet by the undercurrent of this terrible soul-damning teaching of evolution." In addition to a spiritual threat, Walker also appealed to parents by promoting the benefit of a high school degree that allowed young people to move beyond unskilled manual labor and win better jobs, or perhaps even enter college.

Mildred Blackwell was the first high school teacher, but the school was most shaped with the hiring of R. R. Walker. A graduate of Mississippi College and former Baptist pastor, Walker was working as the superintendent of a Mississippi high school when he was baptized with the Holy Spirit and subsequently joined the Church of God. The next year he moved to Cleveland and took the reins as the high school's first principal. The influx of younger students quickly doubled BTS's overall enrollment. The high school shared faculty, classrooms, resources, chapel services, calendars, promotional materials, and the dining hall with the other departments of the school.[28]

Because BTS housed so many enterprises, and because the church shared expenses between the school, Publishing House, and other endeavors, the school's financial history remains murky. Few BTS-specific records remain, leaving only summary balance sheets from General Assembly minutes as evidence. Unfortunately, those records have limited value. Their accounting methods vary widely, as do the income and expenses assigned to the school. Further complicating the picture, the Publishing House sometimes appears to have shouldered some of BTS's expense, and from 1930 or earlier the church paid the school superintendent salary from the separate general tithe fund. What is clear is that the school struggled to break even, running regular deficits as high as $691 (48 percent of income) in the depression-burdened 1931–1932 school year ($1,473 of income against $2,164 of expenses). Add the $1,330 superintendent's salary to those numbers, and the deficit swelled to 137% of income for the year. However, even when it did not make good financial sense, the church remained committed to education.

While the school in Cleveland struggled, the Church of God opened competing educational enterprises. The most important of these became known as the Northwest Bible School. Approved by the General Assembly in 1934, it opened in Minot, North Dakota, the following year. Its superintendent, F. W. Lemons, had a good eye for marketing. As a result, the pages of *Evangel* soon sported feature advertisements of a quality that suggested to casual readers that Northwest Bible School was the premier Church of God school. Within a year Northwest had attracted eighty-seven students from the United States and Canada—students who once might have made the journey to Cleveland. The church also sponsored numerous regional and state-level summer Bible schools, with the first of these six-week-long programs taking place in Florida and New England.[29]

Just as BTS seemed to be finding its footing in Cleveland, a new opportunity arose that would be critical in establishing a distinct identity for the school. In the summer of 1938, creditors put the campus of the defunct Murphy Collegiate Institute in Sevierville, Tennessee, on the auction block. The church seized the moment. As the hammer fell for the final time, the church had won its prize for $29,990, a meager 14 percent of its assessed value.[30] The price was almost too good to be true. J. H. Walker,

The BTS campus at Sevierville, Tennessee, where the school made its home from 1938 to 1947. (Courtesy of the PRC.)

general overseer since 1935, captured the excitement of the moment when he wrote to the church, "We all appreciate, beyond expression of words, the thought that this school is OURS. It is OURS to admire. It is OURS to appreciate. It is OURS to enjoy."[31]

Featuring a central academic building flanked by a pair of dormitories, the new sixty-three-acre home of BTS immediately accomplished two important things. First, it physically separated the school from the other Church of God institutions, while keeping the school in Tennessee and within one hundred miles of Cleveland. This distance was sufficient to provide separation from the daily operations of the press, orphanage, and headquarters, but close enough to maintain the school's ties to the denomination's birthplace. Second, it provided students and faculty a real home. Built of red brick, set on a hill, and identified by the tower and silver dome of the academic building, the new setting met visitor expectations for a college campus. A circular drive ran uphill to the school, and elsewhere the property fell away into cultivated farmland. Situated along the Little Pigeon River, the new campus rested comfortably in the shadow of the Great Smoky Mountains National Park. No longer would BTS scramble for space in structures that had started life as auditoriums, churches, or commercial buildings. Purpose-built, the campus's two dorms could house 324 students, allowing the luxury of only two (not the customary four) students in each room.

The move sparked the school's first major capital campaign. They borrowed $10,000 from the church's general tithe's fund, $8,000 from a private individual, Ola Hatcher, and $5,000 from the Merchants Bank—all with 5 and 6 percent interest rates. An appeal to the church started with the announcement that sixty-four top church leaders had promised $50, or a week's salary, then published a list of 158 other pledges to the cause. To maintain momentum, church leadership challenged each congregant to give the value of one day's wages to the school no later than the Sunday before Thanksgiving.[32] By late October the list had grown to 468, but when the Merchant's Bank note was due, the church still lacked sufficient funds. A special appeal was made for congregants to rush their offering to the school and help satisfy the debt. To boost giving, the *Evangel* even went so far as to publish top per capita giving congregations, with a church in McVeigh, Kentucky, taking first place with $52.88 per member. The appeal worked and the church retired the outside debt.[33]

In Sevierville, BTS prospered under the leadership of Zeno C. Tharp. At age thirty-nine, Tharp took over the school in 1935 after J. H. Walker was elected as general overseer. A 1923 graduate of BTS, Tharp entered the ministry and led congregations in Chattanooga, Tennessee, and

Zeno C. Tharp, president of BTS, 1935-1944.

Greenville, South Carolina. Like all BTS presidents Tharp lacked serious academic training and had no administrative experience outside his churches. A very conservative, holiness Pentecostal, he proved a capable—if stern—school administrator. Tharp was a determined disciplinarian, preferring blunt confrontation to graceful reconciliation. This was on full display during a chapel service that started the spring 1944 semester. Although he avoided names, Tharp called out one student as a thief, announced one girl had been sent home for writing notes to her boyfriend, suggested that the person who took milk from the cafeteria might contract rabies, and chastised married students for being seen "armed-up" in town.[34]

In 1942 the school narrowly dodged a crisis in leadership when the church fathers selected, and the General Assembly approved, R. R. Walker as the new superintendent—without input from the school board. The announcement brought an immediate and unexpected pushback from the normally compliant BTS faculty and staff. Five women, including three teachers, approached the board and church leaders with their reservations about Walker's leadership abilities. While not questioning Walker's Christian character, they cast doubt on his teaching skills, subject knowledge, willingness to discipline students, academic standards, and administrative abilities—in all, a damning critique of the man who built the high school program.[35] The leadership not only gave the school representatives a hearing, but they asked R. R. Walker to resign as superintendent before taking office. They then reorganized the church's educational arm, returning control of local Bible schools to the state overseers and creating the office of President of the Bible Training School. To ensure input from those closest to the school, the school board selected the president. However, this did not mean an independent board decision. The Bishop's Council (the church's pastorate) chose the board and the church leaders and General Assembly confirmed the decision.[36] Tharp, who hoped to leave BTS to join church administration, reluctantly agreed to become the school's first president.

During an era marked by the Great Depression and World War II, Tharp presided over one of the school's three major periods of accelerated growth. The school's physical growth coincided with increased prosperity in the church at large. This, in turn, brought about efforts to adapt the school to internal and external audiences. How did the Church of God prosper in an era of depression and war? Church growth, while steady, does not provide a ready answer. In 1935, denominational membership in the United States and Canada stood at 49,644. Over the next decade, it grew to 72,096—an average 4.5 percent annual increase. More importantly, after suffering during the first five years of the depression, the church grew wealthier; giving to the central tithe fund rose from $29,351 to $249,740, a startling 53 percent per year increase when adjusted for inflation.[37]

One can trace this incredible improvement in circumstances to a pair of factors. First, the church had been quite poor for its first three decades; there simply was not much economic floor below its members. Second, church membership was still concentrated in the southern states, where massive government spending programs during the Great Depression made an enormous positive impact. In particular, the New Deal's Tennessee Valley Authority, Rural Electrification Agency, and Works Progress Administration helped transform the South. Not only did these programs bring immediate relief, but they also brought long-term employment, economic development, new schools, and general improvements in the quality of life of common people. Those trends continued as World War II accelerated government spending and gave another impetus to economic growth in the region.

The church's newfound resources helped raise its social status. Church publications of the period regularly celebrated mortgage burnings, as well as the dedication of newly built sanctuaries and parsonages. Congregations moved into the homes of failed mainline denominations or raised structures of brick, a sign of status in the South. General Overseer John C. Jernigan, in articles published only eighteen months apart, aptly illustrated the promise of prosperity as well as its dangers. In January 1945 he celebrated the success of the church and pushed aside notions that prosperity had lessened Pentecostal fervor:

> Some of our greatest churches, with their large brick buildings and well-furnished parsonages, with plenty of money, were once a little handful of members pushed back into the alley or out to some isolated section of the suburbs of the town, worshipping in some old dilapidated building.... Sometimes we talk about getting back to where we once were, but, really, I do not think that is what we want, and I doubt very seriously we had any more religion twenty or thirty years ago than we have now.... The Church of God has come out from obscurity and isolation, to declare her position in the world. We always had a great deal of boldness and confidence. Sometimes we might have demonstrated more zeal than we displayed knowledge, but we have been an honest, sincere, and hard-working band of people. We have moved to the front...[38]

At the September 1946 General Assembly, his tone had changed to one of caution. Jernigan reported a growth in membership of over 17,000, the construction of new churches, and a gain in church property value of over $3 million. He also noted that the church had won the respect of the public, had opened new opportunities for the spread of the gospel, and had taken its place among the great denominations of the nation. However, "we are in danger of losing our evangelistic zeal by putting our trust and hope in the wealth of our congregations, in our fine church buildings, comfortable parsonages, salaries, luxuries of life, and such things that appeal to the lust of the eye and the pride of life.... It would be easy to sell out to Satan, compromise with the world, and allow our hearts to become engrossed with pride."[39]

Jernigan would go on to suggest that the church stood at a pivotal point in its history, one on which other denominations had stood before backsliding (succumbing to more worldly standards). He hoped for better for the Church of God, but feared the worst as he realized the denomination had moved past its modest Appalachian roots.

This new prosperity came just as the church transitioned from the founding generation—a major challenge in any institution's life. A new generation of leaders had grown up in the church and many, like Tharp and Jernigan, attended Bible Training School while it was still in its infancy. Dedicated to the church, Pentecostalism, and holiness, they were largely reflections of the founders' beliefs. They were certain that Christ would soon return, faithful to classic Pentecostal theology, and dedicated to holiness. However, in this last characteristic, a life set apart from the world, each succeeding generation would hold fast to certain essentials (no alcohol, tobacco, or opioids), but found a bit more room for the latest social trends, styles, and attitudes. These leaders, in turn, helped the school attract the youth of a more prosperous, upwardly mobile, and educationally ambitious generation who took a slightly less austere view of holiness living.

So, on one hand, the rhetoric and practice of the school in Sevierville looked similar to earlier iterations. General Overseer and former BTS Superintendent J. H. Walker left no doubt as to the school's mission at the 1940 General Assembly, stating, "There has long been a need of more advanced training for our ministry. There was a time we could stamp our foot and shout glory and put it over; but that time is past—it takes more than that. IT TAKES TRAINING IN THE WORD OF GOD to meet the scientific attacks on the everlasting gospel.... There is only one place we can be certain our young men and women, the backbone of the church of tomorrow, will receive this training and that is in a CHURCH OF GOD SCHOOL." And what was a Church of God school, but an institution "with Church of God teachers, with Church of God management, with Church of God rules, with a Church of God name, and with Church of God students."⁴⁰

Students, in church publications, continued to extol the virtues that set the school apart from its secular competition. One wrote that for "those who have experienced life amidst the evils of public schools the Spirit-filled teachers are highly appreciated." Others wrote that Spirit-led moments continued to be commonplace. Charles W. Conn, who later would go on to become general overseer and president of Lee College, enthusiastically reported, "Last week a half day was used by the Spirit to pour out His blessings. From early morning till noon the rooms and corridors were filled with weeping, shouting, laughing and dancing students, full of the Spirit and fire." And the 1940 commencement ended with a "service that developed into an old time, shouting, Pentecostal meeting. Tears! Laughs! Tongues! Groanings! Joy! Bliss! And all that accompanies the Holy Ghost."⁴¹ No visitor would confuse BTS with a Baptist school, much less a public one.

On the other hand, life at BTS had started to look like many other schools—at least from a distance. By the time of the Sevierville move, BTS had already taken on a number of academic trappings, including a baccalaureate service, graduation gowns, a school newspaper, and an alma mater:

> On Sevierville's southern border, reared against the sky,
> Proudly stands our Alma Mater as the years go by.
> Praise to thee, our Alma Mater, moulder of mankind;
> Greater glory, love unending, be forever thine.
>
> Balmy breezes gently wafted through inspiring halls,
> Mem'ry's leaflets closely twining shall fore'er recall
> Yesterdays that waken in our hearts a tender glow,
> Making greater still the love that we have learned to know.
>
> "Ever onward" be our watchword, conquer in each test;
> We owe a life of loyal service to old B.T.S.
> Praise to thee Alma Mater, moulder of mankind;
> Greater glory, love unending, be forever thine.⁴²

In 1942 the students published their first yearbook, the *Vindagua*, and its pages offer a different perspective on the school and a fuller picture of student life. Whereas in 1932 J. H. Walker contrasted BTS to schools "where so much time is taken up with non-essentials and various societies and frivolities ...," those same non-essentials were very present a decade later.[43] Students organized a number of clubs, ranging from the pious Ministerial Association and Missionary Society to academic ones for music, speech, Spanish, and the library. Both men and women participated in intramural sports, including volleyball, baseball, softball, tennis, and, for men, football.[44]

The early administrators of the Bible Training School had once tried to suppress any romantic activities among students, but over time that prohibition steadily eroded. That is not to say, however, that the school administration did not attempt to strictly regulate contact between the sexes. The church made it clear that while "Most schools have set student life in practically the same mold—they date, they drink, they dine and dance at sorority houses and night clubs . . . this school has always tried to promote a clean everyday life, free from the vices which threaten to destroy the Christian faith and virtue of our boys and girls in this evil day."[45] At Sevierville, the school encouraged students to leave their cars at home; opportunities for on-campus dating (known at BTS as socials) were carefully controlled community events. "Students are encouraged to meet on terms of friendly social fellowship, but intimate and improper association of co-eds is strictly forbidden. All social functions are under the direct supervision of the Dean of Women."[46] The yearbooks contain photographs of three such on-campus functions. One shows couples sitting on blankets on the school grounds, another has couples paired up in the auditorium's seatbacks, and the third pictures a social in a dorm lobby. In order to have a date at such a social, the male student sent a written request to the dean of men. The dean of men then sent the request to the dean of women, who sent it to the female student. If the student approved, the process was reversed and a date was arranged, usually a shared Friday or Sunday meal in the dining hall. At some events, students without a date could drop their names in a hat to draw a "pot luck" partner for the evening. Of course, some students found ways around those rules. Evelyn Walker-Holcombe later recalled how she would open her window, play a special song, and her boyfriend would appear at the window for a hug and kiss. They were caught once; each received 99 demerits—one short of expulsion.[47]

At first glance, BTS students looked like most other students of their time. Wartime styles had raised the hems on skirts, but for the most part Pentecostals found the fashion trends of the 1930s and war years quite compatible with their holiness lifestyles. For men, changing cuff, lapel, and tie sizes or shoe styles and pleated pants rarely threatened holiness standards. Women's hemlines, sleeve lengths, hairstyles, and accessories came under more careful scrutiny and regulation. After the scandalous flapper-influenced dresses, makeup, and bobbed hair of the 1920s, young Pentecostal women found 1930's fashion more amenable, and 1940's style even more so. By the time the *Vindagua* had begun publishing photographs of students, women wore modest, stylish skirts and dresses that were cut just below the knee. Blouses and dresses were always long or three-quarter sleeved and were often paired with sweaters (some bearing a BTS logo) or short-waisted coats. However, even those styles sometimes came into question. In 1943 an all-male church committee, concerned with concessions to fashion, required female students over the age of fifteen to wear full-length hose, skirts that fell below the knees, and dresses with at least half-length sleeves when appearing in public.[48]

While fashion may have changed, many of the school's longstanding traditions did not. Each year, an administrator would announce, with certainty, "that this had been the best term in all the history of the school."[49] Students still started their school days kneeling next to their desks in prayer, and the daily, mid-morning chapel service was still mandatory. *Hurlbut's* was still in use, Friday afternoons continued to be reserved for students to practice their sermon skills, and prayer meetings were still held at night. The students also continued to use their weekends for chores, church services, and ministry outreach, including elder care and home visitations, Sunday afternoon services at a nearby federal prison, and Saturday afternoon services on the courthouse lawn. Those public services were meant for "mountain folk in this section who cannot be reached by the church," and hundreds would gather to hear the students sing and preach.[50]

The school had a tradition of reaching into the community through its numerous musical groups. These performed in local churches and larger church gatherings, but by the 1930s, technology broadened their reach. From 1938 to 1948, the school hosted a radio program, one of the first regular uses of that medium by the church. The *Church of God Hour* was "Conceived in faith, born of hope, inspired by love, wholly dedicated to the service of Christ, and to the ultimate task of bringing man into fellowship with God."[51] The program featured a Pentecostal gospel message, but depended almost entirely on students for its musical content—especially the

Radio Choir. The school's pioneering efforts were soon a standard feature of the church's outreach, with at least twenty-nine programs being broadcast by the summer of 1940.[52]

In a milestone decision, the church officially approved the establishment of a two-year liberal arts junior college in 1940. The opening of the junior college and a concurrent decision to pursue accreditation from a secular agency had major ramifications for the school's future. Although not evident at the time, the new program marked the beginning of the end for the Bible Training School model, which used the Bible as its primary textbook and incorporated only those courses that made students more effective preachers, teachers, and missionaries. That decline was not intended. The General Assembly made this clear when it approved the junior college, "if it can be done without adversely affecting the Bible Training School."[53] Nevertheless, the move reflected new expectations and aspirations among church members, added a new constituency, and in the longer term served as a stepping stone to an accredited four-year program that would close the high school and consolidate BTS's diverse offerings into one college.

Like the move to large main-street sanctuaries built of brick, pursuit of accreditation signaled the church's steady move from outsider status to the mainstream. It also opened the door for a new set of decision-makers to influence nearly every aspect of the school: its curriculum, organization, faculty, financing, and leadership. Until 1940, the school was a department of the Church of God. As such, it had only to please that one audience. For a church that was proud of its Pentecostal, holiness, counter-cultural message, this independence from worldly institutions was a critical element of the school's identity. Other schools might sponsor sports, allow fraternities, encourage dating, and scoff at daily chapels, but not BTS. Likewise, accredited schools might demand certain qualifications of faculty, books in a library, and courses in the curriculum, but BTS could chart its own path, a path bound only to the church's traditions, needs, prejudices, and aspirations. When those aspirations included right-standing with the larger higher educational world, the school added a new constituency that would steadily reshape the school's academic life, and, over time, its particular social and religious culture.

At first, accreditation did not appear to significantly challenge the BTS model. When the high school won accreditation from the Tennessee Board of Education in 1941, little changed in the school's culture or curriculum. At the junior college, accreditation served to improve the program. From the beginning, leadership intended the junior college to offer a curriculum similar to other schools of its type. To this end, administrators took steps to improve resources at the school. The most notable of these was the creation of a library. When it was learned that the state required the library to house eight thousand volumes, church members were urged to donate any type of book to fill the shelves.[54] Additionally, for the 1941–1942 year, the junior college lengthened its school year from six to nine months in order to match best standards.[55] Ultimately, the junior college sought accreditation from the Southern Association of Colleges and Schools (SACS), but first looked to win approval for its hours to transfer to the University of Tennessee. Such approval, won in May 1947, allowed BTS students to use their classes toward four-year degrees at the public schools in the state and served as de facto in-state accreditation. In 1948, SACS accredited the high school, and in 1951 the junior college added membership in the American Association of Junior Colleges.[56] Approval by SACS for the junior college program took longer, with its endorsement finally coming in 1960.

Similarly, the addition of the liberal arts program appeared to be simply another entrepreneurial move that had little to do with the school's core identity. By 1943, BTS advertised six departments: the two-year College of Liberal Arts, the School of Secretarial Sciences, the Academy, the School of Music, the School of Theology, and the Christian Workers' Course. The first four need little explanation, but the last two merit some clarification. The Christian Workers' Course encompassed the original BTS mission of short-term, Bible-centric curriculum that was essentially vocational in nature. Promotional material described it as serving "young ministers and other Christian workers who cannot meet the entrance requirements of the School of Theology." The short-lived School of Theology, which first appeared in advertisements in 1942, may have been the foundation for a future four-year Bible college or, alternately, an advanced version of the Christian Worker's curriculum. Open exclusively to BTS junior college graduates, the School of Theology was "an intensive two-year course embracing a comprehensive study of the entire Bible and related subjects."[57]

As the Bible Training School struggled to gain accreditation and broaden its curriculum, the school stood on the cusp of one of the institution's three periods of accelerated growth. Buoyed by the move to the new Sevierville campus and the rising expectations of church members, the school opened the 1941–1942 year with a total enrollment of 216, with 35–40 students in the new junior college and eleven faculty teaching across all divisions.[58] The Second World War would soon embrace the United States, however the challenges of the war years did not slow growth. Instead, the school prospered, reaching a fall 1946 enrollment of 535 students.[59]

As war spread through Asia and Europe, the United States instituted a draft. In response the Church of God maintained, but did not vigorously defend, its standing policy against combatant service. However, like many organizations and individuals with pacifist or isolationist leanings, the attack on Pearl Harbor significantly changed their mood. The church encouraged members to register as conscientious objectors, although it is unclear how many men achieved that status. As the nation mobilized, the church's publications largely ignored the progress of the war, but quietly supported the war effort, arguing that it was necessary to secure religious and political freedoms. As the war ended, the general assembly altered its statement of beliefs to allow members to engage in combatant services and stay in good standing.[60]

For BTS, the war created challenges ranging from a relative scarcity of male students to difficulty procuring building permits from the War Production Board. To make up for missing men, BTS targeted the wives of servicemen for recruitment. Advertisements read, "Many young married girls who did not get to finish their schooling are taking advantage of their opportunity and coming to school this term while their husbands are in the Army."[61] Furthermore, advertisements suggested that thanks to the school's inexpensive tuition, room, and board, "The allowance from

BTS students, c. 1944. (Courtesy of the PRC.)

the Government will more than pay their expenses."⁶² It is not certain how many women took advantage of the opportunity, but it is important that the Church of God openly courted government dollars to support its school, especially given many church leaders' skepticism over federal government programs, expansion, and power.

On the BTS campus, administration and students actively participated in programs to aid the war effort. These ranged from somber events, like an Armistice Day ceremony that remembered the suffering and loss of war, to a patriotic event that marked the first anniversary of the attack on Pearl Harbor where students sang the service anthems and put on patriotic plays. In February 1943, BTS held a public event in cooperation with the American Legion during which they sold thirteen hundred dollars in war bonds. The next year the faculty and students raised eleven thousand dollars to support the war loan drive—enough to purchase six ambulances.⁶³ The school community's desire to support the war was made more immediate by the departure of faculty and students into the service. By the summer of 1943, three faculty members, sixteen students, and forty-eight former students had joined the armed forces.⁶⁴

Despite the exigencies of the war, BTS grew at such a rate that administrators struggled to accommodate the increased enrollment at the Sevierville campus. Typical was the experience of third-term student Claude Phillips, who reported that "Three of my roommates had arrived before I did and another one came the next day. Yes, this did seem a little crowded."⁶⁵ Class sizes pushed limits as well, with one visitor reporting fifty-four students in one class and forty-three in another.⁶⁶ President Tharp apologized for the overcrowded conditions, explaining that the jump in enrollment had caught him completely by surprise and totally unprepared. To give students some breathing room, Tharp purchased a large house near campus on Prince Street. This became Marple Hall dormitory and housed fifty women. Many married students moved off BTS grounds and found lodging in town. Here, the war slowed the school's ability to adjust, as the delivery of much-needed beds, dressers, and other furniture was a low priority on wartime railroads.⁶⁷ Hardest hit was the understaffed cafeteria, whose efforts to feed so many resulted in what one visitor described as "burnt offerings."⁶⁸ By the end of the term, Tharp judged that he needed three new dorms and a recreation building in order to keep pace with growth.⁶⁹

The call for a major building campaign came just as the school completed an extension to the main administration and academic building. Approved by the General Assembly in 1941 and finished in time for the spring 1942 commencement, the four-story Zenobia Hall cost $75,000. The building featured a first-floor kitchen and dining room as well as a second floor of classroom space for students in the junior college and Christian Worker's department. The third floor housed a 7,500-square-foot, thousand-seat auditorium. Circling the auditorium on a fourth-floor mezzanine were twenty-six soundproofed music practice rooms, most with new upright pianos.[70] In 1944 the War Production Board provided approval for the construction of a gymnasium, and construction started on a new women's dorm in 1945.[71] It was a reasonable choice given the high percentage of women attending the school, some of whom were housed on the third floor of Sevierville's Central Hotel.[72] Completed in 1946, the three-story, eighty-two-bed dormitory only eased the overcrowding. For married students, a more creative solution presented itself. For $150 apiece, the school purchased camper trailers from Alcoa, Tennessee, where the trailers likely had housed the overflow wartime workforce at the Alcoa aluminum plant. The school jury-rigged water and electric service, built a bathhouse, and created what students called "Simmonsville" in a field on the edge of campus.[73]

As enrollment exploded, the school underwent significant administrative changes. J. H. Walker briefly returned as BTS president for the 1944–1945 year before giving way to E. L. Simmons, who ran the school for the next four years. Simmons's resume looked like many other presidents: he pastored several churches, organized the Young People's Missionary Association, chaired the Orphanage Board, was editor of the Publishing House from 1939–1942, and authored the first denominational history, *History of the Church of God*.[74] He served as a state overseer and assistant general overseer, sat on the Executive Committee, and was a delegate to the meetings that organized the National Association of Evangelicals.[75] Simmons' time as president of BTS was a short chapter in his long history of service to the church.

In 1946, the General Assembly approved an expansion of the Board of Directors from three to five members. The assembly granted the board, in consultation with the president, the final authority in hiring, firing, and tuition decisions. Raphael Stephens, in his 1981 study of governance at Lee, argues that the board's most important function was to guarantee doctrinal orthodoxy at the school, and to otherwise ensure that secular academic measures did not undermine church teachings. That interpretation might make more sense in later years, for Walker and Simmons were traditional Pentecostals who matched the board's commitment to orthodoxy.[76]

The assembly also created two new administrative positions: a controller, and a vice president and dean of the college. In combination, the two cabinet-level positions had the potential to bring professional competency in support of the church leader sitting in the president's chair. The first vice president and dean of the college was Earl M. Tapley, who took on the job in the fall of 1946. Tapley grew up with twelve siblings in rural Georgia, where he, like most children of tenant farmers, stopped his formal education after sixth grade. Unable to attend high school, Tapley nevertheless found time after work to study at home. At age twenty-one, he traveled to Cleveland to attend BTS, which only whetted his appetite for learning. After being called to a church in Nashville, Tapley continued his education. He graduated from Lipscomb with a junior college degree in 1943, a bachelor's from Vanderbilt in 1945, and a master's in education with an emphasis in school administration from the Peabody Graduate College in 1946.[77] This background made him the first senior administrator to join the school based on academic credentials, not seniority in the Church of God. Tapley's education also developed his critical thinking, leading him to question some of the church's more extreme doctrines and placing him firmly on the progressive edge of a very conservative denomination. Tapley would provide leadership in the school's drive to win accreditation and standardize its offerings, but his progressive leaning would not go unnoticed by traditionalists in the church.

At the same time, in 1946 the church formalized expectations for faculty, requiring "every teacher of the Bible Training School and College to sign a contract annually, agreeing to teach nothing contrary thereto, and shall permit no person unable or unwilling to accept the said declaration [of faith], in good faith to be employed."[78] The faculty signing the new contract grew to meet the new enrollment, but also had better credentials than in past years. In 1942–1943, the school had fifteen faculty who collectively earned $13,271, an average of $884 a person. As the school's *Teachers Guide* put it, the salary would not make you rich, but would give you a living; besides, "If God has called you to this work, you will receive your reward at the proper time."[79] Seven of those called to the school were former BTS students. Six held bachelor's degrees, and one, Mary Elizabeth Harrison, earned a master's degree from Duke University.[80] Just three years later, twenty-two faculty earned a total of $31,665, averaging $1,439 per teacher (the school president was paid $3,500 that year).[81] Inflation accounted for 10 percent of the increased salaries, but a more likely explanation was the employment of more full-time, and fewer part-time faculty.

As the war ended, BTS seemed well-positioned to take advantage of what Dean Tapley identified as "a bigger and greater educational awakening, promoted by our government and the sentiment of the American people."[82] The GI Bill of Rights, formally entitled the Servicemen's Readjustment Act of 1944, gave millions of returning veterans a chance to start or complete their education. The bill's generous stipend paid up to $500 in tuition each year and provided a living stipend of $75 or $105 to single or married veterans, respectively. This aid easily covered BTS's yearly costs, which for the 1946–1947 year totaled $288 for room and board and $190 for tuition.[83] Fifty-six veterans enrolled by the spring 1946 semester and many must have echoed the words of one veteran, who said, "after the experience of four years in the Navy, I find school to be much like a vacation."[84] Soon the school included direct appeals to veterans in its advertising, and the catalog devoted pages to explaining how to access GI Bill funding. The acceptance of indirect government aid would be an important step in the school's history in that the money, like accreditation, would come with expectations that would shape the school's academic and cultural life.

At the May 1947 commencement, the school celebrated the graduation of over one hundred students: twenty-one from the junior college, thirty from the Department of Religious Education, and fifty-eight from the High School. The Dean of the University of Tennessee, Dr. Fred C. Smith, gave the keynote address, but the high point of the proceeding came when President E. L. Simmons approached the microphone to make a pair of historic announcements. First, he informed the audience that BTS was moving back to Cleveland. Bob Jones College was vacating its campus, which was significantly larger than what BTS had at Sevierville and only three blocks from the original BTS location. The school was returning home. One can imagine Simmons pausing to let the audience settle before he announced that credits from the junior college had, on May 17, won acceptance by the University of Tennessee. The audience responded with thundering cheers and applause—BTS, and by proxy the Church of God, had won a measure of respect and approval from the state.[85]

Over the course of two decades, BTS had grown from a small band of students and teachers dedicated to preparation for ministry into a diverse entrepreneurial enterprise of over six hundred students. In some ways the school shaped a distinct identity within the church by adding a school board, moving the campus to Sevierville, creating the office of school president, and winning the approval of accrediting bodies. Upon closer examination, however, behind a neon sign that welcomed visitors to the Bible Training School, the institution looked more like an improvised educational medley than an orchestrated enterprise. The school had grown as its leaders, men with little or no experience in school administration, saw opportunities to meet needs in the church with their limited resources. With no long-range planning and rarely with an eye toward broader educational standards, the campus grew to house a high school, junior college, music school, secretarial school, and Christian education department. Not only did those divisions share faculty, classroom space, and other resources, but the campus provided room and board to students from age fourteen to forty. Binding this ungainly collection together was a shared faith, rooted in the Church of God, and carefully guarded by school and church leaders. These leaders might not have understood education standards, but they had no doubts about the importance of their Pentecostal, holiness traditions.

Chapter 3

YEARS OF PROMISE AND CRISIS

Lee College, 1947–1960

In 1947, the Bible Training School relocated from Sevierville to Cleveland, a move that brought with it a change of name to Lee College and promised new growth for the Church of God's flagship educational institution. There was renewed reason for hope. While in Sevierville, BTS added students, a junior college, and new facilities. The move to Bob Jones College's campus brought the school back to the denomination's home base and offered improved facilities for the school's 630 students and twenty-seven faculty. Over the next fifteen years, the promise faded until the school reached a crisis point in 1960, when only 294 students enrolled. The rapid decline in the school's fortunes stemmed from a combination of factors. First, the school adapted too slowly to a fundamental shift that was taking place in the Church of God. There, the faith, practice, and educational needs of its founding generation were being reimagined to meet the needs of a new, more affluent generation. The school paralleled this shift by moving from a Bible training school model of education to a Bible college. Second, such transitions are rarely easy, and Lee's was made more difficult due to high turnover among its leaders, most of whom had no experience or ambition to stay in higher education. Instead, the office served as a resume builder for up-and-coming church leaders. During the period 1946 to 1960, Lee College had five presidents who, despite having strong support from the church, soon faced a financial crisis caused by dropping enrollment.

In the immediate post-war years, the school grew steadily on a diet of federal aid by way of the GI Bill, but as that pool of students dried up, the school struggled to find replacements. Simultaneously, the school's second major source of students—those in BTS's Christian Workers' Department—steadily declined. Improved public schools had resulted in high school graduation rates jumping from 16 percent when BTS began, to 65 percent in 1960. As more Church of God young people earned high school degrees, fewer sought narrowly-couched training for the ministry. Additionally, better public schools meant fewer students for the academy.[1]

With no idea of the hardships that lay ahead, there was nothing but optimism from school and church leaders when the school moved to Cleveland. School leadership expected this success to continue and remained committed to training and equipping young people of the church for effective service and ministry. On the very eve of the move from Sevierville, President E.L. Simmons celebrated the opening of a new dormitory and an educational program which included a high school, a religious education course, music classes, commercial classes, and a junior college for students who had the goal of "finishing in other and higher institutions, after having been well established in the evangelical faith."[2]

Why then did the church relocate? For three reasons. First, the Cleveland campus offered improved facilities for the school.[3] The new campus could accommodate some 800 students and included over a dozen academic buildings and dorms.[4] Second, the church welcomed the opportunity to house its flagship educational institution, denominational headquarters, orphanage, and publishing house in one city. Those four

Old Main, the central building of Centenary College (1885-1929), Bob Jones College (1933-1947), and Lee College until its demolition in 1962. At various times it housed a swimming pool, classrooms, student housing, and administrative offices. (Courtesy of the PRC.)

entities were the institutional heart of the Church of God, often sharing personnel, financial resources, and facilities. It is important to again remember that the school was viewed as an integral part of the church, not an independent entity. As the *Evangel* put it, "Lee College is caused by the Church of God as a whole and can justify its existence only by the service it renders to the church in general."[5] And third, BTS was becoming an important barometer by which the church measured and insured its commitment to holiness. Moving the school two blocks from denomination headquarters would help ensure orthodoxy and temper any independent thinking or decision-making by the administration.

The move came with a new name that better represented the church's aspirations for its school. Vice President Earl Tapley led the campaign, testing the Lee name on colleagues and church officials before submitting a formal proposal to the board of directors. In that proposal, Tapley argued that the school should be named in honor of Flavius Josephus Lee, a beloved church patriarch who served as general overseer and, briefly, superintendent of the school. Tapley also noted that the school sat on Lee Highway and that the Lee name carried a measure of prestige amongst the white population of Southern states, from which the school drew most of its students.

The proposal represented Tapley's ambition to transform the Bible Training School into a more mainstream educational institution, and it won the approval of most church leaders, although former-president and arch-conservative Zeno Tharp fiercely opposed the change. To that end, Tharp led a group of pastors from South Carolina (where Tharp was state overseer) in a protracted fight to keep the church in the forefront and name the school the Church of God College.[6] The church leaders eventually confirmed the Lee name, but Tharp's dissent was only the first of many interventions by traditionalist elements dedicated to maintaining the college's holiness standards.

The return to Cleveland took place as the Church of God made an important transition in the denomination's history. After decades of faithful service, the denomination's founding generation was passing. Consider that during the period 1946 to 1955, the church lost several key leaders, including J. B. Ellis (1947), Alda Harrison (1948), T. S. Payne (1951), and Nora Chambers (1953). Others, like E. J. Boehmer, retired. As with any institution, the loss of that collective memory, authority, and leadership posed challenges to the Church of God. Those figures had defined the church by establishing its Pentecostal culture, marking behavioral boundaries, defining doctrine, and setting priorities. Many had come from a particular

A neon sign welcomed visitors to Lee College. (Courtesy of the PRC.)

demographic. They were poor, rural, white, Appalachian southerners with little formal education. They embraced the primitivist, holiness life that defined the early decades of the church, and most, including A. J. Tomlinson, believed that a commonsense, Holy Spirit-led reading of Scripture was the core of an educated life. This belief permeated the entire denomination. While the Church of God supplemented its General Assembly minutes with a list of approved teachings and practices, the church fathers consistently resisted any sort of creed or confession, which they considered a work of man and a hindrance to the moving of the Holy Spirit.

Due, in part, to the church's lack of a carefully defined systematic theology, a significant debate over sanctification arose in the church. By the early 1940s, questions regarding the doctrine of sanctification subsequent to justification had built to a crisis point.[7] As church archivist and historian David Roebuck ably puts it, "The historic anti-creedal approach of the Church of God . . . allowed for the development of some diversity on theological matters. This has been especially true regarding the doctrine of sanctification."[8] Many members of the church adopted a belief in progressive sanctification after conversion—a sanctification that gradually conforms believers to the will of God and image of Christ. This view allows that salvation could be in jeopardy if not tended to properly. Others cited Romans 6 and argued for definitive sanctification, in which there is a sharp split between the old life and new. In more extreme versions, some Pentecostals cited 1 John 3:9 ("Whoever is born of God doth not sin . . .") to argue that the believer is fully sanctified in this life and would not sin after conversion.[9]

The church fathers, spurred by a need to clarify doctrine, decided that the denomination needed a formal statement of faith other than the teachings contained in the general assembly minutes. The 1948 Declaration of Faith, which reads suspiciously like a creed, became the doctrinal standard for the Church of God.

We Believe:

1. In the verbal inspiration of the Bible.

2. In one God eternally existing in three persons; namely, the Father, Son, and Holy Ghost.

3. That Jesus Christ is the only begotten Son of the Father, conceived of the Holy Ghost, and born of the Virgin Mary. That Jesus was crucified, buried, and raised from the dead. That He ascended to heaven and is today at the right hand of the Father as the Intercessor.

4. That all have sinned and come short of the glory of God and that repentance is commanded of God for all and necessary for forgiveness of sins.

5. That justification, regeneration, and the new birth are wrought by faith in the blood of Jesus Christ.

6. In sanctification subsequent to the new birth, through faith in the blood of Christ; through the Word, and by the Holy Ghost.

7. Holiness to be God's standard of living for His people.

8. In the baptism with the Holy Ghost subsequent to a clean heart.

9. In speaking with other tongues as the Spirit gives utterance and that it is the initial evidence of the baptism of the Holy Ghost.

10. In water baptism by immersion, and all who repent should be baptized in the name of the Father, and of the Son, and of the Holy Ghost.

11. Divine healing is provided for all in the atonement.
12. In the Lord's Supper and washing of the saints' feet.
13. In the premillennial second coming of Jesus. First, to resurrect the righteous dead and to catch away the living saints to Him in the air. Second, to reign on the earth a thousand years.
14. In the bodily resurrection; eternal life for the righteous, and eternal punishment for the wicked.[10]

Upon its adoption, the fourteen tenets were to be posted in every church, every classroom, and every office of the church. At Lee, the board, administration, and faculty had the Declaration written into their contracts and were prohibited from teaching or publishing anything contrary to its standards. While writing the formal statement may have raised eyebrows among the church's oldest generation, the document's Pentecostal theological positions remained consistent with those of the church's founders. The Declaration joined the church teachings published as a supplement to the assembly minutes. While laying out the church's theological foundations, the Declaration left the question of sanctification undefined, and thus a matter of conscience. The supplement also contained the rules that governed lifestyle, but the Declaration did not attempt to organize the accumulated collection of decisions governing life and practice.[11]

As the church formalized its beliefs, it also continued the socioeconomic shift that began during the New Deal years. World War II brought industry, migrants, and military bases to the south, and the postwar years saw continued urbanization, modernization, and prosperity (gross national product grew by 250 percent between 1945 and 1960).[12] Members of the church enjoyed rising incomes and aspirations; many entered the middle class, while others would join the church from the middle class. At the same time, the Church of God began moving from its primitivist, radically Pentecostal, rural roots to a more modern, evangelical, suburban institution. In his social history of the denomination, Mickey Crews labels these the traditionalist and progressive wings of the church. That nomenclature seems both fair and useful in thinking about the church during the 1950s and the decades to follow.[13]

The progressives had different values, aspirations, and notions of respectability than the traditionalists. They remained distinctively Pentecostal in their theology and practice, but in the postwar years they also found a comfortable place within the generally conservative mainstream national culture. This change included new measures of success and new expectations for the school's educational enterprises. BTS, like dozens of other Bible schools across the nation, had emphasized pragmatic education that eschewed the liberal arts model in favor of Bible study that prepared students for the ministry. The school offered complementary courses like geography and history and remedial classes in reading, writing, and arithmetic, but as Nora Chambers had put it, the "object of the Bible school is to train young men and women for Christian service; and to understand the plan of salvation as revealed in Scriptures."[14] This model made perfect sense to the church's founding generation and to traditionalists, who sought a commonsense reading of Scripture, expected the imminent return of Christ, focused on a narrow definition of "kingdom work," and widely disdained traditional models of higher education. BTS's original model also made sense if, as one observer noted, many Lee students were first-generation college students from underprivileged homes.[15] It made less sense to the progressives, who viewed education as an important credential for ministry, but also a stepping stone to social and economic success.

In these transitional years, the progressives controlled the church media. So while responses to traditionalist critiques of the school are available, a fully developed critical argument was not published. Occasionally, however, traditionalist voices do appear in support of stronger holiness standards in the church as a whole. A wonderful example of this is found in a 1947 *Evangel* article by Mrs. P. E. Day entitled "Repent and Get Back to God." Day's jeremiad argues that the church had fallen asleep, and that the power of the Holy Spirit was being driven out because "People have gone wild after money and fine clothes." The rising economic status of church members posed a threat, but Day's focal point was the immodest dress of women: "We cannot distinguish some of our Church of God women from the world. The only difference is the paint on their faces." And more particularly, "How can we expect the Lord to bless us when our dresses are above the knees and the sleeves almost gone?"[16] She certainly would not have approved a photograph in the 1948 college catalog showing female students, on the student council no less, in summer dresses with short sleeves and hems that barely dropped below the knee.[17]

For many reasons, Lee College was an important focal point in the holiness debate. To start, graduates of the school began filling key church leadership positions. General Overseers Zeno Tharp, H. L. Chesser and John Jernigan, as well as many members of the church's top councils were graduates of the Bible Training School, and the school's culture and teaching was shaping the next generation of leaders. Additionally, the school was one of the jewels in the Church of God's institutional crown. Highly visible, heavily promoted, and the recipient of significant church funding, the college was a tangible symbol of the church's rising status. As that status rose, the faculty became better educated. While many once attended BTS, gone were the days when a BTS degree or pulpit experience won a place on the faculty. Among the thirty-five faculty who settled into the new Lee campus, twenty-six had at least bachelor's degrees; twenty of those were from secular colleges (ten bachelor's, nine master's, one doctorate).[18] The students, however, were the real prize—and pawn—in the holiness debate. Their dress, social activities, zeal or lack thereof, and, most of all, participation in Pentecostal religious experiences became important markers of the school's orthodoxy—and that of the next generation of leaders as well.

As for the college, traditionalists were suspicious (and from their perspective, for good reason) of the move from the Bible training model to the new, aspirational Lee College. To avoid unnecessary division, school leaders worked to allay those fears. Church publications featured articles and advertisements affirming the school's commitment to traditional values, while promoting the importance of higher education and defending it against an anti-intellectual culture. Here the school administration carefully positioned Lee between the church's competing traditionalist and progressive elements. They reassured the faithful that Lee stood for Pentecostal faith and practice, but wanted the college to reform its curriculum, win acceptance and status in the broader academic world, and reconsider the purpose and value of a college degree. As a result, the school steadily moved away from its Bible school roots while consistently reaffirming its Pentecostal identity.

From 1947 to 1956, Lee administrators demonstrated their commitment to orthodoxy with a pair of new advertising slogans: "Putting First Things First," and "God's School for God's Business."[19] The college catalog put it this way, Lee College "believes that the world is ill from the effects of sin and that a means of recovery is to be found through the preaching of the gospel of the Lord Jesus Christ and through a personal Christian work. This task is to be accomplished through God-called, consecrated men and women. It believes that these ministers and Christian workers should be thoroughly trained and educated for this great work. . . ."[20]

A third major slogan, "Fundamental in Belief, Pentecostal in Emphasis and World-Wide in Perspective," connected the Church of God to the broader post-war fundamentalist and evangelical world. This subject deserves a more thorough treatment than can be given here, but those ties were important. The use of the term *fundamental* clearly signaled that the church and school remained committed to core orthodox beliefs. Historian Joel Carpenter has shown that the fundamentalist movement had not simply disappeared after the 1925 Scopes Trial.[21] Instead, largely out of sight of mainstream America, fundamentalists built their own network of schools, publications, radio networks, and other institutions. Pentecostals and the Church of God took a parallel path, and together these emerged in the 1940s to form the backbone of a new evangelical coalition, in which the Church of God was very much engaged. Notably, the Church of God was a significant participant in the National Association of Evangelicals (NAE) from its onset. Church representatives attended the 1942 organizing meeting, sent a committee of five church leaders as delegates to NAE's constitutional convention, and served on NAE boards and commissions. As church historian Charles Conn put it, "there was an eagerness to join forces with other fundamentalists in the protection and promulgation of the evangelical precepts."[22] At the same time, the Church of God and its flagship college also shared the fundamentalist's unease with modernity. In 1950, Lee's president, J. Stewart Brinsfield, made it clear that "In this day of materialism, modernism, and secularism ... we are HOLDING THE LINE and are dedicated without any reservation, and certainly without any apology, to the advancement of the cause of Christ."[23] In holding the line, the church sought to remain holy, a people set apart. A year later, President Jernigan understood that "Our acceptance of the full-gospel truths, our consecration, and our manner of life make us a peculiar people. We are misunderstood by some, but our adherence to the doctrines of the Bible does not, in any way, disqualify our school in pursuit of higher academic standards."[24] For the school, the challenge would be to hold that standard while also measuring success against a secular model.

Yet, despite these assurances, responses to traditionalist discontent regularly emerged in the pages of church publications. *Evangel* editor Charles Conn warned against church members who held "extreme attitudes" and greeted visiting "students with suspicion and cynicism." He wrote, "Any opinion of the student which does not follow the generally accepted course of thought is disdained and the school, then, is accused, at the greatest, of corrupting young people's minds."[25] The *Lighted Pathway*, a youth-focused monthly magazine, published a variety of supportive articles with titles such as "Does Lee College Help or Hinder One Spiritually?" and "How Lee College Helped Me Become a Christian."[26]

In 1952, the *Evangel* published the provocatively-titled "Is Lee Dead Spiritually?" in which a Lee student refuted accusations that "Lee College is a dead school, spiritually, and that the chapel services at Lee College are lifeless."[27] School advocates also pushed back, giving evidence of prayer meetings in the dorms, Spirit-filled faculty, Biblical instruction, pre-class prayer, off-campus ministry, and, most of all, campus revivals.

These times of spiritual awakening had always been a central part of life at BTS and Lee. The earliest student reports emphasized the spontaneous outpouring of the Holy Spirit, which interrupted classes—sometimes for days—with Pentecostal worship. Over time these school revivals became less spontaneous, and by the 1940s, revivals on campus were planned events featuring a week of special services and guest speakers, followed by a dutiful report of the number of students saved, sanctified, and/or filled with the Holy Spirit during the event. The programmed nature of chapel and revival time left some students unsatisfied with the spiritual life on campus, which explains why school and church leaders reported in glowing terms the campus revival of February 1950. For those like former Publishing House Editor J. D. Bright, who had been "travailing in prayer that it [Lee] would meet God's standards of acceptance" as successfully as it had SACS's standards, the week-long revival was evidence of God's approval. Bright's report gave a sense of an old-time Pentecostal revival, when "the fire of the Lord fell," "certain things happened . . . a brief message in English, in other tongues, interpretations of the messages, confessions, repenting, restitution, students saved, sanctified, and filled with the Holy Ghost, sick bodies healed, and God's will revealed. . . . [T]he spirit of this great revival is . . . in [a] genuine, old-fashioned Church of God manner." Bright's testimony was confirmed by other church leaders who attended the revival. Charles Conn wrote that "the Holy Ghost began to speak through His vessels of flesh an exhortation to the congregation. Suddenly, with spontaneous conviction of sins and hunger for God, sinners began to leave their seats and kneel at the altar, praying, weeping, and rejoicing . . . until well after midnight." President Brinsfield reported that the Holy Ghost was in full control as the altar filled; General Overseer Chesser called it a "great burn-out"; church general secretary R. R. Walker called it a great visitation by and anointing of the Holy Ghost; and former-president Zeno Tharp believed it to be the start of a general revival in the church. Here, then, was testimony that satisfied any question regarding the spiritual health of Lee College.[28]

At first glance, traditionalist-progressive tensions were not readily evident on Lee's campus. Lee's administration took seriously its job to assume parental duties, with a distinctly Pentecostal flare. Lee expected students to maintain strict holiness standards in both behavior and external appearance. The school's position was clearly stated in its catalogs: "Parents who send their sons and daughters to this school may expect that their associations shall be with young men and women of good moral character. Anyone void of this essential trait need not apply for admission. A student whose ideals and manners are out of harmony with those of right living, becomes a menace to the influence and reputation of a school of this kind."[29]

One can easily guess the college's key behavioral standards: no smoking, no drinking, and modest appearance. Men were expected to keep their hair off their collar, wear slacks and not jeans, and not wear shorts or sleeveless t-shirts (even when playing sports). Women wore skirts and dresses (never pants), kept their hair below their shoulders, and wore no jewelry or makeup of any kind. And, for the period from 1946 to 1960, those standards were not seriously challenged by Lee students, perhaps because the styles of the period easily incorporated Pentecostal norms. Students attended four required chapels a week (one day a week was now reserved for clubs and organizations), Sunday night services, prayer meetings in the dormitories, and enjoyed active lives on campus. The school fielded numerous intramural teams, including basketball, softball, volleyball, and football (in full pads), but did not play teams from other schools. Many students participated in clubs, including the Mission Club, Athletic Club, Speech Club, Beta Club, Spanish Club, Future Teachers of America, and Ministerial Club. The administration attempted to monitor and limit off-campus activities. Students were expected to receive written permission to travel to off-campus events, and were prohibited from attending football games, dance halls, and movie theaters.

One club that became a major feature of campus life was Pioneers for Christ. The club's driving force came from its faculty sponsor, Charles Beach. Beach converted to Christianity while on active duty in the Pacific during the Second World War, graduated from Lee in 1948, and finished his bachelor's degree in foreign languages at the University of Tennessee at Knoxville. He returned to Lee in 1954 as an instructor and began working with Pioneers for Christ, which grew from three dozen students in its first year (1956) to 120—almost one third of the student body—by 1960. The group emphasized personal evangelism, especially door-to-door witnessing, and regularly sponsored "invasions," in which they targeted a town or community for a focused evangelistic effort. They first went to Athens, Tennessee, in 1958, and soon expanded to out-of-state targets.

The Pioneers also held street services, visited jails and prisons, worked with children, and offered training in evangelism. By the early 1960s, the group was making trips to over twenty states and the West Indies.[30]

School administrators were especially interested in monitoring students' social life—a euphemism for dating. On-campus rules limiting contact between the sexes (same-sex relationships were prohibited) were strict, if not perfectly enforced. Through the years, the administration created and discarded rules in an attempt to maintain a culture of purity. At one time, a six-inch rule was instituted to keep couples separate, while at another, men and women were told to leave gym classes from separate doors. Administrators even took measures to literally draw a line between the sexes by painting a white stripe in front of the women's dorms to keep men at bay. The school preferred regulated socials and sponsored events that allowed couples to pair off in public spaces, where chaperones could keep watch and ensure wholesome behavior. These events ranged from formal mixers to the popular fall and spring picnics. The college allowed off-campus dates, but students had to secure an accompanying faculty chaperone. In the mid-1950s, President R. Leonard Carroll's enforcement of traditional holiness standards for dating provoked one of the few student protests on campus. A group of students gathered outside Carroll's office and demanded an end to the chaperone rule. Unamused, Carroll confronted the students and sent them back to their dorms. At Lee, holiness was the rule, and rule changes came from the administration, not the students.[31]

As is often the case, school leadership was generationally removed from the students and tended to be more conservative than the students' parents. Lee's presidents represented a more traditional view of holiness, orthodoxy, and the place of the school as an arm of the church. Furthermore, the presidents cycled in and out of Lee with alarming frequency. The presidency was an important posting for church leaders, but leading the college was never considered a career. Much like army officers serve a tour of duty in the Pentagon, Lee's presidents viewed Lee as an important, short-term posting in their path through the church's highest councils and committees.

One of these transient presidents, E. L. Simmons, took office in 1945. He served three years as president before asking the church to relieve him of his post in 1948.[32] The college board of directors selected former General Overseer John C. Jernigan as Simmons's successor. In 1948, term limits had forced Jernigan out of office as general overseer of the denomination, and he reluctantly accepted the job at Lee College. By June he began the annual presidential recruiting circuit of state meetings, and the *Evangel* printed announcements by the new president. His work in the summer months convinced Jernigan that he was unqualified for and unsatisfied with his ability to do college work.[33] Only months into his new position, Jernigan resigned and the church selected J. Stewart Brinsfield as his replacement. The thirty-five-year-old Brinsfield had no experience in higher education and had not served at the executive level of the church, but was a rising star in the denomination. A former pastor, he served as state overseer of Pennsylvania, a member of the orphanage board, a world missions board member for five years, and the Director of World Missions from 1946 to 1948. Appointed with Earl Tapley's strong backing, Brinsfield was a young, energetic, and innovative leader, but proved a controversial choice.

After years of traditionalist control, the president's office underwent a drastic change with Brinsfield, whose worldview was liberal by the Church of God standards of his day (if terribly conservative by any other measure). His vice president and progressive ally, Earl Tapley, wrote that Brinsfield "encouraged fellowship and freedom in social and spiritual activities on the campus."[34] That innocuous phrase, freedom in social activities, meant that Brinsfield took a more relaxed approach to dating

J. Stewart Brinsfield, president of Lee College, 1948-1951. (Courtesy of the PRC.)

and community engagement. His student handbook omitted the list of specific regulations that governed student life, including strict rules on dating, dress, and physical intimacy.[35] On one occasion, four students accused of attending a local high school basketball game appeared in his office. When questioned if they had attended the game at the high school, the four denied it. Then, under further questioning, they admitted attending the game at a different location. Brinsfield burst out laughing and let the four escape without even a warning.[36]

In addition to allowing young sports fans to indulge their sporting passions, Brinsfield also hired teachers from outside the denomination (although not outside the faith) in order to better position the school for accreditation. These attitudes put him squarely in the crosshairs of the traditionalist wing of the church. Former BTS president Zeno Tharp, who had been working to gather support for a call to the general overseer's chair since he left the school in 1942, rallied conservatives against Brinsfield. In Tharp's view, the new president was a significant threat to the traditional holiness culture at the school, to the denomination, and to Tharp's goal of becoming general overseer. Brinsfield later denied any ambition to become general overseer, but freely admitted his progressive leanings. "God knows I've never been a liberal when it comes to theology," he said, "[but in] social things I may be considered liberal."[37]

At the fall 1950 General Assembly, Brinsfield learned that the school's board of directors was meeting secretly—and had been discussing his ouster. He interrupted the board's private session and offered his resignation, which they refused to accept. Soon after, Brinsfield heard that the board had met a second time. Having been approached by a church that was interested in having him as their pastor, Brinsfield again offered his resignation; it was again refused. The fall semester passed without major incident, but in January the board met secretly in Cleveland and fired Brinsfield mid-term for disregarding their guidance in accounting for the school's petty cash fund.

After leaving Lee, Brinsfield filled a pulpit in Detroit before taking on a full-time position in Pittsburg, Pennsylvania, but the traditionalists, led by Tharp, worked to ensure Brinsfield never sat in another position of power. In 1952, the progressives rallied eighty-four votes to place Brinsfield on the Supreme Council. While a valiant effort, they fell well short of victory and revealed their relative weakness to the traditionalists' strength. Brinsfield eventually left the Church of God to pastor an independent church before new, more progressive leadership sought reconciliation in the 1980s.[38]

Following Brinsfield's mid-year ouster, Earl Tapley stepped in as interim president during the spring 1951 semester. Well aware of his difficult position, he began the spring semester by calling for a "Spiritual Emphasis Week," no doubt, at least in part, to hold traditionalist critics at bay.[39] In April, the board again invited John C. Jernigan to serve as president, which he did for a single year. Deliberate, popular, and folksy, Jernigan reassured traditionalists when he wrote, "With all our additions and improvements, we still held to the old Bible School which is in existence today."[40] Three months later, he returned to the theme, this time reversing the formula to assure progressives that traditional beliefs would not hinder academic improvements. "Our adherence to the doctrines of the Bible" he said, "does not, in any way, disqualify our school in pursuit of higher academic standards."[41] He appears to have served, in effect, as a longer-term interim, stabilizing the office before giving way after the spring 1952 semester.

The transition appears to have been contested in a way that again spoke to divisions in the church. According to Tapley, the chairman of Lee College's Board of Directors offered him the presidency in March 1952, but the official vote was delayed until their next meeting in six weeks' time. In that intermission, Zeno Tharp and other traditionalist leaders in the church organized to reverse the board's decision. Tapley describes how a church official walked back and forth between the board meeting and the church headquarters. At the end of three days of meetings, the board elected Leonard Carroll, a Tharp protégé, as president. Tapley agreed to stay on as academic dean but understood that Tharp had labeled him a dangerous progressive force at the school. The divisions did not heal after Tharp won his long-coveted position as general overseer. When Tharp defeated moderate Jernigan for the general overseer's seat in a hotly contested vote in 1952, the progressives adopted the acronym LS/MFT, or "Lord save me from Tharp."[42]

Carroll was only thirty-two when he took office as president of Lee College. He had joined the church in 1942, pastored in Tennessee and South Carolina, and held a bachelor's degree from Furman University. While president, he earned a master's degree from the University of Tennessee. He brought with him a no-nonsense personality, highly conservative perspective, and sometimes bellicose view of Pentecostal holiness. For Carroll, Lee promised a safe haven to which Pentecostal parents could send their children. Why, he asked, would parents send their offspring to secular colleges, where they would "be exposed to the slurs of agnostics and forced to overcome the criticism directed toward his beliefs by unbelieving professors?"⁴³ In contrast, "Lee College," Carroll wrote, "stands without apology for 'old time Pentecostal religion,' principles of righteousness, and an aggressive, fervent testimony."⁴⁴ In a meeting of administrators, division heads, and dormitory supervisors, Carroll, a strict disciplinarian, expected employees to speak with one voice while enforcing school regulations (which he returned, in detail, to the student handbook).⁴⁵ He paid special attention to interactions in mixed groups of male and female students, reinforcing chaperoned dating and specifying that only teachers could serve as chaperones.⁴⁶ In his five years as president, Carroll brought a commitment to holiness to Lee, but he did not leave the school a better place than when he first arrived. As the school struggled, Carroll tightened his grip. He required students to take a loyalty pledge and faculty mail was delivered to him to be opened and reviewed.⁴⁷ It was no wonder that Lee slid into a sad state that Charles Conn later characterized as "depressing," a "nadir," a "malaise," and "discouraging."⁴⁸ Enrollment, which is examined in more detail below, had dropped, and further accreditation was stalled. In the midst of this turmoil, the board named Rufus Platt the new college president in May 1957.

The thirty-seven-year-old Platt was an unusual choice in that he was the first president who was not also a religious leader in the Church of God. At age fourteen, he left school to support his family. He then attended BTS for a short time in 1940 before serving in the war.⁴⁹ He took religious education classes at Lee in the 1946–47 school year but left to earn bachelor's and master's degrees from Nashville's George Peabody College. Platt joined the faculty at Lee as a social science teacher and dean of men in 1950 and served as assistant dean to Earl Tapley in 1952. In 1953, when the progressive Tapley left for a job at the University of Chattanooga, the administration was reorganized, eliminating the position of vice president and dean of academic affairs. At the same time, the board instituted four divisions: Religion, Junior College, Academy, and Library. Platt was serving as the dean of the junior college division when Carroll stepped down. The faculty, who believed an educator, not another church leader, might reverse the school's fortunes, petitioned church leadership to promote Platt to president.⁵⁰ The board obliged. As president, Platt guided the school to two major accreditations: the Accrediting Association of Bible Colleges (AABC) approval for the Bible college in 1959 and SACS accreditation for the junior college in 1960. Regardless, enrollment plummeted during Platt's three years, and the school reached a low point in its history.

As with the college's presidents, a similar pattern of turnover existing

Table 1. Faculty Credentials.[51]

YEAR	SOME COLLEGE	BACHELOR'S DEGREE	MASTER'S DEGREE	DOCTORATE
1937	6	2	0	0
1948	4	17	10	1
1959	4	10	16	0

among the faculty—a faculty with qualifications that, while perfectly acceptable in a Bible training school model, were minimal for a college. In 1937, only two Lee faculty had bachelor's degrees. Assessing the faculty in an institution that shared full- and part-time personnel between administration, college, junior college, high school, and non-class instruction is difficult, however the faculty's size and credentials did improve over time.

Remembering that the school was committed to hiring from within the denomination, the growth in qualified faculty again suggests that the denomination, at least in part, had moved from the margins of society into the mainstream. However, the commitment to hiring within the denomination also caused the faculty to be less qualified than those at neighboring schools. At the University of Chattanooga, 35 percent of faculty held doctorates, and 22 percent of Southern [Adventist] Missionary College faculty had doctorate degrees in 1957. Qualifications were not the only issue. Due to low pay (one faculty member reported being offered $1,000 more a year—an almost 30 percent increase—by the University of Tennessee) and dropping morale, Lee also experienced a high turnover rate, with only four faculty persisting from 1948 to 1958.[52]

Even with these challenges, there was significant positive change underway at the school, spearheaded by two capable administrators. Earl Tapley hoped to start the SACS process in 1947. Having won approval for Lee credits to transfer to the University of Tennessee, he confidently predicted success and academic growth that would lead to a bachelor's degree program at Lee.[53] SACS officials advised that before the junior college proceeded, the high school should first gain accreditation. Here the high school principal, Mary Harrison Green, took the lead. Green attended the Bible Training School, then went on to earn a bachelor's from Maryville College and a master's from Duke University. She returned to teach in the high school in 1942 and took over as principal the next year. The high school, which had been accredited by the state in 1943, won

SACS acceptance in November 1948. Green's success with SACS did not immediately translate to the junior college, but in the interim Tapley successfully applied for membership in the American Association of Junior Colleges in 1951.[54]

While the junior college struggled to win SACS approval, the pressure mounted for Lee to expand its curriculum and offer a four-year degree. The exact nature of that degree reflected the progressive-traditionalist tensions in the church. Tapley accurately pinned the problem when he wrote, "More and more of the young people of our Church and of other Pentecostal groups are becoming interested in college training. If their own church does not provide the facilities for such training, these young people will find it elsewhere."[55] The desire to offer a bachelor's degree was further fueled when a survey found that the junior college was "not meeting the needs of church constituents. Many of those who attended the college expressed their desire to finish their undergraduate program in this church-related institution."[56] The question, then, was not if a bachelor's degree should be offered, but when the expansion should take place and what model the school would follow.

Conservatives in the church favored a Bible college model that updated, expanded, and improved upon the old training school. The traditional BTS mission, "preparing students for the ministry," would remain unchanged, and the college would hold fast to the school's original promise to use the Bible as its "primary textbook."[57] Scripture would remain the foundation of all aspects of campus life: academics, volunteer work, social organizations, and holiness traditions. The curriculum would include some liberal arts elements, but the school would offer degrees centered on an education in Bible. Progressives promoted the expansion of the junior college, long defined as a liberal arts program, into a standard bachelor's program. Rather than focus narrowly on Bible education, the liberal arts curriculum had students study a wide range of topics through a Christian, Pentecostal worldview. The school would require a core of religion and Bible classes, but those would anchor the broader degree program, not be its focus. This option would continue the junior college's philosophy of providing "a general education designed to develop within its pupils such appreciations, understandings, abilities, and attitudes as are needed for responsible Christian living."[58] Faced with the two options, the church chose not to decide between the two. At the 1950 Church of God General Assembly, General Overseer H. L. Chesser called for "a four-year, fully accredited college and a fully accredited Bible College," the latter of which he viewed as a natural evolution of the religious education division. The school administration dutifully attempted to create both new programs, but implementing such major changes, while also seeking to maintain and expand accreditation for its existing programs, proved difficult.

In 1953, Lee began an unaccredited Bible college that offered a Bachelor of Arts degree in biblical education. It was meant to prepare graduates for ministry in the Church of God. The 126-hour curriculum included thirty-eight hours of liberal arts core classes in English, history, speech, and biology during the first two years, and fifty-eight hours of Bible and religious education in the last two years. The program also required graduates to complete one summer of supervised ministerial work and pass a comprehensive Bible examination.[59] In 1955, the school added a bachelor's degree in Christian education. This degree program shared 78 percent of its curriculum with Bible education, but did not require New Testament Greek and offered electives in Christian education such as Sunday School Administration, Preparation of Youth Programs, and Church Administration.[60] The new degrees immediately proved attractive, and around 100 students enrolled for the fall 1956 semester.[61]

The Bible college sought and gained accreditation through the Accrediting Association of Bible Colleges in 1959. The AABC's evaluative study, while focused on the Bible college, pointed out several of Lee's greatest challenges and one issue in particular. They objected to the school's muddled organization, in which the Bible college, junior college, Department of Religious Education, and high school shared faculty, administrators, meetings, and finances. The church viewed these as branches of its educational enterprise that naturally shared resources. The conglomeration had grown naturally as the Church of God's entrepreneurial impulse caused the denomination to embrace a number of divisions in order to meet a challenging student demographic. As noted by the AABC evaluators, many of Lee's students were first generation college students from underprivileged homes. Lee sought to raise "the sights and standards for the denomination, but . . . cannot be too far in front of the educational and cultural level of its people."[62]

Within Lee's quickly shifting framework, two other notable changes took place. First, Lee opened an unaccredited four-year liberal arts college in 1956. The college began with a limited curriculum and only two majors, English and social studies. To ensure the new program stayed tied to the teachings and doctrines of the church, all students would minor in Bible. Rufus Platt, while serving as dean of the liberal arts division, argued the new venture met the needs of junior college students. Importantly, it also would allow students to train for professional careers without finishing their education in schools where "many of our young people faced secularistic philosophies and influences that were not easy to combat."[63] This experiment graduated two classes but closed when SACS recommended Lee focus on the junior college accreditation.[64]

Second, the school underwent a series of administrative changes. In 1958 the church, likely on the advice of accrediting agencies, added laymen to the Board of Directors. Unlike all previous board members, the new additions were church members but not church leaders. What they lacked in church leadership they made up with new expertise and fundraising potential. Top administration under the president was reduced from a high school principal and a dean of the college and religious education divisions (1949) to a single vice president and dean of academic administration (1951). It then transformed again to fit a divisional structure (School of Religion, Junior College, Academy, and Library) in 1953.[65]

After thirty years of operation as a loose affiliation of schools, which included correspondence courses, a high school, a music school, a religious education program, a junior college, a Bible College, and a liberal arts College, the church had stretched its offerings at the Cleveland campus to the limit. Yet, even with this broad range of offerings, in the mid-1950s the school began a steady decline in enrollment that threatened its very existence. The survival of official school records from this period allows for better accounting of enrollment. Although the school often published numbers that included part-time music and correspondence students, it makes more sense to consider only students enrolled in Lee's five core divisions.

Table 2. Core Enrollment at Lee College, 1948–1960.[66]

YEAR	TOTAL	HIGH SCHOOL	JUNIOR COLLEGE	RELIGIOUS EDUCATION	BIBLE COLLEGE	LIBERAL ARTS COLLEGE	VETERANS
1948–49	643	200	218	225	0	0	200 est.
1951–52	440	102	217	121	0	0	173
1954–55	504	134	218	63	89	0	88
1957–58	368	91	154	27	80	16	nd
1960–61	294	42	155	9	88	0	nd

The most notable losses were in the Religious Education Division. Created after the junior college opened to replace BTS's Christian Workers' Department, the religious education program continued the traditional Bible training model. It offered a three-year program for literate adults without a high school diploma who wanted training for ministry or the mission field. When BTS became Lee College there seemed no reason the traditional model would not remain an important option. Its 225 students made it the strongest division in 1948, but steadily shrinking enrollment left it with only nine students in 1960, and it finally closed in 1965.[67] What caused its demise is not entirely clear, but a number of factors seem to have been in play. Lee had promoted the importance of accreditation by making it a feature of advertising and promotional materials. Prospects must have balked at the idea of spending three years to earn an unaccredited diploma recognized only by the Church of God. Additionally, the recruiting pool for the division decreased as the high school diploma became the standard measure of education for most Americans. The numbers also do not show a shift in students from religious education to the liberal arts college, which one might expect if high school graduation rates factored heavily. Instead, junior college enrollment trended down alongside that of religious education. A more likely culprit was the GI Bill.

The impact of the GI Bill on higher education was tremendous. Nationally, participation peaked in 1947, accounting for 49 percent of all college admissions. By the time the original GI Bill ended on July 25, 1956, 7.8 million of the nation's 16 million World War II veterans had participated in an education or training program.[68] Both BTS and Lee College eagerly recruited former servicemen, featuring GI Bill funding in promotional materials and in their catalog. In the decade following the war, veterans became a mainstay of the student body. At Lee, they made up around one-third of all students between 1948 and 1951, before falling to an average of 17 percent between 1952 and 1956 (when the school records stop noting their number). Those veterans brought their wives and young families to the school. So many came that in 1948, the school committed three dormitories to house them.[69] The drop in the number of veterans at Lee parallels the collapse of the Religious Education division. Correlation is not causation, but almost a third of white servicemen had only a grade school education, and the average veteran had completed only a single year of high school.[70] Therefore, it seems likely that many GI Bill recipients at Lee were enrolled in the Religious Education Division—and that their declining numbers played an important role in the division's demise.

Though they may explain trouble in the religious education division, missing veterans cannot explain the high school's decline. Started in 1932, the high school, or academy, enjoyed an influx of students that effectively doubled enrollment. In 1949 registration peaked at 219 students, or 38 percent of the total institutional enrollment. From there, the number dropped to forty-two students in 1960, a mere 14 percent of total enrollment. Part of the problem may have been a loss of leadership—particularly that of Mary Harrison Green, who had worked closely with Brinsfield and Tapley. In 1950 the school eliminated Green's position as high school principal, and she left the next year. Then the school board closed the ninth grade in 1958 in order to concentrate on the accreditation of the Junior College and Bible College.[71] Predictably, enrollment tumbled as students began and finished their high school education elsewhere. The academy continued to operate until 1965, when pressure from SACS to separate college and high school operations delivered the final blow.[72]

There was, however, something more happening on campus than the loss of high school and religious education students. The generational shift and related traditionalist-progressive tension in the Church of God continued to impact the school. The transition undermined the old Bible training school approach and caused the church to back away from its high school enterprise. It had also given birth to the liberal arts junior college, which came to dominate the school, enrolling an average of 47 percent of all students in the 1950s. Both the Bible college and abortive liberal arts college also reflect that tension. The former showed a commitment to expanding and updating the training school model with a new, more rigorous Bible-centered program to train ministers and missionaries, but the Bible college failed to show sustained growth or the capacity to carry the school's goals for a bachelor's program. Opening with eighty-nine students in 1954, the Bible college averaged eighty-nine students for the next seven years. One could say that it successfully replaced the religious education program, but it showed little long-term promise and did not appear able to capture junior college graduates.

As one would expect, falling enrollment put the school under tremendous financial pressure. Since moving back to Cleveland in 1947, the school had taken on one-and-a-half-million dollars in debt. Retiring that debt was a point of emphasis for both church and school administrators. The church did its part, raising money from the Publishing House, fundraising appeals, and, for two years, a one-dollar per capita fee from the churches. In 1952 the college retired its debt to outside creditors by borrowing the final half million dollars from the denomination's tithe fund. Falling enrollment, however, caused school officials to cut budgets, raise fees, and appeal for even more church funding.[73] Tuition, board, and fees raced ahead of inflation, rising from $254 a semester in 1950 to $516 in 1960.[74] In 1956 the church ended generous Publishing House contributions to the school that averaged over $40,000 from 1941 to 1948. The denomination, however, did increase funding by committing 15 percent of annual donations to the tithe fund to education—with 80 percent of that funding earmarked for Lee.[75] By 1960, the church was providing 28 percent of the school's operating budget, but Lee still could not make its $416,328 budget. The church again bridged the financial shortfall with a special appropriation of $30,000 to cover the school's budget shortfall.[76] With too few students to fill the campus and a physical plant suffering from years of deferred maintenance, the church leadership seriously considered selling the campus for half its $1.5 million purchase price, then building a new, smaller facility.[77]

While the college presidents struggled to find students, they also kept a wary eye on a movement they viewed as a destabilizing threat to the struggling college. By 1955, African Americans were rallying behind a new social justice movement to bring ever-increasing pressure against both the formal structures of Jim Crow segregation in the South and de facto racial inequities present throughout the nation. This new energy in the struggle for civil rights bore fruit over time, but not without facing and overcoming determined, organized, and sometimes violent opposition by white segregationists and their allies in government. Tennessee shared this experience, with the white population adopting a host of tactics aimed at preventing integration. From violence in Clinton to harassment of black children in the slowly desegregated schools of Nashville, the state's most resistant districts held out until the Civil Rights Act of 1964 forced their hands.[78]

Sadly, Lee College was far from the vanguard of the civil rights movement. In 1954, the U. S. Supreme Court's *Brown v. Board of Education* decision established that racial segregation in public schools was unconstitutional, effectively nullifying Tennessee's 1901 law that segregated higher education. However, like most colleges and universities in the state, both Lee and the Church of God allowed the inertia of tradition to prevent them from accepting—much less embracing—racial integration for another twelve years. And while this slow move toward integration was not unusual for colleges and universities in the South, Lee and the church not only missed a chance to lead, but they also regularly took positions of active resistance to civil rights. When change did come, it was led by a college administration that understood that integration was inevitable and prodded the denomination into action—for without the approval of the Church of God, no change was possible at the college.

In 1958 the Church of God had around 5,000 black members (or about 3 percent of U.S. congregants), most in southern black congregations under the jurisdiction of the Overseer of the Church of God Colored Work.[79] Until 1958, black members enjoyed substantial autonomy within the church, holding their own state and national conference meetings under the leadership of a black administrator. However, that year the church's leaders appointed a white minister to head the colored church, citing a need for better accountability and an issue with "personalities" in leadership. Despite strong protests from the African American congregations, the church not only upheld the appointment, but again appointed a white overseer in 1965.

It should come as no surprise then, that Lee chose not to take advantage of a golden opportunity to step to the forefront of civil rights when Philip B. Simmons appeared in person before President Carroll, the registrar, and the business manager to request admission to Lee for himself and his wife, Marjorie, for the winter 1956 term. Mr. Simmons was pastor of the local African Methodist Episcopal Zion church, a presiding elder in the Chattanooga district, and a leader in the African American community.[80] Their application was denied, as was that of another African American, Vernon Springer, the next year.[81] The college's record on racial issues then goes largely silent for several years. Even after the *Brown* decision and Martin Luther King's movement gained momentum, the college and denomination did not officially take a stance on civil rights or actively consider changes in their segregated structures. If anything, it appears that the Church of God hoped to justify its educational system by creating black-only institutions and opportunities. In short, the school planned to respond to the *Brown* decision with segregated facilities. Here, again, the school missed the point and an opportunity to lead.

The 1950s brought significant change to Lee; change brought new challenges, and those challenges, when not managed well, brought the college to its knees. For Lee, the most important transition was the move from a Bible training school and junior college model to that of a four-year college. The change took place at the same time the entire Church of God was shifting in relationship to its founding generation, a generation that had known, loved, and embraced a non-accredited degree in religious education. The move to Cleveland and the new Lee brand became symbolic of the reorientation from Bible school to college. The new four-year, accredited degrees accommodated the higher educational goals of a post-war generation, but the development took place as enrollments dropped—so in part the move was also meant to bolster enrollment. At the same time, the denominational flagship aspired to improve its academic reputation by moving to the new campus and seeking the approval of secular accrediting agencies. The challenge, of course, was to manage change in a way that simultaneously attracted the church's youth and stayed true to the church's traditions. To manage that transition the school needed well-trained, dedicated faculty and visionary, flexible, professional leaders. Both were in short supply until the arrival of a new president in the fall of 1960.

Chapter 4

REBIRTH AND CONSOLIDATION

Presidents Ray Hughes and James Cross

Sixty years after Ray Hughes became the fourteenth president of Lee College, his name elicits a variety of responses from those who have worked in or around the school and the Church of God. Inside the church, many remember his long and faithful service: general overseer on three different occasions, twice the president of Lee College, president of the National Association of Evangelicals, president of the denominational seminary, a member of the Executive Committee for twenty-two years—and those are just the highlights of a life well spent. At Lee there are those on campus whose opinion is shaped by his second term as the college president, when he represented reaction, retrenchment, and tradition, as well as opposition to the nomination of Paul Conn to the office of college president in 1984.[1] A third group, however, does not remember the man, his achievements, or his limitations. They only know the dormitory that bears his (or her?) last name, and that the unknown Hughes must have had some importance to Lee. They would do well to remember Ray Hughes.

When he accepted the call to Lee in 1960, thirty-six-year-old Hughes was one of the brightest young stars in the Church of God. Raised in Ohio, Hughes was a second-generation member of the church who in 1940, at the age of sixteen, graduated from BTS and preached his first revival. In 1942 he married Euverla Tidwell, the daughter of a prominent church leader. Although Hughes pastored two churches, he made his mark as an evangelist. By the mid-1940s he had become known for his long-running revivals, which often lasted for weeks at a time. One marathon in Illinois went on for eighteen weeks straight, and a South Carolina revival continued for forty-nine consecutive nights. The climax of this early phase of Hughes's ministry came on September 27, 1948, when at age twenty-four, he preached to over 21,000 at a Full Gospel Youth Rally

Ray H. Hughes, president of Lee College, 1960-1966. (Courtesy of the PRC.)

at the Hollywood Bowl—two years before the Los Angeles revival that launched Billy Graham's career.[2]

In 1952 the church drafted Hughes into leadership, and he served as the denomination's National Sunday School and Youth Director until 1956, then as a state overseer from 1956 to 1960. Hughes never lost his passion for evangelism, remaining one of the church's most popular speakers at summer camp meetings. To see and hear Hughes in full voice, proclaiming the Christian plan of salvation and the Pentecostal call to sanctification and the baptism of the Holy Spirit, is to understand his passion, drive, and ability to hold an audience. His evangelistic experience and work with the church's youth caused the church to choose Hughes to save its failing college, despite having no experience in higher education or holding even a bachelor's degree in 1960.[3]

As Lee's president, Hughes faced daunting challenges. Foremost was the financial crisis caused by dwindling enrollment. When Hughes arrived on campus, he found only 294 full-time students, of which fifty were in the Religious Education and High School divisions. Morale was low, the physical plant suffered from deferred maintenance, and the school remained open through emergency infusions of church funds. The school's ongoing expansion plans and the demands of accrediting agencies further complicated the problem, as did the need to manage change in a manner that simultaneously attracted Church of God youth and stayed true to the church's traditions. Furthermore, Lee and its sponsoring denomination faced a reckoning on an issue they came to call the "racial problem."

Faced with internal and external demands, immediate and long-term pressures, and a rapidly changing national context, Ray Hughes emerged in 1966 as one of the two most successful presidents in Lee's history. In six years, he led the school into one its greatest periods of growth and advancement. Abandoning the broad variety of educational enterprises that had defined BTS and Lee, Hughes began to consolidate the school's offerings. He closed the faltering High School and Religious Education divisions and began preparations to merge the junior and Bible colleges into a single, four-year, liberal arts college that could win SACS accreditation. At first glance, these changes might suggest that the new president was following a track taken by many of his peers at struggling, church-related schools—saving the school at the expense of its religious traditions and identity, finding new students and faculty from outside the faith, and turning toward a secular model that would ensure accreditation, respectability, and funding. Nothing could be further from the truth. Hughes managed the transition, grew enrollment, expanded and improved the faculty, worked to meet SACS demands, and oversaw the construction of two new buildings, all while strengthening Lee's Christian, Pentecostal, Church of God culture.

Hughes brought to the presidency energy, optimism, drive, and a leadership style that leaned toward the authoritarian. His secretary, Evaline Echols, recalled that when he arrived, "it was like a tornado just blew in."[4] His strong personality played into a no-nonsense, hard-driving administrative style that could easily irritate others. But that was common in his era, and it produced results. He worked tirelessly for the church and Lee College, and he expected others to do the same. Hughes's correspondence is littered with invitations to speak at camp meetings and conferences—he accepted many, traveling the country speaking, preaching, and promoting Lee to Pentecostal and Church of God audiences. He also doggedly pursued the college's goals, looking beyond surviving the immediate crisis to building a modern college. "Onward to Six Hundred" was his first goal. Although some laughed at the idea, Hughes was undeterred and drove the school forward. Sometimes that meant pushing others beyond their comfort zone, and sometimes Hughes was forced to move beyond his own.

Table 3. Leadership Cadre Service, 1950–86.[5]

	GENERAL OVERSEER	PRESIDENT, LEE COLLEGE	ASSISTANT GENERAL OVERSEER	EXECUTIVE COMMITTEE	PRESIDENT, SCHOOL OF THEOLOGY
James Cross	1958–62	1966–70	1954–58	1954–62	
Wade Horton	1962–66, 1974–76		1960–62, 1968–74	1960–66, 1968–76	1975–76
Charles Conn	1966–70	1970–82	1962–66	1952–56, 1962–70	
R. Leonard Carroll	1970–72	1952–57	1964–70	1964–72	
Ray Hughes	1972–74, 1978–82	1960–66, 1982–84	1966–72, 1976–78	1966–74, 1976–82	1984–86
Cecil Knight	1976–78		1970–76, 1982–89		1976–82

Hughes's arrival also marked the ascendancy of a new generation of leaders in the Church of God that included Charles Conn, R. Leonard Carroll, James Cross, Wade Horton, and Cecil Knight. These men served in the church's top offices, rotating in and out of seats on the Executive Committee as well as serving as general overseers, assistant general overseers, and presidents of the denomination's seminary.

These six men shaped and defined the Church of God for over two decades. Four of them served as president of Lee, two on their path to general overseer and two with experience as general overseer. Church leadership had direct personal experience with the challenges and opportunities facing the school, and Lee's presidents likewise understood the currents, politics, issues, and challenges facing the church. Together, these men's popularity in the church, close-knit personal relationships, and common vision provided continuity and ensured the college and denomination would work in concert. Some, especially Charles Conn and Cecil Knight, represented moderate, progressive voices that sought to ease the denomination away from the strict codes that governed appearance and behavior, while still holding fast to the church's core commitment to Pentecost and holiness. Others, most notably James Cross, Wade Horton, and R. Leonard Carroll, represented the traditionalist wing of the church that was willing to improve academics but not at the cost of strict holiness standards.

As Lee progressed through the 1960s, four themes emerged: growth, identity, accreditation and desegregation. Historians, given their belief in a multiplicity of interdependent variables, shy from separating such themes. For this period, however, the narrative may be best served by doing just that, at least in part. Growth and Lee's identity are so closely entwined that they shall be taken together in this chapter. The next chapter will consider the paths toward accreditation and desegregation. Those two narratives run parallel to one another throughout the decade, ending with the admission of African American students in 1966 and SACS accreditation for a consolidated, four-year liberal arts school two years later.

In 1960, the most pressing issue Hughes faced was critically low enrollment. His answer was a recommitment to Church of God traditions and improved marketing to draw Pentecostal students to the campus. He rejected the idea that the enrollment crisis could be resolved by looking outside the church for new students, arguing that "If we endeavor to be liberal enough to attract a number of outsiders—I mean by that, those not of our faith—then we will for the most part lose those who are looking for a Church-of-God-centered school. . . . [W]e cannot expect to build Lee College from outside people. Therefore, if we are to exist, we must be distinctively different. We must be a strong Church of God, holiness, pentecostal [sic] school."[6] Despite Hughes's views toward "outsiders," part of his success in rebuilding enrollment came from attracting those very students. Only a year after Hughes's departure, President James Cross acknowledged that the school had been attracting an increasing number of recruits from outside the denomination. In a private letter, Cross wrote, "I am sure you are bearing in mind that as the school grows there will be more of those who are non-Church of God in Lee College. In fact, last year 22 percent of those who attended Lee College were not Church of God people. While we want them to be Church of God, we cannot force upon them our way of life. We can only ask that they respect our teachings and uphold those things which we love and cherish."[7]

The denomination's holiness traditions were increasingly tested by church members, both on and off the Lee campus. Even in the late fifties, church progressives began challenging holiness codes, and in 1958 one part of that code defined the traditionalist-progressive battle lines: the wedding ring. The Church of God had long forbidden its members from wearing jewelry, including wedding rings. The 1915 General Assembly passed a rule "against members wearing gold for ornament or decoration;

such as finger rings, bracelets, earrings, lockets, etc." In 1930, the assembly reaffirmed the rule, allowing for the expulsion of members who refused to conform. Progressives challenged the rule on several occasions, which resulted in some missionaries gaining permission to wear wedding bands. However, leadership rejected an energetic attempt during the 1942 assembly to allow engaged or married women to wear rings. At the stormy 1958 General Assembly, the church amended its rules to allow married men and women to wear wedding bands, but not before a dramatic confrontation over the issue.[8]

The decision was a major victory for progressives, but traditionalists felt it represented a liberal wedge into church culture. As a result, church leadership appointed a three-man commission to draft a resolution on holiness for consideration at the 1960 General Assembly. Chaired by Charles Conn, the commission wrote a statement that avoided any attempt to carefully define the parameters of the holiness culture. Rather, the statement reaffirmed a broad commitment to holiness principles and called on members to focus on their own lives, not the choices of others.[9]

For a time, the defense of Lee's holiness standard was aided by relative harmony with the broader culture, but that accommodation began to crumble in the mid-1960s, when the church's holiness standards started to contrast markedly with the popular culture. At the 1964 General Assembly, General Overseer Wade Horton preached that the nation was in crisis marked by crime, alcoholism, racial tensions, and international crises, but "perhaps the swiftest slide toward absolute moral degradation is the fleshly and sinful desire for bodily exposure.... Short shorts, tight-fitting slacks, and bikinis are already in vogue.... One can only wonder what will happen next."[10] In the face of rising hemlines, long hair for men, and short hair for women, the Church of God recommitted itself to traditional holiness standards—and that meant, of course, that Lee College did as well.

Throughout the 1960s, Lee presidents personally responded to any suggestion that the school was drifting from its Pentecostal roots. Their correspondence is peppered with letters refuting claims that Lee students wore makeup, went to high school football games, wore sandals, bared their shoulders, or otherwise violated holiness standards. When challenged, the presidents responded aggressively, investigating specific charges and assuring church members that they would enforce "God's standard for His people in this world."[11] In one letter, President Hughes reassured a worried pastor that Lee was theologically orthodox. He was "not in sympathy with this spirit of compromise that exists in many of the Pentecostal schools" (although one wonders what school he believed might have so erred). To further reassure the pastor, Hughes played a trump card, claiming that all full-time Lee faculty had the ultimate mark of God's approval: the baptism of the Holy Spirit.[12]

President Hughes saw the threat of outside influences, but argued that "we must be patient with those who are not members of our church. . . . Some will be saved, others through association will leave off the make-up, and all concerned will be helped."[13] Of course, the presence of non-church members offered presidents a ready-made excuse. When asked about non-conforming students, the presidents might reply that there was a Baptist on the team, choir, or club. The Church of God, however, did not have that excuse in its own pews. As Hughes wrote to one pastor, "There is one thing that you and all of those in the Church of God must remember, and that is that we did not raise these young people, nor did we set their standards of living. They are Church of God members who came to us from Church of God pastors and are typical of most Church of God young people."[14] Hughes believed that "Lee College exists for the Church of God and extension of the kingdom of God; therefore, it becomes our responsibility not only to teach our students how to think, but what to think as it relates to the Church of God."[15]

Holiness standards and Spirit-filled faculty cannot explain the remarkable turn-around Hughes engineered in the early sixties. A number of factors contributed to his ability to more than double on-campus enrollment in six short years. The growth could be written off as part of an overall increase in enrollment at private colleges and universities during the sixties. However, while national enrollment grew by 39 percent (1,459,000 to 2,041,000), under Hughes Lee tripled in size from 344 to 1081.[16]

One might also attribute this growth to the school's newly accredited junior college (1960 by SACS) and Bible college (1959 by the AABC), but the college worked to close both those divisions, not expand them. In his role as denominational historian, Charles Conn argues that the Church of God's 1962 Report on Christian Education demonstrated a renewed commitment to higher education in particular. Conn, along with Cross, Hughes, and two others, recommended that the church focus its efforts on two goals: sponsoring a single, four-year liberal arts college and sponsoring a school of theology. Both would be housed at Lee.[17] Denominational support was also a key component to Lee's rebound. The church had long been a booster, financial supporter, and recruiting ground for the school. However, there is little evidence to indicate that another round of public support from church administrators made any real and immediate difference in enrollment.

In 1964, an updated neon sign for the space age proclaimed that Lee was "a campus of Christian Scholarship."

In the end, President Hughes deserves the lion's share of the credit for the resurrection of the college. Upon taking the presidential post in January 1960, Hughes laid out his program to breathe new life into the campus. He planned to promote Lee at summer church camps, during on-campus "teen-age days," through alumni and current students, by setting state recruiting goals, and through its traveling choir.[18] Hughes used his formidable speaking skills to boost the school at church gatherings—and having worked with the youth for four years, he had good instincts in reaching them. He was aided by Lee's singing ensembles, especially the Touring Choir, later Lee Singers, which traveled extensively and served as the school's most important ambassadors to the church and broader public. The school also revised its branding, abandoning the well-worn "God's School for God's Business" with "A Campus of Christian Scholarship." And, with the alumni association, the school even produced a recruiting film, "Decision for Destiny," which traveled with recruiters to church and camp meetings.[19]

Most importantly, Hughes built on the tradition of state-themed days for visitors to Lee, such as Georgia Day or Louisiana Day, by holding an all-encompassing College Day in 1964.[20] For College Day, later known as Lee Day, Hughes invited prospective students and their families to campus for a day or two of carefully planned events designed to bring them back in the fall. Lee Day allowed the college to put its best foot forward—grounds tidied, a full program of events in place, and Hughes at his persuasive best. The event also made it possible to correct misperceptions about the students, faculty, facilities, and programs by bringing students, parents and alumni to a campus that was—at least for two days—crowded with people and full of energy. The first College Day took place on April 25, 1964, with over twelve hundred high school juniors and seniors in attendance. The event included campus tours, individual meetings with faculty, an address from the president, a dinner banquet, and concluded with a religiously focused youth rally. College Day was so successful that it became a Lee tradition that continues to introduce prospective students to Lee's culture, campus, and people more than six decades later.[21]

After a year in office, Hughes took advantage of steady increases in enrollment to advance a number of agenda items which made the school more attractive. He extensively renovated the gymnasium, then went about modernizing the school's appearance from the adjacent Lee Highway. He started by razing the grand, but dated and hard to maintain, Old Main building, which was the last remnant of Centenary College and Music School, which operated from 1885 to 1929. He replaced it with the Higginbotham Administration Building (1963), then oversaw the construction of the much-needed Beach Science Building (1965). Additionally, Hughes strengthened library holdings and encouraged ongoing professional development by faculty seeking advanced degrees. As is so often the case, success bred success. Increased enrollment, new buildings, better salaries, and strong morale brought positive energy to the campus. There developed a new sense of what was possible and the ability to think hopefully about the future.

Hughes had taken on a great deal during his six years. In doing so he had worked himself to the point of exhaustion. The job of pulling the college back from the brink of failure had stretched him to his limits. Hughes had promoted the school, raised money, and defended the college against traditionalist criticisms. As will be detailed in the next chapter, he also advanced the process of SACS accreditation process and struggled with the question of desegregation. He did all of this while also earning three college degrees. He finished his bachelor's degree at Tennessee Wesleyan in nearby Athens, and then earned a master's and a Doctor of Education degree from the University of Tennessee at Knoxville—all in six years. Always the evangelist, Hughes also preached every Sunday night at Lee during the school year, and he regularly preached at state-wide camp meetings in the summer (for each invitation he accepted, he turned down several others). As if this was not enough, Hughes directed the denomination's weekly radio show, *Forward in Faith*. In 1966 he left Lee and was elected assistant general overseer, which was considered a stepping stone to the general overseer's seat.

When Hughes resigned, the church chose a former overseer, James A. Cross, to lead Lee College. Cross, the son of a Church of God pastor and administrator, had attended BTS, served as a pastor and evangelist, and at age twenty-four was selected as a state overseer of Nebraska. From 1950 to 1954, Cross served on Lee's board of directors. He then was chosen as an assistant general overseer. Four years later, he was elevated to general overseer, a position he held until 1962. Like so many presidents before him, Cross had little formal education, but he was deeply committed to the Church of God and to the college as an integral part of the denomination. Charles Conn describes Cross as popular, cautious, fair, consistent, respectful of opposing views, and conservative.[22] Those qualities were an effective follow-up to Hughes's burst of energy. As president, Cross brought an even-handed, if tight-fisted, consistency to the campus. Lee's growth in enrollment plateaued, but the school consolidated its structure, completed its accreditation process, admitted its first African American students, improved its faculty with new doctoral hires, and built two new dormitories, Hughes Hall (1968) and Cross Hall (1969).

As Lee grew under Hughes and Cross, several developments came to further define the school's identity. The first was the elevation of musical ensembles to a place of greater prominence. Since the founding of the Bible Training School, music had been valued, primarily as an important tool for evangelism. In 1930, the school gave musical training a new emphasis when it hired Otis McCoy and opened a distinct music department. BTS ensembles became a regular feature at any significant Church of God gathering, making the program an important part of the school's outreach and promotion. By the time the school moved to Cleveland and rebranded in 1947, Lee College had a thriving music program that offered lessons to both Lee students and residents of the surrounding community. In 1968, when Lee consolidated its various educational enterprises in preparation for SACS accreditation, the School of Music offered a Bachelor of Music Education and a Bachelor of Arts with emphasis in applied music or church music.[23]

The arrival of a dynamic new personality on campus provided a spark that elevated the music program and secured music's place as one of Lee's cultural pillars. Delton Alford joined the faculty as the chair of the music department in 1962. He represented a new generation of Lee faculty. He was raised in the Church of God, attended Lee's junior college, received a bachelor's degree in music from the University of Chattanooga, and earned a master's degree from Florida State. When he arrived at Lee, the school sponsored the Campus Choir and the more selective Touring Choir. Led by A. T. Humphries, the Touring Choir started a tradition of extensive travel, which served the church and promoted the school. Alford rebranded the choir as the Lee Singers and over the next thirteen years toured with group, elevated the music program, directed the choir for the denomination's *Forward in Faith* radio program, and made time to earn his doctorate from Florida State.[24]

It is hard to overstate Alford's importance in elevating music's place at Lee. What John Wooden did for basketball at UCLA or Bear Bryant did for football at Alabama, Delton Alford did for music at Lee. At age twenty-five, he inherited an established music program with a long history of sending vocal ensembles to sing at church events. By the time he departed, he had cemented vocal music as a cornerstone of the school's

Delton Alford, the founder of Lee Singers.

The Lee Singers, 1965.

identity. The change started with Alford's creation of the Lee Singers in his second year on campus. He brought to the group youth, energy, and a new standard of excellence. "For me," one student said, "Dr. Alford was like a bucket of cold water in the face. Here I'd been singing all my life, with everybody telling me how good I was.... [W]hen I auditioned, I really showed him my stuff; and the more I sang and kept watching the shadows creep over his face, the less stuff I had. Doc said that he could see ... a little potential if I'd work. So I worked."[25]

The Singers toured extensively. On a typical weekend they would board a Trailways bus on Friday, sing that night, and then make two more engagements on Saturday. Often driving overnight, they would sing at one church service on Sunday morning and again that night before another overnight drive back to campus. Alford and his singers often had just enough time to drop their bags and change clothes before making it to Monday morning classes.[26]

Alford expanded the scope of the Singers' tours, taking them across the nation, to the Bahamas, and in 1967 to Europe. The European tour established the Singers as the top ensemble in both the college and denomination. The *Evangel* covered the trip extensively, from the Singers' departure on an Alitalia DC-8 from New York's Kennedy Airport to their return to the states. Eight pages of detailed reporting were given to the Singers' concerts. Testimonials by participants boosted the high-profile group—and the music program they represented—to the college's most important constituency.[27] The trip set a new international standard for the college's traveling groups, ultimately making travel abroad a regular part of their program. The Singers' time in Europe also became the foundation of Lee's later study abroad program. One young singer, Paul Conn, was deeply influenced by the experience and, later, as Lee's president, he made the opportunity for students to study abroad a centerpiece of his administration.

The Singers were joined by the Ladies of Lee and the Evangelistic Singers as Lee's ambassadors. Mary Smith Morris founded the Ladies Choir in 1964, and in 1968 director Roosevelt Miller rebranded the ensemble as the Ladies of Lee. Miller led the group for seventeen years and shaped a culture that included extensive travel, original compositions, and a repertoire grounded in sacred music. Evangelistic Singers (EVS) was formed in 1969 by five African American students who had joined Pioneers for Christ. While accepted by the evangelistic group, they were not always welcomed in white congregations and neighborhoods. The next year, students formed the Evangelistic Crusade Team, which preached and sang the gospel in black churches. The team's ensemble, which became known as EVS, sang Black Jubilee, sacred, and contemporary music. They later expanded their ministry to include campus events that highlighted black culture and history.[28]

A second important element of campus culture was the growth of fraternities and sororities. At Lee these clubs did not affiliate with national organizations and were called social service clubs, concessions that allowed the school to argue that their fraternities and sororities were not stereotypical Greek clubs that might undermine the college's Pentecostal tradition. That argument was partially true, for while the clubs largely operated within the bounds of Lee's culture, they were exclusive and required participation in common Greek rituals, including pledging and, sometimes, hazing.[29] Lee's sororities and fraternities sponsored campus-wide events, provided networks that generated student (and future) school leaders, and assumed a prominent place on campus. The first men's club, Upsilon Xi, was founded in 1962, and was soon followed by Alpha Gamma Chi (1963) and two women's clubs: Delta Zeta Tau (1964) and Sigma Nu Sigma (1966). By 1978 the four clubs combined for around 125 members, or 12 percent of the total student population. Surprisingly, the denomination endorsed the clubs, publishing positive stories in the *Evangel* that highlighted the Greeks as ministry and service oriented.[30] Relationships formed in the clubs created social networks that would

The ladies of Delta Zeta Tau, 1965. (Courtesy of the PRC.)

extend into members' professional careers, and the prevalence of club members in Lee's administration guaranteed their support at the highest levels.

A third culture-defining development was the introduction of varsity sports, which played an increasingly important role in students' lives. When the school published its first yearbook in 1942, it featured a five-page section dedicated to music. The only mention of athletics was a pair of snapshots featuring men playing sandlot football in street clothes during a free hour in the afternoon schedule. Five years later, the publication had a separate section dedicated to intramural sports. This section featured men's softball teams named the Tigers, Hurricanes, and Codgers (no doubt the older men of the religious education division), as well as women playing table tennis and volleyball during physical education classes. By 1957, intramural sports at Lee had taken on many of the trappings found at other colleges. Students played on uniformed men's and women's basketball teams, and cheerleaders worked the sidelines. Non-uniformed, but no less competitive, men's and women's softball and volleyball teams also represented the various school divisions. As one student saw it, "Sports hold a special interest for everyone at Lee College. Being one of the most important activities on campus, they have a definite and integral place in intra-school relations."³¹

Lee sponsored its first varsity sport, men's basketball, in 1959. They began play as the Lee College Dragons, but the next year settled on the Vikings as their mascot and hosted their own invitational tournament.³² Students also had a strong interest in football, fielding three intramural teams that played in full pads through the 1962 season. Despite student love for the gridiron, the church was wary of the sport, as it resulted in too many injuries. Therefore, basketball, not football, would be the

The holiness uniforms of the Lee College Vikings and neighboring Bryan College, 1966. (Courtesy of the PRC.)

school's premier sport.³³ Initially, the college's varsity basketball team played a mixed schedule of local colleges and amateur teams, including church and VFW teams. Basketball gained traction when the church, with reservations, allowed Lee to join the newly formed, eight-school Southern Christian Athletic Conference (SCAC) in 1967. When granting permission, the church's Executive Committee warned that Lee's participation "must be controlled carefully enough that the holiness image of the Church is not hurt."³⁴ The following year, the college joined the newly formed National Christian Colleges Athletic Association (NCCAA) in time to compete for its championship in 1968, but new athletic initiatives stopped there. When asked, church leadership rejected the board of directors' request for Lee to sponsor intercollegiate baseball.³⁵

Winning teams build their own fan bases. During Lee College's first conference season, the basketball team generated enormous energy and excitement on campus. Under former player and third-year coach Dale Hughes, the 1966–67 Vikings averaged over one hundred points a game on their way to a 14–0 conference record, Lee College Invitational crown, SCAC conference tournament championship, and a 29–2 overall record.³⁶ The next year the team pushed the bar even higher. They again won their own invitational before defeating Tennessee Temple in a playoff game to claim the conference championship. The SCAC title sent the team to the 1968 NCCAA tournament in Detroit, where the Vikings won three straight games by an average of twenty points on their way to claiming the national championship.³⁷ The next two seasons cemented basketball's place at Lee, with two conference regular season and tournament championships, a combined 48–14 record, and two third-place finishes at the NCCAA tournament.³⁸ In eleven seasons under coach Hughes (1964–1975), the team compiled a 254–65 record, won seven conference championships, took the conference tournament title eight times, and won NCCAA national championships in 1968 and 1973.

As the school moved to intercollegiate competition, it developed new rivalries and intensified old ones. None burned hotter than the annual series with the Crusaders of Tennessee Temple College. Only thirty minutes away, Chattanooga-based Temple was a fundamentalist, independent Baptist school with three times Lee's enrollment. The school had a strong basketball program, but had a difficult time defeating its smaller, upstart neighbor. The hotly contested games caused fans to pack the gym two hours before tip-off, and the schools moved the games off campus in an attempt to dampen emotions and find larger venues to fit all the fans. By the early 1970s, overly zealous fans prompted the administrations to agree to a two-year hiatus in play before resuming in the fall of 1973. A year later in Chattanooga, a hard foul on Lee star Larry Carpenter cleared both benches, and Temple threatened to withdraw from the conference. Administrators smoothed the waters, and the Lee-Temple rivalry remained the defining contest on both schools' sports calendars for another two decades.[39]

One final potential shaper of campus culture demands consideration—the Vietnam War. President Lyndon Johnson introduced ground forces to the war in southeast Asia in 1965 and dramatically escalated American commitments there. At the same time, he changed the Selective Service System's draft policy so that it threatened college deferments. This resulted in a marked increase in student protests against US involvement in the war. Although antiwar students were a minority on American campuses and active protesters were a minority within that group, popular history remembers a period rife with campus protests, marches, sit-ins, teach-ins, and occasional violence. A typical interpretation comes from PBS's *American Experience*, which explains that students "marched by the thousands, on campuses from coast to coast. At different times they chose different targets. . . . But the students all acted from a common belief that the Vietnam War was wrong. As that conflict escalated, the protests grew in strength, and some turned violent."[40] Nothing in the PBS narrative is incorrect; however, it exaggerates the breadth and depth of protest on American campuses. In reality, nearly two-thirds of institutions did not report anti-war protests during the 1967–68 school year.[41] Contemporary press coverage of protests at prominent universities and ongoing academic interest exaggerate the prevalence of anti-war protests on college campuses.[42] That does not suggest that students blindly supported the war. As evidence, a November 1969 Gallup Poll showed almost 70 percent wanted to de-escalate the conflict. However, the statistical rarity of protests and violence, when compared to media reports of the time, suggests a skewing of the popular narrative.[43] Scholars have shown that, like most things, campus protests defy stereotypes. In the South, Joseph Fry found that protests "began later, were less numerous, and attracted fewer participants than those in other regions."[44]

The Church of God, a largely southern denomination, did not officially oppose or support the war. Instead, the church supported its members in uniform, and the ministry of its chaplains echoed the denomination's generally conservative tone. At the 1968 General Assembly, the church honored soldiers with a tribute that mixed patriotic themes, service to the church, and mourning for lives lost.

> In the darkened amphitheater ... the haunting strains of taps dolefully tolled an exequy. It was an accolade to the chaplains and fighting men of the Church of God. While one spotlight illuminated a golden American eagle painted on a huge banner, another spotlight strikingly highlighted four chaplains of the Church of God who stood at attention in tribute to the church's sons who are in the military service of their country. ... As the people stood in the darkened auditorium, muffled sobs of grief could be heard as ten thousand hearts reverently pondered what these young men represented.[45]

On campus, the Vietnam War took its toll but did not spark open dissent. Instead the story of the war is muted at Lee, its most poignant echoes found in desperate parents' letters to the administration, begging for help in securing deferments for their sons. Hughes did what he could to keep students from having to "fight a useless war." Cross empathized with parents. In 1968 two of his sons had completed service in the Air Force and a third was deployed in Vietnam. Yet, all that Hughes and Cross could officially do was write letters to the Selective Service Board requesting deferrals from service.[46] As Don Aultman, vice president for academic affairs, put it, in the face of the "blood, violence, and death in Vietnam," Lee's best response would be to offer faith-based hope for a better, brighter future.[47]

As Lee celebrated its fiftieth anniversary, the future looked bright. Only eight years previously, the college teetered on the edge of failure, but under the leadership of Ray Hughes the college rebounded. Enrollment tripled from 344 to 1,058 students, and those students enjoyed a campus with new buildings and a vibrant student culture. Academically, under Hughes and Cross the credentials of faculty improved markedly, library holdings increased, and the four-year program stood on the verge of accreditation. Notably, these improvements took place without loosening ties to the Church of God or lessening the commitment to the denomination's Pentecostal, holiness tradition. It might be trite to say that the sixties were a decade of change, but at Lee those years were indeed transformational.

Chapter 5

ACCREDITATION AND DESEGREGATION

The revival of Lee's fortunes was remarkable, but as the transformation took place Lee also came to grips with two critical issues: race relations and the linked problems of consolidation and accreditation. With deep roots in the racist Jim Crow South, the denomination was segregated, as was Lee College. Church and school leadership followed and understood the demands of civil rights activists who demanded racial justice, however, even those sympathetic to racial justice issues acted with caution when faced with a majority that resisted change. As a result, Lee reluctantly responded to African American demands for justice; the school missed an opportunity to apologize for past discrimination or advocate for change.

Unlike desegregation, an accredited, four-year liberal arts college was an important institutional goal for Lee's leadership. Accreditation held the promise of validation for the school, but Lee struggled to meet SACS standards for bachelor's-granting institutions. Administrators found that conforming to secular standards threatened to change Lee's educational culture, especially the continued operation of the Bible College. At the same time, those standards helped them improve the school's quality and allowed them to consolidate the school's diverse educational enterprises into a single liberal arts college.[1]

In 1960, the church appointed a committee to study the educational arm of the church. This included not only Lee, but also the Northwest Bible College in Minot, North Dakota, the West Coast Bible College in Fresno, California, the International Bible College in Moose Jaw, Saskatchewan, Canada, and diverse Bible training programs associated with missionary efforts abroad. Lee also experimented with extension campuses, taking over operation of the Mid-West Bible Training School in 1962 and a second extension in Phoenix, Arizona. Extension campuses offered the traditional religious education model, but also included an opportunity to earn credits in the Bible college division. The experiment was short-lived but again showed the church's entrepreneurial view of education. In late 1962, the Church of God's Coordinating Committee on Education produced a report arguing that Lee College should "sponsor one four-year Liberal Arts college, strong in education and the arts . . . and to sponsor a strong school of theology and Christian training."[2] The recommendation was a clear endorsement of Lee as the centerpiece of the church's educational aspirations and showed a renewed interest in a liberal arts bachelor's degree. However, it left open the question of how the school could continue to operate, reconcile, and accredit so many educational enterprises under the Lee College name.

By 1963, Hughes, in harmony with church leadership, was systematically preparing the ground for a fully accredited liberal arts school. Sometime in 1964, Hughes and Academic Dean J. H. Walker met with SACS representatives and informally discussed the move to a four-year liberal arts program. Their advisors noted several areas that needed attention. Fortunately, the administration had already addressed some of the problem areas in a five-year plan that promised—and eventually delivered—three new buildings (science, administration, and dormitory), 20,000 new books for the library, land purchases, and a steep increase in enrollment. Further, the school encouraged faculty to work toward advanced degrees, employed a development director, conformed business practices to industry standards, and worked to bolster the endowment. The aspirational plan concluded with the goal of opening a four-year liberal arts school in 1967.[3]

Following a year-long self-study, Lee's drive for accreditation hit full stride in 1966. In January, Hughes and Walker traveled to Atlanta to meet with SACS representative, Dr. Bell. Hughes hoped to win initial approval to enroll a junior class in the fall 1966 semester, but Bell dampened that hope by noting four major areas of concern. First, he pointed out the difficult relationship between the Bible and liberal arts colleges. He indicated that the two schools should not share the same campus (an idea one SACS representative called "preposterous"). Rather, he suggested the Bible college become a department in the liberal arts college. Second, Lee needed to increase expenditures per student from the $200 minimum for junior colleges to at least $300. Third, Lee had not met the SACS standard of having at least one faculty member with a doctorate for every major offered. And finally, Lee needed to grow its endowment and build new student housing.[4]

These recommendations gave Lee's administration good cause to improve the quality of the institution, but the proposed closing of the Bible college renewed the traditionalist-progressive debate at Lee. Hughes thought it was logical to "transplant the Bible college program . . . into the liberal arts college." However, he recognized the move could be seen by some as weakening the school's commitment to biblical studies. Furthermore, as he informed Bell, the Church of God wanted to operate both programs, and the college had no jurisdiction over such policies.[5] The Bible college's future reflected larger tensions between the school's various divisions. In a faculty meeting devoted to the future of the Bible college, Christian Education instructor Martin Baldree concluded that the Bible college was unlikely to survive on the same campus as the proposed liberal arts school. He warned that without the Bible college, the school's Christian identity would weaken. Hughes responded with a lengthy and wide-ranging speech to the faculty. In part, Hughes addressed the school's "divided interests and emphases," pointing out how those divisions could create "a tendency to discredit what another is doing by feeling that his field of endeavor is not quite so important." Hughes did not, however, offer his thoughts on the liberal arts school, accreditation, or the future of the Bible college.[6]

Ultimately, Ray Hughes would not see the accreditation question through but left the final resolution to his successor, James Cross. Cross came to Lee with no experience in higher education, but he had the qualification that mattered: a lifetime of ministry experience in the denomination.[7] As had been, and would continue to be, the case, the church valued loyalty and orthodoxy in its presidents and administrators, not academic credentials. In part, this was a logical outcome for a denomination that had only just begun producing academics. There simply were not experienced candidates in the church. More importantly, the church continued to view the school as a division of its broader ministry, which made the college a logical destination for its top leadership. Fortunately for both church and school, Cross proved an able president who saw to completion three major undertakings begun by Hughes: SACS accreditation, consolidation into a liberal arts college, and desegregation.

In the fall of 1966, Lee closed its junior college and admitted third-year students to its new liberal arts college which consisted of six departments: education, music, social sciences, business, natural sciences, and language and literature. The administration hoped SACS would extend initial accreditation by the time the first class graduated, but December 1967 brought devastating news. SACS informed Lee that a planned spring

1968 site visit would be delayed for a year. As a result, the first graduating class would receive diplomas from an unaccredited college. In explaining its decision, SACS cited old concerns about faculty credentials, library holdings, and the school's relationship with the Bible college. They also added new, faculty-related issues.[8] This was a major setback for the school, especially given the extensive efforts made to address deficiencies. The church had increased giving (from $129,000 in 1965 to $292,680 in 1970) to meet a SACS requirement that the school spend more per student. The administration had also been diligent in its efforts to recruit new faculty with earned doctorates and had extended generous sabbatical leaves for faculty pursuing advanced graduate degrees. Yet despite these gains, SACS raised new questions about the faculty, including tenure, salary levels, and academic freedom.

While deeply disappointed, Lee administrators put a positive spin on the delay and redoubled their efforts to conform to standards. As Dean J. H. Walker bluntly put it, "The cost of accreditation is expensive yet the alternative is unthinkable."[9] General Overseer Charles Conn agreed, stating that accreditation "is the responsibility we have today. We cannot ignore it, for the task is thrust upon us. We cannot defer it, for to fail now will retard our progress for years to come. We can only accept the responsibility and thank God for making it possible."[10]

The future of the Bible college presented a more difficult problem. The administration and board considered three paths forward. The first was to create a fully independent Bible college with its own campus. This was publicly promoted by the general overseer in February 1968, but then abandoned.[11] The second idea was to keep the Bible college alongside the new liberal arts school, which both SACS and the AABC rejected. The third option, creating a department of religion within the liberal arts school, was ultimately adopted.

Within the faculty and administration, strong divisions developed between supporters of the Bible college and those who aspired to a single liberal arts school. R. Hollis Gause, dean of the Bible college, led the fight to save his program. As late as January 1968, Gause promoted the Bible college in the *Evangel*, arguing that it produced graduates able to "present the Word of God in an effective manner—a manner that is acceptable academically, theologically, and spiritually."[12] Gause had the support of President Cross and, predictably, more conservative leaders in the Church of God. His best vehicle of protest, however, was found in a team of outside observers from the Accrediting Association of Bible Colleges.

Members of an AABC accreditation team provided a sympathetic audience for Bible college defenders during a 1968 visit. Informed by conversations with faculty, the AABC's post-visit report pulled few punches. It pointedly warned that Lee was forsaking its birthright by choosing secular accreditation at the expense of a traditional Bible education model. The AABC report predicted (correctly, as it turned out) that "the Bible college will before long become a fading memory in the annals of the denomination." Furthermore, it foresaw that the new liberal arts school, with its concern for SACS accreditation, "may be crowding out the Bible college program and leading the school away from its basic purposes." This transition would come sooner rather than later if the school increased enrollment from outside the faith. While evaluators conceded that there could remain an evangelical Christian spirit regardless of the chosen path, the AABC's final judgment was that "the school as a whole has departed from its original purpose; or perhaps more accurately, it has expanded its educational program so as to overshadow almost completely such purposes."[13]

The AABC report was scathing, but did Lee desert its original purpose by expanding its programs and leaving the Bible school model? If so, then the Church of God approved, for the school was tightly controlled by the denomination; it was not an independent actor. Lee may have abandoned its original mission of training pastors, missionaries, and Christian workers, but it had expanded its horizons to meet the changing needs of its Church of God constituency. President Cross understood why the church moved to a liberal arts model, writing, "I think we must recognize the fact that not all young people are called to be ministers, missionaries or musicians. I fully feel that God has called some to be schoolteachers, businessmen, and, in fact, every walk of life."[14] Rather than send its junior college graduates to other schools, the Church of God developed a broader definition of ministry and expanded its curriculum to meet that definition. Organizational changes, new programs, and the push for accreditation were not used to move the school away from its historic Christian, Church of God roots. While intentionally Christian schools often stray from their mission, it was not so at Lee.

If the AABC saw Lee as becoming more liberal, a SACS advisory committee saw things very differently. SACS's evaluation of Lee focused on academic standards, but did not neglect the school's unusual religious environment. "One who spends any considerable time on the campus will observe a pervasive and quite distinctive spirit of religious commitment among faculty and students, a spirit which sets them apart from common society in personal habits and attitudes. The discipline of the Church of God guides and controls personal conduct to an extent that would be oppressive, if not intolerable, to a college community not dedicated to this religious faith."[15]

The SACS report found this dedication admirable, and it understood that "the officials of Lee regard this attempt to gain accreditation as a matter of desperate urgency, not only within the College but also throughout the Church. A heavy blow to morale will be the effect of failure, and morale is particularly important to this institution which has survived and developed more on morale and faith than on cool calculation."[16] Though complimentary of the college, SACS insisted that Lee make significant changes to win accreditation. One was to gain a measure of independence from the Church of God in order to become a true liberal arts college. Predictably, the church resisted such separation, but they were willing to make cosmetic adjustments in order to win accreditation.

SACS's guidance bumped up against the church's vision for Lee at two particular points. The makeup of the board of directors was one such place. SACS wanted (or perhaps even assumed) a board of directors made up of members who could raise money. This was met with resistance from school administration and church leadership, both of whom were tasked with protecting church interests rather than being what they called "money men."[17] Another point of friction was Lee's definition of academic freedom, which SACS found highly restrictive. While the administration acknowledged that faculty needed a measure of intellectual freedom to allow an exchange of ideas, any such freedom had to operate within social and religious restraints imposed by the church.[18] Lee required its faculty and administrators—a few were not members of the denomination—to sign a pledge to abide by the Church of God's Declaration of Faith. In addition to common standards of Protestant Christianity, the declaration required faculty and administrators to, as part of their contracts, accept Pentecostal standards, including baptism with the Holy Spirit as evidenced by speaking in tongues. SACS reviewers found this level of doctrinal purity troubling to the point that they doubted any "genuine academic freedom exists at Lee College."[19]

The question of academic freedom had significant implications as, for the first time, SACS intruded into an area with the potential to undermine Lee's strong, sectarian identity. Lee's representatives agreed that limitations existed but argued that the faculty understood and accepted that a commitment to the church's doctrinal position necessarily limited their freedom. A reasonable measure of academic freedom, they reasoned, could still be found inside those boundaries.[20] Nevertheless, the board of directors approved its first statement on academic freedom in

1968, simultaneously adding the following new language in faculty members' contracts: "You further agree that your conduct will not be contrary to the standard of the Church of God and that you will refrain from propagating any religious theory or doctrine which is contrary to the established doctrines of the Church of God. You will work in harmony with the administration and faculty of Lee College at all times in achieving the spiritual, cultural, intellectual, and social objectives of the institution."[21] A year later, the board revised the contract again to make faculty acceptance of Church of God doctrine more—not less—explicit.[22] Any academic freedom, then, existed in careful defined parameters that did not meet the spirit, much less the letter, of the SACS report recommendations.

In March 1968, Lee's Board of Directors voted to end the fifteen-year-old Bible college by merging it into the liberal arts college.[23] The new school would operate with three distinct divisions: arts and sciences, religion, and education (Lee won approval from the state to start a teacher education program in May).[24] To dampen criticism of the consolidation, the board required all students to complete an eighteen-credit-hour religion minor, which became a standard talking point for administrators when they promoted, and sometimes defended, the new structure. The board, rather tardily, also hired Don Aultman as a new vice president and tasked him with overcoming the hurdles facing the transition.[25] A rising star in the church, Aultman had attended Lee, earned a doctorate at the University of Tennessee, served as the church's director of youth ministries, and been the president of Lee's alumni association. Despite misgivings about SACS approval of the new structure, the school crossed its Rubicon. In November, administrators informed SACS that they would not seek reaccreditation of the junior college program. Instead, they were staking the school's future on successful accreditation of the four-year program.[26]

This future seemed uncertain in 1968 when the university received devastating news from SACS; the association once again denied Lee's request to accredit the new college. Although desperate to reverse that decision, the administration saw no road forward until Delton Alford, chair of the division of Arts and Sciences, met with Don Aultman. In the school's moment of crisis, Alford told Aultman of an old associate, David Kelly, who worked at SACS. Perhaps Alford could contact Kelly and ask for advice?

It was already late in the afternoon, but Aultman did not hesitate. He asked Alford to set a meeting for that evening. Kelly generously agreed to meet the two men in his home. Aultman and Alford gathered their materials, drove to Atlanta, and arrived on Kelly's doorstep at nine that evening. With paperwork spread across the living room floor, the three men talked through the problem until deep in the night.

Aultman and Alford spent the night in Atlanta and were at the SACS offices when they opened at nine that morning. There they met with a second SACS representative, John Barker. Barker created a path for Lee to save its accreditation by giving Aultman and Alford a list of issues the school needed to address. If President Cross would sign a commitment to remedy them, perhaps something could be done. The two Lee representatives wasted no time getting the president's signature and returning it to Barker. Letter in hand, Barker took Lee's request to the accreditation committee for reconsideration.[27]

Over the next year the administration and faculty worked to satisfy the conditions set by SACS. One major reform was in faculty teaching assignments. Over the past decade the college had made great strides in adding faculty with doctorates. They recruited a handful of PhDs, but most of the improvement came from Lee faculty commuting to the nearby University of Tennessee and earning a doctorate in education. So, while reports showed an increasing number of faculty with doctorates, most of them taught in areas outside their degree specialization. Aultman took on the unpopular task of reassigning faculty, but he also led the way in meeting the other SACS requirements that made success possible.[28]

On December 3, 1969, Lee won accreditation for its new liberal arts college. Cross canceled classes for a day, and students, faculty, and administration celebrated the end of the five-year journey. Through those years, the college made enormous improvements in almost every aspect of its enterprise—faculty, facilities, endowment, and library, while streamlining an ungainly, complex educational conglomeration into a single liberal arts college. Lee's leaders accomplished all of this without compromising their commitment to its religious tradition. In fact, the school simultaneously won accreditation and renewed its commitment to conservative, evangelical, Pentecostal doctrines, and its Church of God constituency.

But those were not the only changes taking place. As Lee faced and overcame its accreditation hurdle, the college was forced to acknowledge, react to, and eventually accept social justice reforms demanded by a growing civil rights movement. Unlike the high-profile, sometimes confrontational integration of several flagship universities in the south (Meredith at Mississippi, Hunter and Holmes at Georgia, or Malone and Hood at Alabama), Lee's integration proceeded with little visible opposition in the community. Lee followed a pattern that may be more typical than those highly publicized examples with which historians are familiar. However, assessing Lee's integration against a norm is difficult because, as historian Charles Padgett notes, "Very little documentation exists of those quiet, successful experiments with desegregation on southern campuses."[29] At the same time, while many desegregation events were quietly successful, that does not mean they took place in uncontested environments. As Melissa Kean has ably demonstrated in her study of the desegregation of Emory, Duke, Rice, Tulane, and Vanderbilt, "to suggest that desegregation . . . was voluntary would be deeply misleading."[30] Ray Hughes, Lee College administration, and Church of God leadership actively sought alternatives to desegregation. Their acceptance of integration only came after the civil rights movement had transformed America's cultural and political landscape.

In 1963, both Lee and the Church of God began to consider the reality and immediacy of the desegregation question. That is not to say that the leadership had been unaware of the civil rights movement. They could hardly miss the marches, sit-ins, and integration of many public schools. Despite this, they only began to officially consider the issue that year. Much of their early effort appears to have been focused on avoiding meaningful integration. On August 12, 1963, the board of directors held a special meeting that immediately preceded a gathering of the Church of God's Supreme Council. The board unanimously approved a motion requesting guidance from the church: "Whereas the matter of integration of races at Lee College has come to the attention of the Lee College Administration and whereas the matter has far-reaching ramifications, be it resolved that we, the Lee College Board of Directors, respectfully request the Supreme Council to advise on behalf of the General Church as to the formulation of policy concerning the matter."[31]

Given that a segregationist policy was already in place, the board appeared to be asking for support for a more progressive policy. However, the Supreme Council's Committee on Colored Work delivered a report the next day stating that "it does not seem feasible to integrate our colleges in the immediate future."[32] Four days later on August 16, the Supreme Council drafted and approved a resolution calling for prayer on the matter, but argued that "Inasmuch as no local situation prevails that would call for immediate action at this time, we feel that it is not necessary for your committee to draft any resolution concerning the racial situation for public consumption." The council furthermore handed the issue back to the college. "[I]t will be left entirely up to the Lee College Board of Directors and the President to take whatever steps they deem necessary and expedient if you are confronted with a crisis relative to the abovementioned problem."[33] Instead of providing actionable guidance, the Supreme Council's response created a series of caveats and conditional clauses. Their response both stopped progress on integration and effectively passed responsibility to the college to act, should a crisis force their hand.

President Hughes's role in this decision-making is difficult to ascertain. On the one hand, he clearly influenced the board's decision to ask for guidance. On the other, he sat on the committee that drafted the denomination's response. (Here again we see the blurred line between church and college.) Sources on Hughes's attitudes are limited and fragmentary, but they suggest that he was reluctant, even resistant, to integrating the school, as well as individual churches.[34] In 1961, he informed a pastor that "the racial tension is very acute here at the present and will not permit us to admit Negroes."[35] At the same time, Hughes appears to have understood the changing racial landscape and wanted to position the college to respond, if necessary, to calls for integration.

In 1963 Hughes allowed seven African Americans from the Church of God to participate in a leadership training conference at Lee. There is no record of the reasoning that went into the decision to open the conference to black congregants, but both context and Hughes's correspondence suggest the decision was deliberate. Hughes appears to have followed the lead of schools like Vanderbilt, which integrated elements of its graduate schools before fully integrating its campus. Lee had no graduate programs, but an event like the leadership conference might have played a similar role. It would have allowed the college to desegregate an event, test the waters, and then move forward or backward based on the outcome. And as Hughes tersely put it, the experiment "had quite serious repercussions afterward."[36]

There is no in-depth record of the feedback Hughes received about the conference, but two letters suggest the range of opinions voiced. One letter to the president expressed the writer's shock to see black people on the college campus and in the leadership workshops. He had heard of Lee's "fine Christian background and principles, but my dreams fell when I saw the school integrated as it was." His concern was such that, despite his commitment to Christian education, he could not imagine sending his two children to Lee. He concluded his letter by warning "that the integration of Lee College would be a fatal mistake to the Church of God."[37] In contrast, some attendees found the presence of black attendees at the conference a positive sign. Bill Watson, the denomination's overseer for

Brazil, hoped that "in the future it can be reported that Negro students are accepted in all departments of Lee College." Watson grounded his opposition to segregation in his personal convictions and hoped that Brazilians with a "high degree of colored blood" would be able to attend Lee.[38]

In his replies to these letters, Hughes was both cautious and conflicted. To the supporter of integration, he was unsure when Lee would open its doors to black students, stating that race relations were "a real problem in this part of the country."[39] To the segregationist, he made assurances that there were no black students enrolled for the fall semester. More tellingly, in a personal letter he wrote, "I . . . do not believe in integration as such, but I do believe in desegregation. By this I mean that all people should have equal rights and equal facilities. Although I do not feel that is the best thing, yet it seems that the integration of our schools is inevitable."[40] Here he seems to take the position held by some segregationists in neighboring Georgia: that races should be separate but that African Americans deserved truly equal facilities. It is no wonder then, that Hughes was loathe to fully integrate Lee, believing that "when integration does come that it will have to be on a limited scale, for a time at least."[41]

In November 1963, the university received a communication from the United States Commission on Civil Rights. The commission was preparing a directory of admission policies and practices of Tennessee's higher education institutions. Specifically, the directory was concerned with admission policies and practices as they pertained to race. Attached was a list of public and private universities in Tennessee and their admissions policies. The report showed that Lee was not the only private college in Tennessee resisting integration—a reality made more evident by the complete absence of a category for schools that had achieved some measure of proportional integration.

Table 4. Segregation Status of Tennessee Colleges and Universities in 1963.[42]

	PRIVATE	PUBLIC
Segregated: All White	19	0
Segregated: All Black	1	1
Desegregated: Predominately White	13	6
Desegregated: Predominately Black	5	0

It is worth noting that desegregation in these years rarely meant real integration. Admitting a handful of minority students was enough to achieve desegregation, but creating a culture of racial diversity took more work. In such a culture, students are seen as individuals to be treated with dignity and respect, rather than members of a group intruding on the majority culture. As 1964 began, both Lee and the Church of God were far from the mark, but instead were considering how to create a Lee College extension in Atlanta for African American students.[43]

Then on May 26, the Church of God's Supreme Council took action. With Lee's board in attendance, the Council approved a motion to integrate all educational institutions of the church. On the surface, the policy and its attendant preface integrated Lee, but that was not the case for three reasons.[44] First, the Council and Lee's Board of Directors clearly believed that opening an Atlanta extension for black students qualified as integration.[45] Second, the Council chose not to send the policy change to the General Council. Doing so would open the integration question to the scrutiny of the broader church membership.[46] Third, the decision had no impact on the segregated operation of Lee College. This hesitancy to desegregate was not limited to the college but was part of the Council's broader confusion on how to engage integration and civil rights. A subcommittee considering a resolution on race relations was equally unsure how to proceed. In a statement to church leadership, they noted the race issue was both a cultural and moral problem. As such, it created a dilemma for a denomination that accommodated a segregated culture, but saw the strength of the civil rights movements, anticipated federal action on the matter, and had just passed a motion to integrate its educational institutions. Faced with such issues and a church that had yet to come to grips with the changing nature of race relations, an exasperated committee asked the Supreme Council to take up the matter as a whole and provide for "at least some inkling" as to the Council's mind on the matter.[47] The leadership, however, resisted change and instead continued to explore a segregated school for African Americans.[48]

On July 2, Congress passed the landmark Civil Rights Act of 1964. Title VI of that act stated that "No person in the United States shall, on the ground of race, color, or national origin, be excluded from participation in, be denied the benefits of, or be subjected to discrimination under any program or activity receiving Federal financial assistance."[49] Lee depended on federal aid. Among the most important were indirect support through students who benefited from work study programs, veteran's benefits, and other federal aid. His back against the wall, Hughes had to act. Within a month Hughes requested that the denominational leadership allow him to formally, and publicly, announce Lee's integration. Hughes proposed a policy that spoke directly to the issue of race: "Applications for admission to Lee College are considered on the following basis: Readiness for effective participation in the life of our Christian college community, character, ability, academic foundation and personality. Applicants being best qualified on the consideration of the combination of these factors will be admitted without regard to race or color."[50] The policy might have, if adopted, effectively opened the doors to all students. However, the policy's language also would have allowed for selective discrimination against people of color based on subjective qualities such as character or ability.[51] While the archives include no formal response to Hughes's request, on July 29 the Supreme Council canceled plans to "integrate" Lee with an extension for African Americans in Atlanta. Instead, church leadership returned once more to the idea of a separate, black Bible training school—a measure preferred by the white overseer of the denomination's black churches.[52]

In the end, it may have been the financial balance sheet that pushed the school and the denomination to the tipping point. Hughes made the completion of a new science building a central feature of his plan to create a reenergized and relevant Lee College. An important piece of the funding puzzle came from the federal government. Under the conditions of the Civil Rights Act, that money was suddenly in jeopardy.[53] A January 18, 1966, letter from the Federal Housing and Home Finance Agency required Lee to show evidence that it was in compliance with the provisions of Title VI. Otherwise, the college risked losing funding. The college immediately and disingenuously assured the government of compliance, citing the May 1964 resolution passed by the Supreme Council, which read:

> Moved, seconded and carried that the measure passed by the Executive Council [of the Church of God] on the integration of Lee College be included in the minutes as a matter of record:
>
> INASMUCH AS the Holy Scriptures clearly set forth that God hath made of one blood all nations of men (Acts 17:26), and it is the declared will of Christ that Christian men be one in Him (John 17:20), and
>
> INASMUCH AS the Church of God believes in the human dignity of man, which is his inherent right as the image of God, and
>
> INASMUCH AS we believe that all races should have equal opportunity in the Church of God:

WE THEREFORE RECOMMEND That the educational institutions of the Church of God be open to all those who meet its spiritual, moral, and educational standards and who can satisfactorily pass its normal admission requirements.[54]

While long in coming, Lee's use of a twenty-month-old resolution was not a public statement meant to announce to the church, the community, or the nation that it had abandoned systematic discrimination against African Americans. Nonetheless, in reporting this private document—which at best might be considered a hope for the future and at worst a contingency against exactly such a moment as took place—Hughes and Lee College turned a corner. Now the school needed to back its position paper with the admission of black students.[55]

The statement was also important in that it provided a clear, faith-based rationale for desegregation that cited the authority of Scripture, not federal law. That stance, which was held by the church's governing body, soon translated to the Church of God as a whole. On August 15, 1966, the last day of its annual general assembly, the denomination passed a resolution that officially desegregated all branches of the church by eliminating any race-based, colored designations.[56] If federal funding provided the proximate cause for Lee's desegregation, then the school's decision had the same effect on the denomination.[57]

When it came to actually admitting black students, Lee's administration took a cautious approach that allowed desegregation to take place with little fanfare.[58] In the fall of 1966, three African American students enrolled at Lee. Deborah Bacon was a local woman who lived at home while attending classes. For Lee administrators, she was likely the per-

Deborah Bacon, Larry Cox, and Hazel Edwards, who desegregated Lee in 1966.

fect student to help incrementally break the color line by separating the classroom from dorm life. Bacon could selectively participate in campus life, minimize race-based tensions, and enjoy the support of her family and Pentecostal congregation. The record is less clear about Larry Cox. Another local enrollee, he dropped out of school after just a few weeks, but would return to Lee the following year.

Hazel Edwards, however, was a different case altogether. An ambitious student and Church of God member from New Albany, Mississippi, Edwards first considered attending Lee during a state meeting of black churches. There she heard a white official from the church extolling the virtues of Lee College, and he invited those gathered to apply to Lee. Edwards took him at his word and sent in an application, complete with her black-and-white school picture. She was excited when Lee admitted her and made plans with her family to make the trip to Cleveland. Upon arrival, Edwards found a different environment than what she expected. She had been unaware that Lee had been segregated until she arrived on campus—one can imagine her surprise. Equally surprised was her white roommate and the Lee administrators, who were unaware that Edwards was black. She was fair skinned and straightened her hair; the application did not ask about race; and the black-and-white photograph was ambiguous. An embarrassed Dean of Women informed Edwards that her roommate's family was unhappy with the situation. Undeterred, Edwards bravely stated that she did not intend to move in order to accommodate their racist attitudes. The dean proceeded to clear the room next door, the roommate moved her belongings, and the two women had adjoining accommodations for the entirety of the school year.[59]

While Bacon and Edwards opened the door for a small cadre of African American students, Lee administrators made no attempt to encourage real integration or more broadly recruit black students. In the early years of desegregation, the college remained far more reactive than proactive on matters of race. Rather than publicly acknowledge the new students, the college attempted—and largely succeeded—in quietly adjusting to the new reality. Between 1966 and 1971, thirteen African American students attended Lee College, a school that was desegregated, but not fully integrated. These students lived on campus, attended class, and joined student organizations. Yet there remained a degree of social separation between them and their white peers. White students generally accepted them and acted with civility toward the newcomers, but with so few black students it was easy to maintain social and physical separation.

Despite the college's history of avoiding integration, a handful of examples indicate the college's sincere desire to commit to protect individual students, especially when those students were directly threatened, insulted, or made to feel unwelcome. In one particularly charged incident, three students dressed as Klansmen led two white students dressed as slaves into the school cafeteria to publicize a "slave auction" to raise funds for a college club. The incident was racist, insulting, inflammatory, and threatening; it was also part of a tradition of students using blackface in college-sanctioned events and spaces. In response to the incident, six students wrote in protest to school President Cross. These students argued that tolerating such events not only violated the Christian mission of the campus but allowed racism to "circulate freely on . . . campus" and fostered student unrest. In reply, Cross personally apologized on behalf of the school. He then forced the club to make a public apology to the students in the college chapel service.[60]

The decision to accept, and even scholarship, African American student-athletes gives another point of reference in Lee's desegregation. Integrating sports teams allowed Lee to access a new pool of talent, but it also removed black students from the bounds of a carefully monitored campus environment and placed them in a highly visible space. Lee alumni and Church of God members who wrote the college president about the hemlines on uniforms could not fail to notice black players wearing those same uniforms. Two of those athletes, Mike Linley and Alfred Barnett, came to Lee in 1967 and 1968, respectively, to earn their degrees and play basketball. Barnett chafed at Lee's restrictive holiness standards and left after two years, but Linley graduated in 1971. Linley's memories of Lee are broadly positive. A Baptist from Georgia, Linley was introduced to Lee by his family's insurance agent, a Church of God member, who drove Linley to campus for a visit and workout with Lee's basketball coach. When offered a scholarship, Linley jumped at the chance. He had already been accepted to a junior college, but he could not pass up the opportunity to earn a four-year degree.

In remembering Lee, Linley recalled the black face incident in the cafeteria, but he emphasized a different set of experiences. When on the road with his team, Linley repeatedly was denied service at restaurants and motels, but his coaches and teammates pushed back against this prejudice. In each and every instance, the vendors either served all the players or the team loaded up and went elsewhere. At least within this community, personal relationships backed by institutional will trumped segregationist traditions and signaled the school's commitment to educate and protect individuals, regardless of the color of the skin.[61]

At the same time, Lee did not publicly acknowledge, much less celebrate, its steps toward racial inclusion. Non-Lee sources such as newspapers and Church of God publications allowed the school's integration to pass unnoticed. Even more telling, Lee's surviving internal communications and reports ignored the landmark enrollment of Bacon, Cox, and Edwards. The school newspaper did not report on their arrival; the *Vindagua* yearbook published their photos, but nothing more; administrators made no effort to explain or even note desegregation. One might conjecture that the college's stealthy approach might have been to avoid antagonizing segregationists in the church's ranks, but even in protected, private reports and communications, desegregation was not noted, much less applauded. When President Hughes made his last yearly report to the church, he mentioned the air conditioning in the science building, alumni support, and evangelistic endeavors among students, but failed to even mention the decision to integrate. Minutes from Lee faculty meetings also show an absence of any official dialogue about integration. And when President James Cross made his first progress report to denominational leadership, he neglected to identify integration as a sign of progress. In fact, Cross did not mention it at all, choosing instead to report on teacher training, plans for a new dormitory, and the success of campus revivals. So, while the college desegregated, it did little to influence the broader culture.[62]

Another landmark was reached in 1970 when Mollye Edmond, Hazel Edwards, and Pauline Washington became Lee's first three African Americans to earn bachelor's degrees. None appears to have sought her role as civil rights pioneers at the small, southern, sectarian school. Instead, they wanted an opportunity to earn a degree from a college that

Mollye Edmond, Hazel Edwards, and Pauline Washington, the first African Americans to earn bachelor's degrees from Lee.

valued their Pentecostal faith. Their quiet resolve in no way reduces the importance of their taking a first step toward racial justice at Lee but does speak a great deal to the strength of their character, perseverance, and commitment to their education.

As for Lee, the school's dedication to creating safe spaces for its new black students should be recognized and appreciated. Yet the school and its sponsoring denomination missed a pair of major opportunities to take a proactive stand for racial justice. When given the chance to take a leadership position in the fight for integration, school and denominational leaders instead chose a cautious, hesitant, and even resistant approach. Nearly a decade after the *Brown* decision, Lee not only remained segregated, but its governing bodies appeared more committed to finding ways around desegregation than finding the courage to take a moral position. When leadership finally acted, they did so in response to a culture shift, a shift due to the efforts of African Americans themselves. Only after marches, violence, sit-ins, lawsuits, and legislation marked the path of the civil rights movement did administrators act. Even when they responded, they did so with caution bordering on timidity. So, while the college desegregated its campus and supported individual black students, it missed an opportunity to apologize, to lead, to advocate, and to celebrate the school's first step toward a more just, welcoming, and truly integrated campus.

Chapter 6

PRESIDENT CHARLES CONN AND THE 1970S

Lee College entered the 1970s as a small, sectarian, Church of God school, standing at the door to a new era. Under President Charles Conn, Lee would enjoy moderately progressive leadership and began conforming to higher education standards. And, while students adopted some of the more liberal values of American society regarding dress, appearance, and lifestyle, the campus remained conservative in comparison to its secular peers. For most of the decade, Lee enjoyed stable enrollment and access to new economic resources. These allowed the administration to expand programs, raise salaries, and better the campus community. At the same time, the college remained a department in a division of the church. As such, it neither had institutional independence, nor did it seek such freedom.

In 1970, church leadership named Charles Conn the sixteenth president of Lee College.[1] He brought to the office the usual resume. A graduate of the Bible Training School in Sevierville (where he met and married Edna Minor), Conn quickly rose into the top leadership of the church. At the age of twenty he served as the head of Sunday school and youth in Louisiana. After pastoring six years in Missouri, he moved to Cleveland in 1948 to work at the Church of God Publishing House. Four years later, Conn became chief editor, a position he held from 1952 until 1962. As editor, Conn brought a balanced, moderate voice to church publications. He also made time to write *Like A Mighty Army*, the official denominational history. First published in 1955, his carefully composed, triumphalist chronicle remains the definitive work on the church and helped win him an honorary doctorate from Lee. Conn went on to author several books on theology and Christian living, including *Christ and the Gospels* and *Pillars of Pentecost*. Like many before him, Conn served on the executive committee and as assistant general overseer before being elected general overseer of the church in 1966. When term limits moved him from the overseer's chair, he followed in the footsteps of his predecessor James Cross and became president at Lee.

The fifty-year-old Conn had no academic credentials, but he did have a longstanding interest in education and engaged the life of the mind. Unlike many of his peers in the Church of God, Conn loved secular art, culture, literature, and music. He collected a personal library of thousands of books, and read the classics, history, and the great works of literature. He appreciated the Red-back Hymnal's gospel hymns, but also loved classical music. As his son recalled, while the church leaders immersed themselves in Bible study, theology, and ministerial preparation, "they didn't care anything about Shakespeare, and they didn't care anything about Beethoven, and they wouldn't know Eratosthenes from Moliere, but Dad cared."[2]

A moderate in a conservative denomination's progressive wing, Conn was a central figure in the denomination's efforts to desegregate and to expand the church's international reach. He spearheaded its ministry to service members and served on the board of directors of the National Association of Evangelicals. As general overseer, Conn stated that the church's "foremost [educational] goal [is] to achieve that academic excellence which we have been pursuing for so long."[3] Throughout his twelve-year tenure as president, Conn proved capable, moderate, and forward-looking. He consistently advanced academic programs, oversaw construction projects, and secured new sources of funding. He also led the denomination and campus through a difficult period in which traditionalists decried the intrusion of secular culture into the church.

Whereas Ray Hughes easily managed the cultural landscape of the early 1960s, President Conn and his predecessor, James Cross, faced more difficult times as secular culture challenged church teachings in novel ways. There was the sexual revolution, counterculture, civil rights movement, Vietnam War, new left, women's rights movement, environmental movement, Watergate scandal, gay liberation, and the *Roe v. Wade* decision. Combined, these cultural movements and moments created what historian Alan Brinkley calls a crisis of authority.[4] A new emphasis on personal freedom, liberation, and choice undermined the collective traditions of the church. Historically, each generation tested the norms of their parents, but the period spanned by the Cross and Conn presidencies (1967–82) was marked by an especially strong impulse to directly challenge conventional standards.

Colleges were the epicenter of a generation's reaction to institutional restraints. Free-speech zones, sit-ins, and demonstrations became a central part of campus stories from the period. Lee College, however, saw little of the popular narrative play out on its campus. The only real campus protest took place after a church official intervened to save his child from disciplinary action. The students reacted by setting a fire in a dorm lobby, harassing administrators with late-night calls, and vandalizing the president's office. In general, however, the Christian, evangelical, fundamentalist, Pentecostal families that chose Lee's peculiar environment understood the rules before they came. Those wanting a different experience had dozens of public and private options that allowed greater freedom and experimentation. The administration knew that the nation was changing, but Lee was a conservative place, with a conservative constituency. Students may have stretched dress codes and traditions that governed personal relationships, but they otherwise accepted assumptions underpinning American socioeconomic order and Church of God culture.[5]

Despite the conservative campus climate, church traditionalists did not have to look far to see the encroaching secular culture. They believed that threat was best judged by church members' susceptibility to the lure of worldly amusements and inappropriate clothing. More specifically, they measured the broader church's holiness by the dress of its women. Traditionalists believed the appropriate standard was always the most conservative measure of the leadership's generation. For men, the bar was low. They were to present a clean cut, wholesome appearance. This meant a collared shirt and short hair and no shorts or jeans. The standard for women, however, was much higher. The denomination's rules desexualized their appearance by limiting exposed skin, the use of makeup, and jewelry. In each passing generation, men could easily conform to cultural norms. The changing preference for cuffs, lapels, pleats, tie widths, and collars rarely clashed with Church of God standards, but women's styles regularly crossed boundaries as the trend of receding hems, sleeves, and necklines revealed more of the woman under the clothing.

At no time was the conflict between fashion and holiness more evident than the late sixties and the seventies. As tight-fitting jeans, miniskirts, pantsuits, short shorts, and halter tops came into style, denominational leadership rose to the challenge. In 1967, they issued a formal plea to pastors. Pastors were to reinforce holiness standards of dress and modesty. "In the wake of an avalanche of sex-oriented fashions which threatens to infiltrate the Church of God . . . [the Executive Council must] speak out against these godless fashions. . . . Generally speaking, the Council strongly suggests that low cut, sleeveless dresses, and the so-called miniskirts, shorts, slacks, jeans, etc., in no way meet the Bible standard of modest dressing and, consequently, have no place in the wardrobes of Godly women and girls."[6] In response, Lee's dean of women led special chapel services, during which female students "were lectured on modesty, they were further given instruction on how to properly be seated without undue display of their limbs."[7] In a separate meeting, the dean of men lectured male students on holiness standards, but the university's focus was clearly on female modesty.

When Charles Conn became president, he stepped onto a campus at the center of the holiness debate. The 1970 school catalog stated that Lee was "a Christian College operated under the auspices of the Church of God. Lee College is firmly committed to the conservative, evangelical and Pentecostal position of its sponsoring denomination."[8] Twelve years later, the language in the catalog had not changed, but President Conn brought a more progressive understanding to the issue.[9] Though committed to modest dress and godly behavior of students, Conn's view of holiness ran much broader. He explained his view at a symposium, hosted by Lee, that examined the Church of God's Declaration of Faith.

Conn took the podium to give his views on the seventh tenet in the declaration, that "Holiness [is] to be God's standard of living for His people." He argued that holiness "has become a catch word that too many use for some personal bias, some personal prejudice, or the notion of the moment." He believed that a fixation on worldly attire and amusements blinded some to a host of less visible, more socially acceptable, manifestations of worldliness. These included unjust business practices, ambition, envy, materialism, anxiety, selfishness, lust, and a desire for power, honor, and recognition. Moreover, he argued the progressive view that it was not enough to hate evil and separate oneself from the world. Rather, holiness demanded love of God, neighbor, and righteousness. To the traditionalist, Conn said that to "pick out one or two parts of it [holiness] and let that become the sum and substance of the worldly menace are fooling themselves and are not doing justice to the church." Instead, he called on the church to remember that simply following church rules did not make a person holy. Holiness, he argued, started with Christ's presence in the heart, and that power worked its way into all corners of life. It could not be limited to the traditionalist dress code. "We should not and we must not prostitute the word holiness by making it something shallow and superficial, or something narrow and something dogmatic, or make it

President Charles W. Conn and his secretary,
Evaline Echols. (Courtesy of the PRC.)

something that is provincial, something that does not belong to our time, because this is the very nature and the very essence of God."[10]

The traditionalists took issue with the progressives' emphasis on principles and love of neighbor. In hotly contested meetings at the 1974 General Assembly, conservatives sought to expand, or "amplify," the church's holiness standard by more precisely defining unacceptable dress and behaviors. One such amplification read, "That the public dress of our female members exclude the wearing of shorts, slacks and dresses or skirts shorter than three inches above the knee, and that male members refrain from wearing sleeveless or see-through garments in public." The progressives countered with measures moving in the opposite direction. They not only rejected the more precise standard but also offered amendments to revise existing language to emphasize principles and avoid parsing the fashions of the day. Regarding dress, they proposed "That our members seek the adornment of a meek and quiet spirit and be guided in their aim by the Biblical pattern of modest personal appearance." In the end, both sides won victories and suffered losses. The progressives passed measures "That our members dress according to the teaching of the New Testament" and that women have long hair and men have short hair. The traditionalists pushed through admonitions that forbade swimming with members of the opposite sex. They also warned "Against members attending movies, dances, and other ungodly amusements," and urged them to exercise extreme caution when choosing which television programs to view.[11]

Back on campus, Conn's progressive view of holiness caused him to moderate the college's stance on some external appearance standards—if not the more important behavioral holiness standards. The catalog still included prohibitions of specific behaviors: stealing, cheating, lying, smoking, drinking, and petting—to name a few.[12] Chapel was held only three times a week, but roll was carefully taken by assigned seats. Students even won the ability to go on unchaperoned dates. Most expulsion and discipline records have been withdrawn from the university archives, but a number slipped past censors and suggest that students regularly strayed outside the boundaries set by the church. The record shows that while Conn loosened some rules, serious offenses resulted in disciplinary action. Violations included visiting a house of ill-repute, dating without permission, peeping-tom activities, pornography, homosexual acts, stealing test stencils, repeated dancing and dating, prowling, and getting married without written permission from the president (in loco parentis indeed!).[13] So while serious violations like drug use were cause for expulsion, a shorter skirt or a touch of makeup were not. Even the president's secretary, Evaline Echols, dared to wear a little jewelry. When Conn noted it, she told him that women had been restricted for so long that they "were just trying to make up for lost time."[14]

The pages of Lee's *Vindagua* yearbook provide ample evidence of changing standards on campus. In 1965, students looked fashionable, if perhaps overdressed for a college campus. Women wore skirts and dresses (never sleeveless), the men slacks and collared shirts. The overall effect was like a scene from *The Donna Reed Show*. Five years later, the students maintained their clean-cut appearance, but men sported impressive sideburns and women's hems crept well above the knee. By 1975, students moved beyond the most generous holiness boundaries. Men had hair to the shoulder, wore beards, and for a costume party one sported makeup modeled on the popular band Kiss. Women now wore pants in-

In the 1970s, Lee College students increasingly challenged Church of God holiness standards.

stead of skirts or culottes when playing sports, and some of their hemlines reached mid-thigh. Church leaders no doubt sighed in relief as hems dropped, men's hair shortened, and a more conservative attire returned in the 1980s.

Lee's varsity sports clearly illustrate the changing standards. Lee had long played a wide range of intramural sports. Only in 1959 did the school field its first varsity team—men's basketball. While Lee's early teams played without conference affiliation or championship competition, their attire is worth noting. When the Lee Vikings took the court, they did so in special, holiness-appropriate uniforms. These included calf-length pants and sleeved jerseys. Lee administration even went so far as to provide matching uniforms for visiting teams. The pants lengths slowly crept upward, but Lee presidents could reasonably say that the team did not wear shorts. By the end of the 1970s, the teams competed in standard uniforms, wearing what the president justified as longer, soccer-style shorts.

Lee added three new men's sports in 1975: baseball, cross-country, and tennis.

At the same time, the administration kept a wary eye on court challenges to Title IX of the Education Act of 1972. Title IX prohibited federally funded educational institutions from discriminating based on sex. For years, Lee avoided the requirement to offer women equal opportunities to play sports, but in 1978, the law compelled the school to either drop sports altogether or field the college's first varsity women's basketball team. By then, the men's team had left their holiness-inspired pants behind. The women's uniforms, though not a throwback to the college's original holiness standards, combined sleeved jerseys with shorts. Aware of the potential conflict, yearbook editors took care to only publish photos cropped at the waistline.[15]

As might be expected, church traditionalists did not appreciate Conn's softening of holiness dress and behavior rules. In response, they waged a vigorous letter-writing and whispering campaign against worldliness on campus. The accusations were many: women in mini-skirts and pants, men with long hair, alcohol and drug use, homosexual behavior, smoking, and women wearing jewelry.[16] One critic lectured the president, implicating him in a "diabolical plot to affect our college." The pastor suggested that the president read *Skimpy Skirts and Hippie Hair* to correct his thinking on holiness (Conn assured him that he was familiar with the book).[17] Another pastor summed up the traditionalist criticism, writing "the rules at Lee do not mean a thing. They are not being carried out."[18]

In 1976, the constant drumbeat of criticism caused General Overseer Wade Horton to sharply question Conn's commitment to a strong holiness standard. Horton wrote, "I thought at the beginning of this new year you were going to be somewhat more strict than Lee College had been before," even if it meant a loss of students. Specifically, Horton noted photographs in the local newspaper showing Lee students in immodest clothing, "hippie-style hairdos on men," basketball players in shorts, and a faculty member's wife in pants. Conn wrote an extended reply. The school, he said, had "the greatest degree of responsible behavior and conformity to regulations that I have ever known of at Lee College." The letter reminded Horton that Conn had authored the 1960 Church of God reaffirmation of holiness and was sponsoring a "holiness week" and "heritage week" to teach students denominational distinctives. Still, he asserted that "there has never before been a perfect solution to worldliness in either the college or church. I am nevertheless looking for a workable solution."[19] Conn kept Horton's confidence. The next year

Conn was asked to chair a committee recommending policy "regarding unseemly or unbecoming conduct, adultery, fornication and homosexuality" among church members.[20]

Conn, who as general overseer approved the 1967 Statement on Modest Apparel, was not leading the young people of the church to perdition. Rather he recognized that the denomination's churches had become more liberal than the school. He stated, "The only students we have at Lee are those who come to us from our churches. The kind of background they have at home is usually the kind of background they bring to the school with them."[21] In picking his battles on the appearance of students, Conn chose a middle ground between the conservative standards of the last generation and the more permissive view held by many families whose children arrived at Lee with longer hair and shorter skirts. In some areas, Conn made concessions to culture. He reasoned that modesty would be better served if women wore pants, not skirts, to intramural games and P.E. classes. Despite official guidance from the church that dresses should be no higher than two inches above the knee, photos of students show that Conn did not make such particulars a point of emphasis on campus.[22] In other areas, such as chapel attendance, he held a stronger line. When students staged a de facto revolt against chapel attendance policies, Conn did not waver. He suspended fifteen offenders and retained chapel as a central feature of Lee's campus culture.[23] And, when a female staffer went beyond the pale by modeling "hot pants" at a charity fashion show, she was fired.[24]

Under pressure from left and right, Conn held the uncomfortable position of many moderates, but he managed it well. Campus may have seemed a den of iniquity to traditionalists, but the administration put significant limits on employee and student dress and behavior. The church hierarchy knew students chafed at school regulations. General Overseer Horton wrote one student, "I know that young people of this day are caught between the trends of the world . . . and the Church of God that stand for the old-fashioned holiness concept."[25] Conn reported that Lee lost students because of its rules. Despite this, he believed he had found the right balance between tolerance and legalism. Regarding the dress code, he wrote, "Naturally, we do not regard this as having the significance of our morals and spiritual codes. We understand that it is a matter of taste and image."[26] His dean of students, Paul Duncan, explained Lee's position this way, "I have tried quite diligently to emphasize that one cannot legislate spirituality and that there is a difference between college rules and Bible standards. . . . We have attempted to avoid the extreme rigidity of certain groups and the unconcerned, 'do your own thing' approach of other groups."[27] In the end, Conn liberalized the dress and appearance regulations on campus in a way that angered traditionalists and frustrated many students. His moderate, progressive approach emphasized principles over regulations and kept pace with the values of most Pentecostal families.

For much of Conn's presidency, enrollment at Lee grew steadily. Lee's particular mission and constituency, combined with a large pool of high school graduates and Lee's improving academic program, made for interesting admission policies and retention numbers. By the early 1970s, admission to the school required a high school diploma with a C average or a seventeen on the American College Test (ACT). In practice, the college admitted almost all students who applied, denying only fifteen applicants in the 1971–72 school year. At first glance, the low admission floor could be viewed as a necessary policy created and sustained by the needs of a cash-poor school. Lee was heavily dependent on enrollment dollars, with student charges accounting for 75 percent of gross income from 1967 to 1972.

However, the school had always welcomed almost any student to its campus. From its first class of students, when BTS admitted fourteen-year-old Jessie Capshaw, Lee maintained minimal, if any, admission standards. Students arrived from disadvantaged families, eager to train for ministry but sometimes functionally illiterate. This open-admission policy, at least on paper, was slowly revised as the school opened its junior college, won accreditations, and consolidated into a single liberal arts college. However, an open-door mentality was imbedded in the school's institutional DNA. Lee's flexible admissions policy gave almost any Church of God person the chance, for at least a year, to attempt college—and in 1971, over 90 percent of students came from within the denomination. As might be expected, the policy resulted in a high rate of attrition after the first year, but school leaders believed that a change to this policy would violate the principles on which the college was founded.[28] In the end, Lee experienced slow, steady growth in enrollment from 1970 in 1,108 to 1,394 in 1979.[29]

The school's budget rose from $2.1 million for the 1970–71 year to $3.8 million for 1979–80—an increase that kept pace with high inflation rates of the period.[30] Three sources of outside revenue bolstered the school's finances. Lee began to win grants from private foundations, and they tapped into new federal funding. At the same time, President Conn successfully lobbied the Church of God for increased funding. Financial backing by the church had long been a critical part of Lee's balance sheet, and from 1967 to 1972 the church provided 19 percent of gross income. Between 1970 and 1982, church funding jumped from 14 to 27 percent of the school's budget.[31] The boost in giving was not the result of a new church commitment to improving the college. It came after Conn persuaded the church to provide cost of living increases, a decision church leaders approved for its ministers in 1972. During years of high inflation, the church contribution rose generously to keep pace with the rising cost of living. Conn also secured the school's first significant foundation grants: $50,000 from the Kresge Foundation and $100,000 from the Benwood Foundation.[32]

The school had long received indirect federal aid from its students, most notably through veterans' benefits and student work-study programs. Between 1967 and 1972, indirect government assistance accounted for 18 percent of the college's income, but direct assistance was rarely sought and not readily available. When the 1970s arrived, new funding and programs made grant dollars both plentiful and accessible. Conn took advantage. In 1972, he corrected a misunderstanding with government officials, who believed that Lee would not accept federal funds. He indicated to the state's higher education commission that Lee would indeed accept federal dollars, and that the college was in the process of building married student housing with U.S. Department of Housing and Urban Development (HUD) assistance.[34] After two years

Table 5. Budget and Income Sources.[33]

YEAR	CHURCH OF GOD CONTRIBUTION	GRANTS	TUITION AND FEES
1973–74	$696,946	$196,380	$1,025,803
1974–75	$440,000	$184,991	$1,193,250
1975–76	$511,329	$305,727	$1,329,904
1976–77	$567,328	$310,944	$1,478,979
1977–78	$722,489	$302,069	$1,805,388
1978–79	$850,600	$324,064	$1,912,898
1979–80	$978,315	$436,060	$2,134,450
1980–81	$1,073,045	$955,210	$2,466,560
1981–82	$1,365,323	$497,067	$2,655,480

of negotiation, Lee won its first Title III grant of $100,000. Title III of the Higher Education Act of 1965 helped schools "become self-sufficient and expand their capacity to serve low-income students by providing funds to improve and strengthen . . . academic quality."[35] The award jumped to $171,000 in 1978 and then to $393,000 in 1980. In 1980 the school won its first Title IV grant of $67,987 to provide financial assistance to students. Altogether, in the period 1976–81, the school received $1,170,320 in direct federal funding, as well as indirect funding from the College Work-Study Program, Pell Grants, veterans' benefits, and other federal support for students.[36]

Over time, most colleges build endowment funds that provide scholarships, fund operations, serve as a reserve, fund faculty chairs, and keep tuition low. When Lee moved to Cleveland, it had almost no endowment and major donors were not in the offing. The school's students hailed from families with limited means, and after graduation they worked in ministry, as educators, and in other jobs with modest incomes. Though supportive of the school, these graduates could not write large checks, but the lack of an endowment was not the fault of the graduates. It reflected the church's belief, no doubt grounded in the limited resources of its first generation, that God provided for needs as they appeared. Additionally, given the church's strong, consistent belief that Christ would soon return, building an endowment for the long-term health of the school hardly seemed necessary. When BTS or Lee did undertake fundraising campaigns, that money almost exclusively paid for new buildings or for the school's purchase of the Sevierville and Cleveland campuses. In 1968 Lee had an anemic endowment of $11,800. By contrast, nearby Maryville College's modest endowment grew from $1.7 million in 1930 to $3.6 million in 1968.[37]

When Lee began to pursue accreditation in the 1950s, the absence of an endowment did not escape the visiting committees.[38] The church's answer illustrated its handling of internal finances and the degree of control the church held over the school. In response to SACS recommendations, the church promised $1 million from the Church of God Publishing House to jumpstart the college endowment. Through the years, the Publishing House steadily grew the fund but withheld the money from the college. On paper, it finally delivered $750,000 in 1972, just in time for a follow-up visit by SACS.[39] In reality, the money was not a cash gift, but a promissory note. On the balance sheet, Lee's endowment had an asset in the note, but Publishing House executives were slow to hand over the funds. After making $200,000 in payments, they successfully lobbied the church in 1974 to renegotiate the note. The new note stated that payments would not start again until 1985, with a maturity date of 2000.[40] Even then, church leaders regularly borrowed money from Lee's endowment to pay for other church initiatives and operations.[41]

The school's lack of independence from the denomination was a major SACS concern. In response the church provided nominal authority to Lee's board of directors, while retaining all real decision-making power in the church's executive committee, which appointed the board and approved all major administrative decisions. Notably, the membership of the executive committee underwent its eleventh, and final, revision in 1968 to include the general overseer, three assistant general overseers, and the general secretary treasurer.

That same year the denomination created the Church of God Board of Education to oversee its various educational enterprises. By 1976, these included Lee College, Northwest Bible College (North Dakota), West Coast Bible College (California), East Coast Bible College (North Carolina), International Bible College (Saskatchewan, Canada), the Spanish Institute of Ministry (Texas), and the Indian Bible Institute (New Mexico). After the reorganization and consolidation of Lee College led to SACS accreditation in 1969, one might suppose that the school gained some measure of distinct identity, if not freedom. Yet the church held the college close. As a nod to SACS, denominational leadership modified language to give Lee's board, not the church executive council, final approval for new presidential appointments. Nevertheless, this did not change practice. The board might choose, but the executive council would confirm new presidents.[42] When the school printed materials in 1974 stating that "Lee College is an independent four-year liberal arts institution," General Overseer Wade Horton asked President Conn to remove the word *independent*, which had "always been objectionable to Church of God ministers and pastors." Conn complied.[43] In fact, during Conn's twelve-year presidency, the lines dividing church and school became less—not more—clear as the school again began sharing resources with other Church of God enterprises.

Conn's building campaigns clearly reflected the school's identity as a division of the denomination. After briefly considering moving the campus to a new site, Conn chose to improve the existing campus instead.[44] His first major project was the construction of a new auditorium to serve both church and school constituencies. The college had outgrown the auditorium purchased as part of the Bob Jones campus in 1947, and the church approved the construction of a new facility at the 1972 General

Assembly. Finished in 1977, the $1.7 million, 1,800-seat multipurpose auditorium hosted chapel services, musical performances, church functions, and cultural events. A year later, the college board named it the Charles W. Conn Center for Performing Arts and Christian Studies.[45]

In a related development, the denomination opened a separate seminary, the School of Theology, in 1975. Lee's board of directors first raised the possibility of a seminary in 1965, when the school was attempting to reconcile its Bible and liberal arts colleges. Charles Conn, while serving as general overseer, renewed a call for a seminary in 1968. He then pressed the issue at the 1970 General Assembly, stating, "We must now turn our attention to a proper seminary.... The question is not whether the youth of our church will pursue learning—they will; but the question is, Shall the church satisfy their need or shall they turn elsewhere?"[46]

The call for a seminary was not generated by a lack of confidence in the qualifications, work, or theology present in Lee's religion program, but was rather the goal of progressive elements within the church. Traditionalists often derided seminary training. They labeled it "cemetery training" that impeded the spontaneous spiritual development associated with Pentecostalism. In response, some sought to resurrect the old Bible training school model in the new seminary. This element looked to the Moody Bible Institute as a model, an institution where church members could receive ministerial training without meeting any academic entry standards.[47] Progressives successfully redirected this impulse by creating Bible institutes, which taught enrichment courses, while continuing to promote a graduate seminary. Serious planning for the seminary began in 1972, and it opened three years later. Named the Graduate School for Christian Ministries, the seminary was led by the general overseer, Wade Horton, as president and Hollis Gause as dean. Initially housed in the remodeled College Arms apartment building, in 1980 the seminary moved to new quarters in the city block separating the denomination's press and the college. Later renamed the School of Theology, the seminary shared facilities and adjunct faculty with the college.

Conn, the church historian, keenly felt the need to preserve the denomination's heritage. In 1971 he created the Pentecostal Research Center (PRC), a special collection of denominational history. Conn hoped to grow the center into the denomination's archive, while also making it a resource for the study of the broader Pentecostal movement. As the collection grew to fill the converted attic of the library, he promoted a plan under which the college and seminary would jointly develop a new facility to house Lee's library and an expanded PRC. The denomination enthusiastically embraced the $2.5 million project, and the Hal Dixon Foundation boosted the effort with a generous gift. After five years of planning and construction, the Pentecostal Resource Center opened in September 1985. The building housed the college's William G. Squires Library and the Hal Bernard Dixon Pentecostal Research Center. Both were under the administration of head librarian Frances Treadway Arrington, who served in that position from 1978 to 2002, with David Roebuck taking on the job of the director of the research center in 1997. Though the college and seminary shared ownership of the new building and both sets of students utilized its resources, Lee absorbed most of its operating costs.[48]

Even while Lee remained deeply emmeshed in the church, Conn and the faculty began creating internal academic structures that more closely resembled higher education norms. Lee's success in winning, by the thinnest of margins, a three-year accreditation in December 1969 came with requirements to fulfill a new round of SACS-mandated work in 1971. The school submitted a self-study in 1972, hosted a team site visit later that year, received the committee's report in the fall of 1973, and dutifully responded to SACS recommendations. They were then awarded a ten-year accreditation, the highest mark a school could achieve. In the same period the college sought, but failed to receive, additional accreditation from the National Council for the Accreditation of Teacher Education (NCATE). Still, they carried on, joining a number of organizations, including the Appalachian Colleges Association, the National Association of Independent Colleges and Universities, and the Christian College Coalition (later the Council for Christian Colleges and Universities). The college also ended its correspondence courses, which had been a staple of its outreach to church members since 1919. As a replacement, Lee created a continuing education program in 1976. Within three years, the program enrolled over 400 men and women, most for ministerial training.[49]

In combination, the accreditation process and new financial resources allowed the college to improve many of its internal structures—especially those affecting faculty. Lee expected faculty members to teach fifteen hours each semester, commit to school and community service, and view their work as ministry. From the first days as BTS, Lee compensated its faculty below their colleagues at similarly sized institutions, but in the seventies the church granted the school generous cost of living adjustments (two were a remarkable 10 percent). Church funds allowed the school to pay a more competitive salary by the end of the decade. Salaries also improved with the faculty's credentials. In 1973, 35 percent of full-time faculty held doctorates; by 1984 that number had risen to 48 percent.[50]

President Conn, unlike his predecessors, was open to reforming policies relating to faculty. Prior to Conn's arrival, faculty could only participate in the denominational pension plan, and their annual bonus was usually a frozen turkey. Conn boosted benefits to include participation in the TIAA-CREF retirement plan (1971) and a cash Christmas bonus equal to a week's salary. Following a 1972 SACS recommendation, the administration also worked with the faculty to write formal faculty constitution and bylaws that clarified rank and tenure rules. The board first granted tenure in January 1962, but it provided no job security and year-to-year contracts persisted. Then in 1969, the board responded to SACS recommendation by approving a more substantive tenure policy that established termination for cause, and with due process. The Conn administration's reform of the rank system helped alleviate a policy that based salary levels on the degree earned and not rank. This previous policy resulted in some first-year assistant professors earning more than those with master's degrees and twenty years of experience. Despite these improvements, the president's office maintained a firm grip on the process. Until 1983, faculty committees played no significant role in recommending or evaluating individuals for hiring, tenure, or promotion. Additionally, the administration gave preference to denominational members when making recommendations to the board. This resulted in a measure of dissatisfaction among non-Church of God faculty. Limits to academic freedom, on the other hand, were widely accepted by faculty as necessary to protect the school's religious distinctives.[51]

Taken as a whole, the seventies were a good decade for Lee College. Charles Conn's leadership benefited almost every aspect of the school's operation. While not a transformational leader, Conn's steady hand, collaborative management style, and ability to identify new sources of funding created a period that some Lee employees considered a golden age. In part, this characterization comes from Conn's ability to secure federal grants, large increases in church funding, and income from steady increases in enrollment. The new funds allowed Conn to provide improved student services, expand the faculty and staff, fund new programs, and pay for renovations and new construction—all of which improved morale. Conn also changed campus culture by applying holiness principles—not strict holiness codes—to the college, and to students in particular. Although this change drew the ire of church traditionalists, his history as former general overseer, popular speaker, and author granted him some much-needed leeway. He was able to soften some standards while maintaining core holiness commitments. Ultimately, this balancing act helped him keep the confidence of church leadership and hold critics at arm's length. The result was a distinctly Pentecostal, less legalistic, more content campus community that accommodated a wider range of lifestyles within the church. As the end of the decade approached, Conn had served both Lee and the church well, but difficult times lay ahead.

Chapter 7

AN ERA OF LIMITS, 1978-1986

In the late 1970s a series of challenges threatened to undermine the advances made by President Conn. The most pressing of these came from external economic and demographic factors which the administration could not control, and to which it had difficulty adapting. Those problems were aggravated by managerial missteps, ill-advised investment strategies, and the ongoing struggle between traditionalists and progressives in the Church of God. The college entered a downward spiral characterized by budget cuts, falling enrollment, and sinking morale that threatened the school's future. Lee would not gain a measure of stability until the mid-1980s.

Perhaps the greatest threat came when the nation's economy faltered after generating twenty-five years of post-war, widespread economic prosperity. During the 1970s, complacent American manufacturers struggled to match foreign competitors who adopted new technologies and benefited from low labor costs. The United States had become dependent on cheap, imported oil from the Middle East, but in 1973 Arab oil producers embargoed the U.S. in retaliation for American support of Israel. Oil prices quadrupled and, even after the embargo ended in 1974, energy prices remained high and drove inflation. The combination of economic shocks resulted in stagflation, an economic phenomenon that coupled economic stagnation with rising consumer prices. Presidents Nixon, Ford, and Carter struggled to find effective policy solutions and the economy slipped in and out of recession as unemployment, consumer prices, and interest rates soared.

For any college stagflation spelled trouble, but Lee was especially vulnerable. The school was heavily dependent on enrollment and annual donations from the Church of God. It ran on tight budgets and had almost no endowment on which to draw in hard times. Even with those limitations, President Conn weathered the worst of the 1970s crises by steadily growing enrollment, accessing significant federal aid, and convincing the church to raise its yearly contributions. However, as the decade ended three new blows added to already-existing challenges and drove the school to its knees.

First, a large recruiting pool created by the baby boom began to shrink. 9 percent fewer students graduated from high school in 1983 than in 1979, and the number continued to fall for the next decade.[1] Lee's enrollment dropped from 1,394 students to start the 1979 school year to 1,090 in 1982, despite the admission of an increasing number of underperforming students on a probationary status. This 24 percent plunge in enrollment was a serious threat to the school, which derived some 60 percent of its operating revenue from enrollment.[2] The problem was amplified when struggling families eyed less costly alternatives to private education. Locally, Lee faced competition from the newly opened Cleveland State Community College. Not only did the community college draw local students, but many Lee faculty supplemented their modest incomes by working for the competitor.[3]

The situation only worsened when, in 1981, the US Department of Education informed Lee that the school had used funds for purposes outside the Title III grant's parameters. Therefore, the college's grant would not be renewed for the 1981–82 year—a loss of almost $400,000 in annual income. Lee lost another $144,000 from reductions in federal student assistance funds. And as if the other losses were not enough, the Church of God, as part of a broader set of budget cuts, decreased its support of the school by $59,000 for 1981–82. The drop in enrollment, broader weakness in the economy, already-tight budgets, and the lost federal and church income made it increasingly difficult to balance the budget through internal spending cuts.[4]

Then Lee made national headlines for all the wrong reasons. On April 16, 1981, ABC's *World News Tonight* reported that "Lee College, Cleveland, Tennessee, a small Bible school with 1,400 students and modest financial means" had taken its endowment and "gambled it on a Miami based investment company which said it could . . . return 40 to 100 percent on each dollar invested." The company, Barclay Financial, ran a pyramid scheme through which the fund management paid early investors (and their own generous salaries) by using later investors' money, not gains from underlying investments. While a few Barclay investors realized high returns, those who joined later in the scheme—the college among them—lost almost everything. ABC reported that "investors, including Lee College, don't know for sure what's happened to their money, but investigators say $30 million or more may have disappeared." The television story was a public relations disaster for the college, even more damaging perhaps than the lost investment dollars.[5]

Lee's decision to participate in the scheme was driven by the pressing need to find investments that might outpace devastatingly high inflation rates: 11.3 percent in 1979, 13.5 percent in 1980, and 10.3 percent in 1981.[6] The college endowment had loaned money to the denomination at lower interest rates and had also forgiven several months of interest payments. Skyrocketing inflation meant that the college was effectively losing money on their loans.[7] The school desperately needed an investment with a high rate of return. Board member and Oklahoma oil man Bill Higginbotham, along with former Lee board member Lynwood Maddox, suggested the Barclay Fund. Maddox, an Atlanta attorney and Church of God stalwart who served as counsel for numerous churches, had invested $2 million of his own money into the fund and attracted millions more in investments from businessmen active in Christian religious groups.[8] He personally presented the investment fund to Lee's board, and it appears that he projected that a $2 million-dollar investment would make over $9 million dollars of profit in just five years.[9] However, to participate in the Barclay fund, the cash-poor school had to find money to invest.

Most of Lee's endowment consisted of loans to the church, so it used the endowment as collateral and borrowed $1 million from a local bank. Higginbotham guaranteed a second loan for another $1 million to be invested in the fund under Lee's name. The bank strongly cautioned President Conn and the board to consider the risks inherent in an investment promising such large returns, especially if guaranteed by the endowment fund, but the board persisted.[10] Furthermore, General Overseer Ray Hughes wrote the bank to certify that the Executive Committee of the Church of God formally endorsed the investment.[11]

When the Barclay fund collapsed, it caught Lee's administration unawares, along with a variety of other investors who collectively put $53 million into the fund.[12] The news reports harmed the school's reputation. As board member Paul Barker summarized the situation, "we have been made to look like the greedy, get rich quick schemer."[13] Conn did his best to limit the damage and soon settled on a standard response. In short, he argued, "we have been innocently defrauded by an agent in a large financial institution and then exploited by a news medium in order to make a more sensational story."[14] His account was not wrong, but it was incomplete. The board was culpable for hastily and recklessly investing almost the full value of the endowment in a fund that promised returns that were too good to be true—even after their own banker warned them to proceed with caution. The school paid off one of the million-dollar loans in June 1981, but relied on Bill Higginbotham's generous, ongoing financial support to manage the other.[15]

Lee's financial footing slipped even further during the 1981–82 school year, when President Conn announced to employees that the school was in a financial crisis that forced him to cut programs, budgets, and personnel. In August Conn slashed the budget by 6 percent, which included savings realized by consolidating divisional deans into a single college dean.[16] Administration also restructured $2.15 million of the college's $3.58 million debt, which included notes on buildings and loans to make good budget shortfalls, as well as a note payable to the endowment fund.[17] Though financial support from the church made up 27 percent of the 1981–82 budget, administration could not balance the books.[18] In a short, direct letter sent on September 10, the board informed Conn that "it is imperative that every possible measure be taken to ensure Lee College's financial solvency. This means that all personnel should be evaluated in view of continued employment and all unnecessary expenditures must be eliminated immediately."[19] That same day, Conn informed the board that he would resign a year later, on September 1, 1982.[20]

Desperate to cut costs, the board suspended the granting of tenure, the administration restructured to eliminate positions, and Conn announced the difficult decision to fire four faculty members at mid-term. Lee's faculty responded to the news with a remarkable act of self-sacrifice. The Faculty Affairs Committee asked faculty and administrators to save the threatened positions by making contributions from their salary. The plan would not go into effect until two-thirds of the faculty and administration agreed to the plan. The successful implementation of the scheme was the result of widespread, shared sacrifice by the university community. Unfortunately, the reprieve was only temporary, as job cuts resumed the following academic year.[21]

While not about to close its doors, Lee was in serious financial distress. This emboldened conservative voices in the church, who welcomed the opportunity to replace Charles Conn. In addition to their usual complaints about relaxed holiness standards, they capitalized on sports-related issues that stirred unrest. During the 1980–81 school year, Lee dropped intercollegiate tennis, golf, cross-country, soccer, and baseball. Only basketball survived budget cuts. The next year, the popular men's basketball coach and athletic director Earl Rowan unexpectedly resigned after winning four district championships in six seasons. Then, in the last chapel of the fall 1981 semester, Conn announced a pending change in the university Viking mascot. After the board approved the idea in April 1982, Conn asked the student body for suggestions. He received twenty-one submissions and winnowed the list to the Chargers, Eagles, Flames, Kingsmen, Knights, Lancers, Maroons, Pioneers, Sentinels, and Warriors. Conn then asked the board to choose from three finalists: Conquerors (an option championed by Ray Hughes), Eagles, and Flames. A tie between the Eagles and Flames ended with Chairman of the Board Paul Walker casting the deciding vote for the Flames.[22]

The decision was not a popular one, and the Lee community pushed back. The director of alumni affairs reported that many former students strongly opposed the change.[23] Students, who rooted for the Viking teams and met in the school's Viking Den for refreshments, joined in dissent, but the administration persisted. During the 1982–83 season, the Lee Flames took the court for the first time. Alone, the changes in athletic programs were not especially significant, but in context they added to a general malaise on campus.

In early January 1982 Conn made public his decision to resign, and the board began searching for his successor. They turned to Ray Hughes, former Lee president and Church of God general overseer. Hughes had demonstrated, albeit two decades previously, that he could revive the college in difficult times. He could also help quiet traditionalist detractors, for not even the most conservative critic could accuse Ray Hughes of being a liberal progressive. In announcing the new president, board chair Paul Walker diplomatically contrasted outgoing and incoming leaders, praising Conn's "progressive leadership" and Hughes's "deep spiritual concern for the ministry of Lee."[24]

The two Hughes administrations demonstrate, perhaps better than any other example, Lee's role as a marker of generational change within the church. When Hughes took the presidency in 1960, he was a young pastor and youth leader—in touch with a new generation but deeply committed to the denomination's holiness tradition. In his first term, Hughes successfully recruited from church ranks and upheld tradition, while simultaneously pursuing accreditation and allowing new developments in campus life. His second term started two decades later and, while the cultural context had changed, Ray Hughes had not. If anything, he had become more conservative. In 1982 he represented the traditionalist church of the last generation. He was a pastor in the old tent-revival tradition, thundering from the pulpit as he called down the Holy Spirit. His leadership style leaned toward the authoritarian, and his views of holiness returned to a strict reading of the rule, not an application of principle.

The school he inherited had changed considerably in his absence. Guided by Conn's more collaborative style of leadership, the faculty had professionalized and had begun to find their voice in campus governance. The students enjoyed increasing individual freedom, if within a denominational context. When Hughes arrived, he found longer hair on men, louder music in the dorms, more open sexuality among students, and real shorts on the basketball teams. And if Hughes's traditional approach to governance and Pentecostal education was not enough to create a challenging presidential transition, his governance style, sensitivity to criticism, and reaction to the school's deep financial crisis only made his return to the presidency more problematic.

Hughes viewed the college as "a service department of the church" tasked with reinforcing church doctrine. Change, if it came, started in the church's executive committee, not on campus. The school's job, then, was to train productive workers to fill the needs of the church, not to educate students in the liberal arts or more academic disciplines.[25] Hughes told the faculty they must "accentuate the lordship of Jesus Christ," better integrate faith in their disciplines, reform student clubs and societies that operated counter to Lee's mission, attend chapel, and refrain from criticizing the administration or church in front of students.[26] He also made denominational loyalty a priority, sidestepping normal hiring and tenure processes in order to increase the number of Church of God faculty and staff.[27]

If the traditionalists wanted a more conservative approach to student life issues, Hughes delivered. To ease budget concerns, and because he saw the presidency as a ministry, Hughes took over the job of campus chaplain, organizing chapels and preaching each Sunday night. He tightened the dress code and campus discipline to conform to the letter of the church's teachings. As he saw it, "we are in a life-and-death struggle at Lee College endeavoring to defend the teachings and doctrine of the Church.... We also have a very critical problem as it relates to dress and lifestyle.... I am not a fanatic when it comes to externals, but things are so far out of hand in some of our churches that many of the young people who come to Lee College are very excessive in their appearance and dress."[28] One such group was the basketball team, who Hughes required to live on campus and attend prayer meetings with their newly assigned chaplain.[29] He went so far as to fire the women's coach when she, depending on the source, either refused to give up her jewelry or refused to discipline team members for alcohol-related offenses.[30] An alumnus recalled that it seemed that the rules mattered more than "what we were learning or how we were learning it." And at the time, students complained that Hughes "sometimes came across as a very strict individual seemingly demanding more than the students were willing to give up."[31]

Hughes tied the issue of holiness to the school's declining enrollment, believing that more liberal standards kept church members from trusting their children to the school. He pushed recruiting in the churches and wanted to satisfy conservative pastors who backed his presidency. The problem of upholding holiness standards, however, paled in comparison to the school's immediate economic problems. Upon taking office, Hughes faced an operating deficit of over $1 million. He wrote one confidant, "I don't think the brethren on the field are aware of the desperate financial condition of Lee College. The shortfall in enrollment and withdrawal of federal aid for students . . . have left us in a very desperate financial situation."[32] To another he said that he needed a miracle to find a way out of the most difficult financial crisis he had faced, and the responsibility was "almost unbearable."[33] Significantly in debt, the school had exhausted its ability to borrow money, but Hughes attacked the problem with grit and determination. He ruthlessly cut expenses, raised money to refurbish the old library into classroom space, renovated the basketball arena, refinanced loans, convinced the church to delay further funding cuts to the school, reduced the debt, and kept personnel cuts to only three faculty, one administrative staffer, and one maintenance worker.[34]

In working to move the school back to financial stability, Hughes's management style often sat poorly with those accustomed to Conn's leadership. A SACS evaluation team rightly put it, "The chief administrator of the college has traditionally been a past church administrator unaccustomed to the more democratic process common to institutions of higher learning. This attitude sometimes follows these administrators to the campus where faculty input-criticism is occasionally regarded as 'lack of support' and perhaps even threatening."[35] As one administrator remembered, when an old-school Pentecostal preacher believed the Lord had spoken to him and was directing his steps, processes like voting and consultation did not seem necessary.[36] In sharp contrast with Conn's collaborative style, Hughes renovated buildings without consulting faculty, had to be prompted to provide an agenda for faculty meetings, required some faculty to teach summer classes without additional compensation, and unilaterally issued directives. And while he did not attempt to roll back academic and institutional gains, he favored immediate action over the sometimes-cumbersome procedures of the academy.

Hughes was a fierce protector of the denomination, the college, and his own reputation. This attitude caused him to have a difficult relationship with the local community—especially the city newspaper, the Cleveland *Daily Banner*. The paper covered the school extensively, but Hughes had little tolerance for stories that he felt undermined his efforts. When Hughes invited the Chattanooga press, but not the *Banner*, to a college press conference, *Banner* editor Beecher Hunter took exception. Hunter wrote an editorial that called into question Hughes's commitment to Cleveland and revisited several older Lee controversies, including the endowment scandal and coaching changes. Hughes responded with a blistering five-page letter to the editor which accused him of "journalistic nitpicking and sensation seeking." He concluded darkly, "the Lord reward you according to your works."[37] Hunter printed Hughes's diatribe, and the editor's more professional response left Hughes bruised; his vigorous defense of the school and his presidency had come across as bitter and petty.[38]

As if his hands were not full enough, Hughes took office as the college prepared for a SACS accreditation review. Work on the self-study began in 1982 and was published in March 1984. The study reported the school's growth in the mid- to late-1970s, while also providing a frank and honest view of the limitations and frustrations of the early 1980s. The SACS visiting team was generally satisfied that the college's work to "present an intellectual experience uplifted by a spiritual experience appears to result in a most positive product, a serious student and a responsible citizen."[39] The report noted several long-standing trends in Lee's history. The school's open enrollment policy continued to admit underprepared students, with nearly half accepted on probationary status. The visitors also had concerns about the budget, especially Lee's heavy dependence on the church for operating expenses. In regards to the faculty, the report expressed ongoing concerns about limits on academic freedom and the credentials of faculty.

Their most serious critiques related to authority and decision-making. The church had too much control of the school, primarily through its close control of the board and ownership of the campus. The board made decisions, such as approving all faculty hires, that were best left to the president and administration, while the president made decisions about faculty, curriculum, and academic policies without consulting the faculty. However, these caveats did not undermine what was otherwise a generally positive report that resulted in a full, ten-year reaccreditation.[40]

In April 1984, Hughes abruptly resigned to accept an offer to become the president of the Church of God's seminary, effective August 1. His second effort to revive Lee's fortunes had been a qualified failure. During his second tenure, Hughes managed to close the books on an $800,000 dormitory renovation, paid for all but $150,000 of an $800,000 gym project, and helped raise money for the new library. He also began the "Partners for Excellence" fundraising campaign, which raised almost half of its $2 million goal by the time he left office.[41] However, Hughes's recruitment strategy failed. As a result, enrollment continued to fall, dropping from 1,134 in fall 1982 to 1,059 the next year.[42] He left his successor the leanest of budgets and a school that operated in a world defined by limits and constraints. Hughes also left behind a demoralized faculty and a frustrated student body that chafed at his authoritarian leadership and enforcement of holiness strictures.

The board's choice of a new president proved both complicated and contested. At an April 15 meeting in Atlanta, the board drew up a list of candidates and selected a search committee. Within a week they narrowed the list to two men, Lamar Vest and Paul Conn.[43] Like many previous leaders of the college, Vest held no academic credentials, but had an outstanding reputation in the church and held a bachelor's in Christian education at Lee. Vest pastored in South Carolina before moving into a series of posts related to youth ministry, first as state director and then as general director of youth and Christian education. He was considered on the fast track to the executive committee, but when term limits pushed him from his office in 1984, no chair on the committee was open. Although Vest had no ambition to lead Lee, this did not deter some church leaders, who, following long precedent, viewed the college as a good place to employ the popular, moderate Vest until he could be further promoted.

Paul Conn, the son Charles Conn, represented the most progressive wing of a very conservative denomination. Raised in the bosom of the church by parents who valued education, Conn excelled in the local public schools. Upon graduation he faced a difficult choice. His grades and test scores opened a wide variety of university opportunities, and schools like Vanderbilt and the University of the South offered an opportunity to escape the parochial bounds of life in Cleveland. On the other hand, his parents hoped he would attend Lee for at least a year before transferring to finish his degree. At the time, Lee had little to offer academically, and he considered the decision to attend Lee a matter of "choosing your religious tradition, your subgroup, over choosing your bright future."[44] Conn followed tradition and enrolled at Lee in 1963. Bright, competitive, and internally motivated, Conn made the most of his college experience. He graduated at the top of his class, traveled with the Lee Singers, edited the yearbook, and helped found a college fraternity. In the process, he also gained a reputation as a liberal who rejected the holiness regulations and separatist culture of the 1960s' church. After graduating from Lee's junior college, he considered transferring but remained at Lee and earned a bachelor's degree from the Bible college. Conn married fellow Lee student Darlia McLuhan before pursuing graduate school. He attended two semesters at Georgia State to bolster his undergraduate preparation before winning a fellowship at Emory University to study psychology.[45]

While at Emory, Conn completed his master's and doctoral degrees before joining Lee's psychology faculty in 1972. There he found an opportunity to pursue a life-long passion for writing. He had been editor of his high school paper, contributed articles to denominational magazines, written for the local paper, and served as yearbook editor at Lee. He also published a short book on the Lee Singers with the denominational press, but his real break came after a friend from Cleveland connected Conn with Revell Publishing. While teaching a fifteen-hour load at Lee, Conn wrote or co-authored twenty books, including collaborations with celebrities like singer Johnny Cash and Pittsburg Steeler's quarterback Terry Bradshaw. Most were successful and four were bestsellers, granting Conn entry into the world of wealthy, famous, and powerful people. These included Richard DeVos, founder of Amway; Jack Eckerd, founder of a nationwide chain of drugstores; and Julian Carroll, governor of Kentucky. All were Christians; none were Pentecostal. On weekdays Conn taught at Lee, but he spent as many as forty weekends a year on the road promoting or celebrating his latest book. His success as an author, popularity as a teacher, and progressive views made him an attractive presidential option for certain members of the board. A potential Conn presidency was not, however, popular among traditionalists in the church, including outgoing president Ray Hughes.[46]

The choice came down to the safe, moderate Vest or the progressive wildcard, Conn. The Church of God's Executive Committee wanted Vest, and they made their choice known in church circles. Board members who served as pastors and state overseers, many of whom owed their positions to the Executive Committee, followed the church leaders' preference. But the committee's influence was not enough to secure an uncontested Vest presidency. By 1984 their votes were balanced against a near equal number of laymen. This cadre of businessmen, led by Bill Higginbotham, sought to use Conn's nomination as a rallying point to exert the board's independence from the Executive Committee. Overseeing the debate was

Board Chairman Paul Walker. Walker pastored one of the denomination's largest and most prominent churches, Atlanta's Mount Paran Church of God, where a younger Conn worked while in graduate school at Emory. The progressive Walker was friend to Charles and Paul Conn, but he was also politically astute. He understood that, despite Lee's bylaws, the final decision on the presidency would be made by church leaders and not the school's board. Walker might have preferred Conn but understood that the denomination would have the final say in the matter.

On April 21 the board met via conference call. A motion to hire Vest was moved and seconded, but some board members balked at the idea. Following some debate, the board agreed to delay the vote until they consulted with the church's liaison, Executive Committee member Robert White. At Walker's urging, the five-man Executive Committee called Conn to the Church of God headquarters on May 7 for a meeting that more closely resembled an interrogation than a job interview. In particular, they wanted to know—or perhaps confirm—that Conn did not abide by the strict holiness code endorsed by the traditionalists. Did he attend movies? Play tennis in shorts? Allow his wife to wear jewelry? Conn answered that he did all of those things and did not intend to stop. Further, he argued against the traditionalists' legalism and exceptional view of Pentecostalism. For Conn, the central value of faith was a personal relationship with Christ as informed by the Bible, not the separatist strictures of past generations. He held his ground, and in doing so guaranteed that the church fathers would not only endorse Vest, but also explicitly reject Conn. Vest's selection seemed assured.[47]

When the board met the following day to finalize its choice, Walker had Conn wait nearby. Walker's plan was that the board would nominate Conn, then committee liaison Robert White would explain why the denomination would not accept him as president. Walker would then call Conn into the meeting, where Conn would graciously refuse the nomination and pledge his support to Vest. In this way the board would make known its will but avoid directly challenging denominational leadership.[48] Conn agreed and waited for the call to join the meeting and withdraw his name. The meeting started at 7:00p.m. and Conn waited two and half hours for Walker's summons—something had not gone as planned. The board had expressed its desire to nominate Conn; and White, on cue, had explained that the church would not accept the nomination. In an unprecedented move, the board exerted their independence by refusing to call Conn to the meeting. Instead, they proceeded with a formal vote in the face of White's vociferous opposition. In an eight to seven vote split largely along ministerial-lay lines, the board voted to nominate Paul Conn as the next president of Lee College.[49]

The following day the board sent their choice to the Executive Committee, which immediately responded to the board's challenge. The committee's decision, however, was not cut and dried. If the church rejected the board's recommendation, they would effectively signal to careful observers—SACS included—that the board had limited power. Rejecting Conn might also alienate and demoralize the board, which included powerful members of the church. In the end, the vote was 3–2 to reject Conn. Cecil Knight and Raymond Crowley voted for Conn, while conservatives E. C. Thomas (general overseer at the time), Robert White, and Robert Hart rejected him. The leadership had decided to exercise its de facto power over the board.[50] That afternoon Lee's board met again and unanimously approved Vest's nomination.[51] Neither Vest nor Conn was happy with the turn of events, rather, both were embarrassed, angry, and placed in an awkward position vis-à-vis the other. That night Vest called Conn and the two men, in a meeting that lasted well into the next morning, talked about their respective futures at Lee. They agreed that Vest would take the job and that Conn stay on the faculty, but the contested transition strained their friendship.[52]

A few days later, church leaders duly approved Vest and in August 1984, he became the eighteenth president of Lee College. Never desirous of or comfortable with the job, he only served two years before the church elected him to the Executive Committee.[53] In that time, Vest made two important contributions to Lee. First, he tempered Hughes's conservative policies and set a moderate tone that improved morale on campus. Second, he approached Paul Conn in November of 1984 about taking a place in the school administration. Vest had no specific role in mind, but Conn asked to be made vice president for institutional advancement, with a portfolio that included community relations, alumni relations, fundraising, and student recruitment. As conditions of taking the job, Conn asked that he be the only vice president on campus and enjoy free access to the president's office. The campus needed a clear signal that he was Vest's number two, with the authority and power to get things done. Vest agreed, and in January 1985 Conn stepped into the administration.[54]

For Conn, the decision was a turning point. After Church of God leadership rejected his nomination, he had been weighing his options. His writing career was in full swing, academia offered multiple career paths—Amway's Richard DeVos even recruited him as the president of a film production company. Rather than hedging his bets, Conn chose to fully engage the challenge of turning Lee College around. He opened his appointment book, canceled all but the most imminent speaking engagements, and put future writing opportunities on hold. At the time, the pause likely seemed temporary, but the decision had permanent consequences. He left the speaking circuit and turned down radio and television appearances, book signings, future royalties, and awards banquets enjoyed by a bestselling author. Out of love for his alma mater, Conn stepped away from the national and international stage to the worn campus, fractious constituencies, financial constraints, and general inertia that defined Lee in 1985. It was a sacrifice of status, money, and opportunity that few would have been willing to make.[55]

Promoting Conn proved to be a wise move by Vest. As vice president, Conn gained experience, honed his administrative skills, demonstrated his abilities, and positioned himself as the frontrunner to become the next school president. Conn made the most of the opportunity, and Vest gave his vice president the credit for a string of new initiatives that stabilized the school. One of Conn's first goals was to repair the damage that the church's separatism, in general, and Hughes's combativeness, in particular, had done to Lee's relationship with the broader Cleveland community. He started by taking out four billboards proclaiming, "We're proud to be in Cleveland."[56] Conn reached out to community and business leaders and mended relations with the *Daily Banner*, to which he had occasionally submitted stories over the years. Almost immediately the paper's coverage of Lee expanded and changed tone. To jumpstart fundraising, Conn started small, seeking—and finding—funding for a new endowed scholarship of $5,000 each month. He also raised $56,000 to honor local businessman, Cletus Benton, with the creation of a memorial fund. While modest, these scholarships created a sense of progress and momentum. In another initiative meant to draw top students to Lee, in July 1986 Conn began the Summer Honors program for rising high school seniors that drew several dozen prospective students to Lee for a two-week, on-campus, residential experience. Under Conn's leadership the college worked to regain lost Title III funding, began an alumni magazine (*Alumnus*), and secured a generous gift of computer equipment for the business department.[57]

Vest and Conn also took a close look at two troubled areas: intercollegiate sports and nursing. A nursing degree was the long-held dream of Lois Beach, who joined BTS faculty in 1944 and became the first female department head at Lee before retiring in 1999. The namesake of the science building, Beach was a formidable and persistent advocate for nursing, and at her urging Lee had begun to seriously explore the initiative in 1979. Advocates raised around $40,000 to promote and explore the degree's potential, and the school hired a program director in 1981. Although the state gave Lee preliminary approval to pursue development, the financial crisis and loss of the director put the program in limbo. Ultimately, the college did not have the resources to complete the project, which it terminated in May 1986.[58]

The financial crisis also took its toll on athletics, which suffered cuts in personnel, budgets, and teams. By 1984 the college sponsored only men's and women's basketball and men's golf. Conn led a task force to assess the future of athletics at Lee, which found that "a superior athletic program has the potential of enhancing the school's image and morale to a degree that is perhaps disproportionate to the intrinsic value of the sport itself."[59] To that end the school recommitted to its existing sports and, while deferring on restarting baseball, pledged to start softball the next year. Unlike past Lee administrators, Conn saw the value of sports in promoting the school, but only if given sufficient funding and a chance to win.

The new administration's efforts, however, would have been in vain had they not been able to reverse the downward trend in enrollment. Vest contributed to recruiting by utilizing the contacts he had made as the church's director of youth and Christian ministry, while Conn led the team that focused on steadying enrollment. One remedy was the new merit-based Presidential Scholarship, which offered students scoring in the top 10 percent of the ACT a year's free tuition. In tandem with the Summer Honors program, the initiative attracted and recruited academically advanced students who were more likely to persist and graduate. Lee also began sending teams, often accompanied by a singing ensemble led by Danny Murray, to special recruitment nights in major cities. These multi-faceted efforts stopped the downward trend. Enrollment moved from 1,059 students in fall 1983 to 1,204 two years later.[60]

Lee was beginning to show signs of recovery. On-campus morale rose as Vest loosened holiness constraints imposed by Hughes. Over two years, Vest gave students freedoms unthinkable under traditionalist rules. He eased prohibitions on women wearing pants, jewelry, and makeup. Whereas Hughes forced *Vindagua* editors to clumsily edit out earrings in photographs, the yearbook unabashedly displayed women wearing necklaces, earrings, and blue jeans during Vest's term.[61] He also moved homecoming to Saturday (a change long opposed on the grounds that pastors would not have time to return to their congregations the next day) and reduced chapel from three to two days a week.

Surprisingly, Church of God leadership did not attempt to slow the changes in Lee's culture. Instead, they approved the board's recommendation to give Vest a new two-year contract. Vest, who admittedly felt out of place in the president's office, accepted the church's call.[62] He was undoubtedly relieved when elected to serve on the Executive Committee in 1986. Lee's board of directors promptly nominated Paul Conn to succeed Vest. This time, after an extended debate that lasted until four in the morning, the church fathers approved the appointment.[63]

The period from 1978 to 1984 had not been kind to Lee College, which suffered on multiple fronts. Declining enrollment coupled with inflation, poor investments, lost federal grant money, and declining denominational support caused the Conn and Hughes administrations to fashion a culture of scarcity. They cut budgets, fired faculty and staff, limited student services, and measured success as limiting loss. In itself the financial crisis hurt morale on campus, but the ongoing struggle between the Church of God's progressive and traditionalist factions further damaged the Lee community. Charles Conn, a moderate progressive in the denomination, led the campus for twelve years, all the while enduring the scrutiny and criticism of those that held to the strict holiness strictures of the church. When he left office under the cloud of the financial crisis, conservatives saw an opportunity to reverse campus culture. The Hughes presidency temporarily restored the traditionalist, sectarian approach to education, but he was unable to check the decline in enrollment and his policies further damaged campus morale. Faculty and students had little choice but to comply with Hughes's directives. His autocratic approach and short tenure, however, helped ensure Charles Conn's progressive legacy would survive the brief return to holiness culture.

Lamar Vest's brief, transitional presidency was most notable for bringing about Paul Conn's move into the college's administration. The traditionalists' victory in rejecting Paul Conn's 1984 nomination proved fleeting. Vest, despite his backing by Ray Hughes, proved more moderate than conservative. He not only created a vice presidency for Conn but also gave him the opportunity to check Lee's financial decline. Conn did just that, and Vest made sure that the campus, board, and church knew Vice President Conn deserved the credit for each successful initiative.

Vest's departure marked the end of an era in Lee's history. Since the school returned to Cleveland from Sevierville, the Church of God, its pastors, and the last generation's holiness tradition had defined the college. The presidents had been church leaders steeped in the denomination's peculiar Pentecostal culture, but had no experience in college administration, and their personal ambitions made their tenure at Lee brief. Some, especially Ray Hughes and Charles Conn, made substantial contributions to Lee's evolution into a liberal arts college. Most served briefly, reluctantly, and with little competence for the task at hand. Typically, these presidents held a narrow pragmatic approach that looked to the past and lacked vision for the future. That leadership created a school of a specific type, a sectarian institution that appealed to a very particular type of Pentecostal person, even in its sponsoring denomination. Within the limits set by that constituency, the school made significant progress in winning SACS accreditation, offering new degrees, improving its physical plant, winning federal grants, bettering its faculty, and generally producing a better product. And Lee might very well have continued on this path for some time longer. However, that narrow sectarian model limited growth and was increasingly out of step with Church of God families who had turned from strict holiness codes to a more progressive view of faith and practice.

Chapter 8

EXPECT SOMETHING GREAT

President Paul Conn

When Paul Conn became the nineteenth president of Lee College, no one anticipated that he would remain in the post for thirty-four years. During that time, he transformed the school from a small, struggling, sectarian liberal arts college to a vibrant university with three and a half thousand undergraduate and five hundred graduate students. He raised millions of dollars, most of which he used to expand the physical infrastructure of the campus, including the construction of more than twenty new buildings. In the process, he raised the school's academic reputation from a virtually unknown denominational college to a respected regional institution. Underlying Conn's success were three intertwined themes: his desire to create a more evangelical institution that attracted non-Pentecostal students and faculty, his determination to loosen denominational control of Lee, and his desire to provide students the sorts of diverse educational and social opportunities that had marked his own undergraduate experience.

Conn intentionally diversified the faith traditions of the student body and faculty, thereby creating a school anchored in Church of God culture, but broadly evangelical in its composition. "I am deeply committed to the place . . . and I loved the Church of God in a cultural way, but I realized how limiting it was and how narrow it was," Conn said.[1] He never sought to break ties with the denomination, but instead wanted to reimagine what it meant to be a Church of God institution. Broadening Lee's culture entailed securing a measure of independence from the political ebbs and flows of the Church of God, whose leaders continued to appoint the board of directors but otherwise were distanced from the school's operations. It also meant moving the school toward a more progressive, inclusive stance, a choice that did not go uncontested.

Breaking denominational control of Lee put Conn in direct conflict with church traditionalists, especially in the first decade of his presidency. Led by Ray Hughes and Wade Horton, the opposition insisted that Conn's effort to diversify the campus would destroy the school's Pentecostal culture. "They didn't trust me," Conn said, "and they were right."[2] From opposing his nomination by placing "Don't be Conned" flyers on cars at a local church to questioning his decisions at budget meetings, the traditionalists resisted Conn's innovations. To the president, his opposition's efforts were "deeply xenophobic and narrow, and intentionally narrow. The Church of God, I felt like, had to choose between having the kind of school we have now [2020] or having a small, chronically struggling, denominationally pure little Bible college—they would have chosen the little Bible college."[3]

Conn never forgot how his own years at Lee gave him opportunities to connect, lead, and succeed outside the classroom. Those formative years convinced him that the on-campus undergraduate experience could be a transformative agent in students' lives. To help students integrate into Lee's community, he created added new sports and campus organizations. He built dormitories and apartments to house the growing stu-

Charles Paul Conn, when he became the president of Lee College in 1986. (Courtesy of the PRC.)

dent population and maintained rules that moderated student behavior without driving them from campus. In the classroom, Conn remembered the role that special faculty had played in his formation. He maintained that teaching undergraduates was the most important responsibility of the faculty and believed his job was to put students in front of transformational teachers. And even as Lee's academic quality and reputation steadily improved, he committed to provide opportunities for marginal students at an accessible price.

Those key strategic decisions, an emphasis on residential campus life, a teaching faculty, and broad access, meant that Lee remained on a course that eschewed certain standards by which the academy judges the success of colleges and universities. While accrediting agencies have increasingly focused on the student experience, university prestige is more often judged on academic reputation within the academy, faculty production of original research, and research citations.[4] Faculty research, a deciding factor in determining whether Harvard, Oxford, or Stanford wins academic bragging rights for the top university in the world, was not part of Conn's vision for Lee. Instead, he believed that the school's success depended on a faculty that was committed to realizing Lee's mission through teaching and service. Excellence in teaching and an investment in students, not the lab, archive, or studio, would be the measure of the faculty at Lee.

That teaching-focused, student-centered model has long been a staple of the small colleges and universities that populate the roster of the Council of Christian Colleges and Universities.[5] As Mark Noll explains in his *Scandal of the Evangelical Mind*, evangelical institutions of higher learning have been especially dedicated to the work of educating undergraduates for practical work in the church and in society at large. For most, this focus not only lives out the vision of their sponsoring denomination, but it also is a practical necessity driven by limited financial resources. Noll laments that this teaching model has resulted in a landscape devoid of evangelical research institutions which lighten faculty's responsibility to undergraduates, but expect them to produce the sort of first-rate, original research that might set new intellectual agendas. He writes, "Virtually without exception, however, they were not designed to promote thorough Christian reflection on the nature of the world, society, and the arts." Schools like Lee "can exert a life-changing influence on their students. But by their nature they are not designed for the kinds of patient, creative study that alters the way we think about the world and ourselves."[6] In 1986, Conn might have agreed with Noll's assessment in principle, but his own undergraduate experience, the expectations of the

Church of God, and Lee's immediate physical and financial needs meant that he would judge success by growing the university's investment in the undergraduate college experience, not endowed research chairs and graduate programs.

In August 1986, any record of success had yet to be written. In his inaugural address Conn signaled that he viewed his presidency as the start of something new. One of his first pledges was to the broader community, with which Lee had a difficult history due to the Church of God's separatist impulses. These habits had long isolated the campus and kept it something of a mystery to the community. More recently, tensions between President Hughes and community leaders exacerbated old grievances, but Conn set out to heal those wounds. Unlike almost every other Lee president, Conn was more than a son of the church. He was a son of Cleveland. He grew up in the city, went to public schools, bagged groceries at the supermarket, and threw newspapers for the *Daily Banner.* He stayed in Cleveland to attend Lee, returned to the community after graduate school, and raised his family there. He told his audience, "It has always seemed to me that Lee College and the community of Cleveland and Bradley County have been unnecessarily distant. We have not known each other well enough, and have not supported each other well enough. With your help, I plan to try to improve that situation. We share too many values, too many things in common, not to know one another better."[7]

In his inauguration speech, Conn recognized that he represented a changing of the guard—one that was notably progressive in its outlook. "It has been said, on several occasions, that this presidency marks the passing of a torch," he said. "There is a sense in which I represent a new generation of leadership, and it is natural that some should wonder whether the Lee College flame will burn as brightly, or as purely, in the hands of this generation." Conn reassured the church that Lee would always be a campus "where Christ is King. A campus where Christ is not merely studied, or discussed, or acknowledged, but where He is Lord and Master in the lives of individual students and faculty." With the Christian faith as the college's controlling worldview, Conn argued that the campus could then pursue more pragmatic goals: increased enrollment, building projects, new programs, and well-educated students in the liberal arts tradition. As president, he would change the college, but he promised the church that "by God's help, we will not squander this inheritance we have received. We will not back away from our birthright."[8]

In his first year in office, Conn began to define his program. In a meeting with administrators in January 1987 and then with faculty that fall, he laid out his priorities and goals. Some were practical and operational. He wanted to raise funds from a broader pool of supporters to renovate the old library, spruce up the campus, and retire the school's $3.5 million debt. Like every president before him, Conn needed to increase enrollment. Unlike his predecessors, he saw retention, not just recruiting, as a means to that goal. Conn argued that the school had an "anti-student" attitude that neglected student welfare. At the time, 40 percent of Lee students were freshmen, but high attrition rates meant that few made it through to graduation. A student-centered approach would improve enrollment and fill seats in small, cost-ineffective upper-level classes.[9]

More intriguing were comments that suggested changes to life on Lee's campus. Conn wanted to allow greater freedom for students. His vision was to welcome evangelicals to a campus that had been narrowly sectarian in faith and practice. While clearly supporting the ministerial programs that provided the church's pastors and leaders, Conn wanted to broaden the school's horizons. Under his watch, students would be free to explore the whole spectrum of evangelical expression. He also loosened the rules that governed student life, believing that students needed the opportunity to make mistakes, accept discipline, and grow from the experience. At the same time, he recognized the need to set boundaries in order to maintain the confidence of parents and of the church. Conn viewed Lee as a progressive change agent in the lives of students and the denomination. He would not abandon the Church of God. However, while he privileged Pentecostal practice in an evangelical setting, he rejected the narrow, legalistic culture espoused by traditionalists. Conn desired a campus where Christ, not the church's expression of holiness, was king.[10]

In his first months as president, Conn made a pair of seemingly insignificant decisions which illustrate the degree to which the denomination controlled Lee, as well as Conn's determination to break that control. The first took place when Conn allowed Broken Heart, a Christian rock group headed by Mylon LeFevre, to perform on campus. Denominational leadership vetoed an earlier attempt to host the band during Vest's presidency, but Conn used the concert to help establish boundaries. During a meeting with the executive committee in his office, Conn put his presidency on the line. When Ray Hughes motioned that the committee order Conn to cancel the concert, Conn refused to back down. As Conn recalls, he said to them, "I believe in spiritual authority . . . and if I'm directed to cancel the Mylon concert . . . I only have two legitimate responses. One is, 'yes sir.' And the other is, 'I quit.' And if you direct me to cancel the Mylon concert, my answer will be, 'I quit,' because if I can't decide who sings on our stage, what good is it to be president?" They relented and Conn gained control of campus culture. Conn's second decision was to hire a soccer coach who was not a Pentecostal. Defending his choice before church leaders, Conn asked whether leadership would prefer an unqualified amateur lead the team or a dedicated Christian professional who, while not Pentecostal, could both win games and mentor his players? The church leaders backed down and Conn would later use the same argument to open the door for more diverse hires on the faculty and staff. Decisions like these, whether to ease curfew rules or to allow women to wear earrings, helped create a healthy distance from the Church of God's more conservative leadership.[11]

Like any CEO taking over a struggling enterprise, Conn faced the daunting task of overcoming institutional inertia. Working with Vest, he had managed to check the school's decline, but for seven years the faculty, staff, and administration labored on a campus defined by scarcity and dedicated to surviving the latest crisis. When Conn took his post, he was the college's fourth president in five years. Church politics still lingered in the background, and the school had become defined by its limits. Under ever-tighter budgets, faculty and staff endured program cuts, came to expect weak enrollment numbers, and watched colleagues lose their jobs. The students occupied a tired, worn campus that was virtually unchanged from Conn's time at Lee and, especially when compared to state schools, the college provided students few opportunities for cultural and extracurricular activities. As the 1986 school year began, there was little reason to believe that change was on the horizon. Enrollment remained steady from the year before, no new construction was planned, and the administrative team remained almost unchanged. To the casual observer, that first semester would have seemed like the same old Lee. But change was coming.

Before any dream could be realized, Conn's administration first needed to recruit and retain the students who made growth possible. He then had to raise money to construct the buildings in which those students could live, learn, and grow. To attract students, Conn believed that Lee needed to offer the "sizzle with the steak."[12] Lacking an academic reputation, Lee needed to attract high school students with other enticements before it could provide them a quality education. Conn suspected that Summer Honors, Lee Day, sports, study abroad, musical ensembles, and Greek clubs would draw students to campus. There they would find ample extracurricular opportunities and a faculty dedicated to undergraduate teaching. In time the university could grow its endowment, reduce faculty teaching loads, encourage research, and improve the academic quality of its program, but first the school had to build momentum.

In his first two years as president, Conn created positive energy that invigorated faculty and staff, excited students, engaged the community, and intrigued donors. The starting point of that change appears modest today, but the $1 million Pass the Torch fundraising campaign was an ambitious goal at the time. Once fulfilled, the campaign promised to renovate the old, vacant library building into classroom space, add parking, and build a new maintenance building. The campaign proved to be the first step in what became a three-decade transformation of the campus. Short on capital but needing to make a visible impact on the campus, Conn started by demolishing an old auditorium in the center of campus. Abandoned after the Conn Center opened in 1977, the auditorium symbolized the past and things left undone. It had to go. Next, Conn asked the city planning commission to close a three-block section of Church Street that bisected the campus. The school had long sought the closure, but the church's separatist culture and the resulting antipathy between the community and school stymied any such efforts. Conn promised to transform the ceded street into a model pedestrian mall, but in 1987 there remained substantial community opposition to the street closure. The decision was uncertain even as the commission cast their votes, but the closure was narrowly approved by a 3–2 vote. Conn, knowing that the city might reverse its decision at any time, immediately set to work to secure his victory. During the early hours of the following morning, he had contractors removed thirty-foot sections of pavement from either end of the street.[13] He then reached out to local property developer Jim Sharp, who volunteered his time to oversee the development of a pedestrian mall. Sharp delivered on a plan that included two plazas, an open-air amphitheater, and careful landscaping.

The campus renovations were a step in the right direction, but the real measure of success was enrollment. Conn took responsibility for recruiting when serving as vice president. In January 1985, his first fall class reversed a four-year slide and the next saw a modest increase that stabilized enrollment at about 1,200 students. Fall 1987's 1,332 students, however, began a surge in enrollment that would continue for two decades. At the time, the 11 percent boost was a critical force in changing Lee's momentum. More students added money to the coffers, but they meant far more than a healthy bank balance. Students have a very short institutional memory that can be measured in a three-year cycle, therefore entering freshmen joined two other classes that never knew the turmoil and lean years of the second Hughes administration. For those classes, Lee was a pleasant, slightly dated place with a student culture dominated by clubs and traditions established by their parents' generation. The upswing in enrollment in 1987 was sustained in future years: 1,534 in 1988, 1,642 in 1989, 1,739 in 1990, and the trend continued.[14]

Enrollment growth created demand for new dormitories, academic space, and service buildings. If scarcity creates demand, then Lee's limited physical plant added its own energy to campus. By 1988 Lee had filled every available bed in campus housing, causing the school to build Sharp-Davis Hall (1989–1990), its first new dormitory in twenty years. Despite the additional 240 beds, necessity forced the administration to start a new tradition. Almost every fall they searched for apartments, motel rooms, houses, and other arrangements to house the overflow of new students.[15] Similarly, despite the repurposing of the old library building into the Vest classroom building, teaching space remained at a premium. As administrators and faculty put to rest questions of survival, they began to consider the best way to manage growth. Conn embraced the old entrepreneurial spirit of BTS, which had been at rest for two decades. In that spirit, he welcomed new ideas, giving faculty, administrators, staff, and students the opportunity to innovate and create.

The steady growth in on-campus undergraduate enrollment was the result of a multifaceted effort that enhanced existing recruiting initiatives and created new ones. One key to growth was a new scholarship program. In addition to his creation of dozens of new endowed scholarships, Conn developed a three-tier system of university awards. These awards drew students, including better-prepared students that had been so difficult to attract in the past. Based on standardized test scores, the Dean's, Presidential, and Centennial Scholarships rewarded prospects for their hard work. Students could earn a lump sum discount, a year's tuition, or for the elite Centennial Scholars, a full four years of tuition.[16]

Even with generous scholarships as an incentive, it was no easy task to convince top students to bypass well-known public and private universities to take a chance on Lee. Conn took matters into his own hands and personally phoned and recruited the first Centennial scholar, whom he convinced to attend Summer Honors. Impressed with the experience, she chose Lee over the University of Alabama.[17] The new scholarships were not only an effective recruiting tool, but they also helped raise the average ACT score from 16.5 in 1987 to 21.1 in 1991.[18] The college also improved its recruiting team and resources, building a separate admissions center on campus, improving the traditional spring Lee College Day, creating a group of student ambassadors, and adding a series of one day, on-campus Frontline events for prospective students.

The college also improved retention. Increased institutional aid helped keep students on campus, but the growth of student programs and a new sense of freedom made retention an easier task. A new generation of students—particularly those from the Church of God—were growing up with a host of new choices and opportunities unavailable to their parents. As Conn put it, "At Lee College, we do not believe that a student should be forced to choose between being a Christian and being a full participant in a well-rounded college life." He continued, "For me, as a high school graduate twenty-five years ago, the ecclesiastical table at which I sat offered a fixed menu. I got what was served, take it or leave it, and God help me if I didn't take it! . . . We intend to offer more experiences, with higher quality, inside and outside the classroom, than any previous generation of Lee College students has seen."[19] Conn was not going to sponsor keg parties and put ashtrays on the cafeteria tables, but he wanted to give students the chance to travel, play sports, take the stage, lead, and hear more diverse viewpoints. He began a semester in Europe program, encouraged the formation of new social and service clubs, and invited guests from outside the denomination to speak in chapel.

Overall, Lee gradually moved toward becoming a less sectarian but distinctly Christian campus in the first years of Conn's presidency. Unlike some change agents at faith-based schools, he remained committed to a distinct, explicit, intentional Christian mission rooted in evangelical beliefs. He also remained committed to Pentecostalism, but created a measure of independence from the Church of God. In part this meant ending long-held practices, such as sharing a computer system with the denomination or housing the university bookstore on campus instead of at the Church of God Publishing House. Conn ended or relaxed many traditionalist holiness rules, and he steadily loosened denominational controls on Lee's governance and budget. In time, Lee ceased being an exclusively Church of God school, staffed by Church of God members, and attended by Church of God students. Conn preferred a campus where Christ was king, and the church was a welcome partner.

Though there were boundaries governing behavior, those boundaries steadily moved away from the holiness rules favored by Ray Hughes and other traditionalists. This retreat from legalism mirrored a similar trend in the Church of God. The denomination first defined *holiness* in its Practical Commitments in 1948. Then in 1974, progressives and conservatives fought to redefine holiness restrictions. Six years later the Church of God began an eight-year process that reevaluated the practical commitments of the denomination. After years of study, debate, and committee work, the result was a clear progressive victory. At the 1988 General Assembly, the church approved a revised set of Practical Commitments which focused on seven principles that should guide the Christian life. These are worth considering, as they demonstrate a new position that allowed traditionalist congregations and pastors to hold the holiness line while granting new freedom to the progressives.

> SPIRITUAL EXAMPLE. We will demonstrate our commitment to Christ through our practice of the spiritual disciplines; we will demonstrate our commitment to the body of Christ through our loyalty to God and commitment to His church; and we will demonstrate our commitment to the work of Christ through our being good stewards.
>
> MORAL PURITY. We will engage in those activities which glorify God in our body and which avoid the fulfillment of the lust of the flesh. We will read, watch and listen to those things which are of positive benefit to our spiritual well-being.
>
> PERSONAL INTEGRITY. We will live in a manner that inspires trust and confidence, bearing the fruit of the Spirit and seeking to manifest the character of Christ in all our behavior.
>
> FAMILY RESPONSIBILITY. We will give priority to fulfilling family responsibilities, to preserving the sanctity of marriage and to maintaining divine order in the home.
>
> BEHAVIORAL TEMPERANCE. We will practice temperance in behavior and will abstain from activities and attitudes which are offensive to our fellowman or which lead to addiction or enslavement.
>
> MODEST APPEARANCE. We will demonstrate the scriptural principle of modesty by appearing and dressing in a manner that will enhance our Christian testimony and will avoid pride, elaborateness or sensuality.
>
> SOCIAL OBLIGATION. It should be our objective to fulfill our obligations to society by being good citizens, by correcting social injustices, and by protecting the sanctity of life.

Each principle was followed by more expansive definitions, but those definitions relaxed the strict holiness codes of past generations. Whereas the old rules stated that the denomination stood "against members wearing jewelry for ornament or decoration," the new guidance suggested that "we must seek spiritual beauty, which does not come from outward adornment with jewelry, expensive clothes, or cosmetics." Similarly, the church removed specific prohibitions against swimming, attending movies, and dancing.[20]

The changes did not, however, alter a number of key Pentecostal holiness positions or distance the Church of God from the conservative evangelical mainstream. In the 1980s, conservative Christians joined a powerful new political and social movement referred to by historians as the New Right. Ronald Reagan captured the political imagination of conservatives, but the New Right reenergized and reorganized evangelical Christians. Dismayed by the rise of "secular humanism," these Christians engaged in grassroot efforts that promoted "traditional family values" and denounced abortion, divorce, feminism, and homosexuality. Baptist Jerry Falwell, Pentecostal Pat Robertson, and conservative activist James Dobson became the faces of the Christian Right. Their organizations (the Moral Majority, Christian Broadcasting Network, and Focus on the Family) helped mobilize evangelicals on a variety of fronts.

The Church of God's new practical commitments dovetailed nicely with the positions held by the Christian Right. The denomination explicitly prohibited sex outside of marriage and homosexual relationships. Within the family, the denomination supported a complementarian, as opposed to egalitarian, view of marriage in which God gives men and women "distinctly different characteristics . . . as well as different responsibilities." This position extended into church politics, where women could not hold elected office and could not, until 1992, vote at the general assemblies. Additionally, the church stated its unequivocal opposition to abortion, stating, "Because the human fetus is sacred and blessed of God, we believe that we have the responsibility to protect the life of the unborn." They also continued to prohibit specific behaviors, including gambling and the use of alcohol, tobacco, or drugs. That list, however, was shorter than the older commitments and differed little from Southern Baptist and other evangelical positions. While the Church of God moved to a more progressive stance vis-à-vis its own traditions, it remained firmly planted in the conservative evangelical world.[21]

While the denomination sat comfortably in the evangelical mainstream, Lee College did not follow paths set by Falwell's Liberty University and Robertson's Regent College. Both Falwell and Robertson sought to politically mobilize conservative Christians—and the schools they founded played an important role in their efforts. Liberty, in particular, regularly hosted conservative Republican politicians, candidates, and pundits as part of its effort to influence the nation's political culture. In contrast Conn, who was once considered as a possible Democratic candidate for governor, did not attempt to elevate Lee's status by engaging the political world. The university rarely hosted debates, office holders, or politicians. The student body and alumni were conservative in their worldview, but Conn did not see Lee as vehicle to promote a particular party creed or platform.[22]

Instead, Conn held fast to core conservative evangelical teachings while focusing on changing campus culture. Restrictions on piercings, tattoos, and hair color—all superficial, but readily observable challenges to convention—disappeared. Conn hired a new, younger group of residence hall directors and extended curfew times. Gone were the days when the dorm matron would flash the dorm front porch lights to call students in for curfew, and forgotten were the days when female students knelt on the ground to check the length of their skirts. At the same time, some rules, like echoes from past generations, persisted. Students could not wear shorts to class, chapel kept its place on Tuesday and Thursday mornings, and dancing was not allowed on campus. For the most part, the campus continued following a rhythm that revolved around old campus traditions. Two-thirds of students lived in the dorms, and they socialized in the cafeteria and post office. Each year they participated in Sadie Hawkins Day, on which women chased men to ask for a date, and the Parade of Favorites, a beauty-talent contest for women. They watched sunsets from the top of Chilhowee Mountain in the nearby Cherokee National Forest and packed the gym when the Temple Crusaders came to play. Students found peer groups in clubs, intramural teams, ministry opportunities, and in Lee's various singing groups (whose membership far outnumbered the campus's music majors).[23]

So while discipline remained strict by public school standards, Conn and his student life staff valued moral principles over legalism and justice tempered by grace and second chances. They were comfortable with students who made mistakes and struggled with questions of faith, but desired a school that could support them, guide them, and help them to own their beliefs. Conn also removed many barriers between the students and the administration by moving in and among the student body. He attended intramural sports, visited the cafeteria, walked the campus, attended basketball games, and taught classes. His administrative staff followed his example, which helped them keep in touch with trends, concerns, and attitudes on campus.

A 1992 exit survey provides a snapshot of graduating seniors, a group who still had many characteristics of past generations of Lee students. Overwhelmingly white (82 percent) and Pentecostal (86 percent), six of ten hailed from hometowns with populations under one hundred thousand and fewer than two of ten came from major metropolitan areas. Half were under age twenty-two when they graduated, but 16 percent were in their thirties. 28 percent were married, a number that reflected both the significant number of non-traditional students at Lee and the tendency for undergraduate couples at Christian colleges to marry rather than cohabitate. Around 20 percent came from homes with a parent who was a college graduate, but a similar number had a parent who had not graduated from high school. A third of the students' families made less than the national median income of $36,000, but 18 percent made over half a million dollars annually. One demographic showed an interesting change: a third of students were not from the Church of God, and that number would grow over the next two decades.[24]

In 1990, buoyed by rising enrollment, the success of the Pass the Torch campaign (which raised $1.35 million), and the energy in the extended Lee family, Conn kicked off his second fundraising campaign, Higher Ground, at a special two-day campus event dubbed Celebration 1990. In what became a regular event, Celebration gave the college a chance to woo donors while dedicating new buildings. At the first Celebration, the college dedicated the 240-bed Sharp-Davis Hall. The event featured on-campus seminars, a service including faculty in full regalia, a procession of fifty class representatives, and special music. During the keynote address, Conn spoke of past success and future plans. In 1990 and then again at Celebration 1992, he made three things clear. First, he would not compromise Lee's Christian identity, mission, and worldview. "Lee College is committed to the principle," he said, "that the human experience, however logically reasoned or brilliantly expressed, is empty and valueless unless it finds its meaning in Jesus Christ."[25] Second, he believed that while the college was experiencing a period of unprecedented growth and optimism, continued progress was not inevitable. And finally, he intended to sustain growth and elevate Lee to a new, prosperous normal with a standard of excellence. Having worked so long with so few resources, most of his audience understood his sentiment that "Lee College will be the kind of place we always thought only other places can be."[26]

By 1993, the campus was entering a seventh year of growth under Conn's leadership. His Higher Ground campaign had an ambitious, two-year goal of $3 million. Success draws donors, and lead gifts from Bernard Dixon and the Watkins Foundation propelled funding for the two construction projects. The centerpiece of the campaign was the Dixon Center (1992), a 500 seat, state-of-the-art performing arts center that included classrooms, faculty offices, and studio space. The campaign also produced the Watkins Building, which housed the school's external ministerial training program, and a series of renovation projects. Additionally, the campaign built the DeVos Recreation Center, a much-needed student life facility that benefited from a lead gift by Richard and Helen DeVos. The gift came as the result of Conn's relationship with the Amway billionaire that developed after working with DeVoss on several book projects, most notably the best-selling *Believe!*[27] DeVos, whose first major donation helped fund the DeVos Tennis Center (1989), once joked about what Conn's promotion to the presidency would cost him. Over time, DeVos proved one of Lee's most generous benefactors.

The new recreation center also was a godsend for Lee's athletic programs, which grew at a rate of almost one per year. When Conn chaired a task force on athletics in 1986, the college sponsored only three varsity sports: men's basketball, women's basketball, and men's golf. Over eleven years, the college added men's and women's tennis, soccer, and cross-country teams, as well as softball, baseball, and women's volleyball. Collectively, some two hundred athletes competed in the National Association of Intercollegiate Athletics' (NAIA) TranSouth Conference. In off years, they also competed for National Christian College Athletic Association (NCCAA) championships. Conn was committed to not only competing but doing so at a high level. To that end, he gave coaches the ability to offer athletic scholarships. He also improved venues, including a soccer field (1989), softball's Butler Field (1991), and baseball's Olympic Field (1996). Men's basketball, Lee's premier sport, led the way in establishing a new winning tradition. From 1985 to 1992, Coach Randy Steele posted a 167–93 record. His tenure included six twenty-win seasons, three NAIA district championships, and six NCCAA district championships. Two years later, new coach Larry Carpenter guided the men to a NCCAA national championship. Other sports also enjoyed notable success, including several of the start-ups. Between 1991 and 2001, the women's volleyball team compiled a 358–146 record under the direction of Andrea Hudson and her assistant and husband Kevin. In the process, the Flames reached the NAIA national tournament in 1988 and 1989. Women's basketball made the national tournament eleven of twelve seasons between 1981 and 1993, the tennis teams dominated conference play, and the softball team won the 1992 NCCAA championship.

Success in athletics encouraged high school students to attend sports camps in the summers. By the summer of 1992, Lee was hosting eleven athletic camps that drew over two hundred and fifty teenagers and children to campus. The athletes joined sixty high school students who attended an annual summer music camp at Lee, sixty-eight Summer Honors students, and forty-three students who participated in Upward Bound, a six-week program that exposed high school students from underprivileged homes to a college environment. Rounding out the summer's offerings was Elderhostel. This program invited four dozen participants over the age of sixty to spend a week taking classes on campus. (Elderhostel later evolved into Lee's Encore program). Collectively, the summer camps further eroded the barrier that traditionalists in the Church of God had maintained for decades. And as the years passed, the summer offerings became a staple of the summer season for church groups, athletes, musicians, artists, and a host of other groups who were invited to campus.[28]

The 1993 school year started with more than two thousand students on campus. They were greeted with the smell of fresh paint and the buzz that accompanies a newly arrived freshman class. The semester progressed apace until, in the early morning hours of November 4, two students returning to the seventy-six bed Ellis Hall saw flames in the window of the first-floor prayer room. They immediately raised the alarm as the fire raced through the wood-framed building. Woken from sleep, the men of the dorm stumbled into hallways as the alarms screamed their warning, but flames blocked the exit for most of the men on the second floor. Residents, gathering outside the dorm, saw a second-floor window open, and called for their friend to jump to safety. He came headfirst out the window and was followed by a string of others, desperate to escape the inferno. Less than ten minutes after the flames were first spotted, the fire burned through the rafters and the roof collapsed. Fire crews could not enter the building, but worked through the morning to simply contain the blaze. The fire had every hallmark of a killer: it took place in the early morning in crowded quarters in an old, wood-framed structure without a sprinkler system. Fueled by gasoline splashed on the prayer room walls by a pair of arsonists, the flames spread with alarming speed. Investigators later said it looked like a bomb had gone off in the room. Seventy-four men lived in the dorm: emergency services treated eighteen for injuries, and helicopters took three men suffering from burn injuries to Chattanooga for urgent care. No lives were lost.[29]

The college community saw the hand of God working in those flames, making the Ellis Hall fire a seminal moment in Lee's history. In chapel

Headlines report the catastrophic 1993 Ellis Hall fire.

three days later, Conn said, "I do not want this lesson to be lost on the least observant one among us. We did not get lucky early Thursday morning. We had a miracle occur in our midst. . . . I offer my great gratitude and praise to the protective hand of God almighty and the person of Jesus Christ of Nazareth."[30] Vice president David Tilley said, "If anyone has the nerve to ask, 'Where was God when Ellis Hall burned?' I'm here to tell you that he was right in the middle of those flames, pulling his children out of danger."[31] Years later Conn said that the Ellis fire was one of those moments that convinced him that God had his hand on Lee in a special way. The escape of those Ellis Hall men had reaffirmed a belief that the school had lost sight of, but which Nora Chambers and BTS pioneers firmly believed: that God had plans to prosper the school, turning losses into gain and tragedy into victory.[32] For people of faith, the sense that one is not only serving God but has found the center of God's will is a feeling that inspires faith that leads to action.

Less than a year after the fire, Lee held Celebration 1994 to dedicate the 130-bed Atkins-Ellis Hall, reflect on God's providence, and close the Higher Ground campaign, which tripled its $3 million goal. The school recognized not only the major donors, but Church of God congregations, local community support, and sympathetic parties who opened their pocketbooks to support the students and raise over $1 million for the new dorm. In many ways, the fire represented how far Lee had come in mending relations with the people of Cleveland and Bradley County, who gave generously of their time and money during the recovery. Many residents donated clothing to students in need. A local defense attorney provided pro bono legal services to Lee students questioned about the fire. And in an act of good will, the planning commission finally granted permission for the college to expand beyond Parker Street, the campus's eastern boundary.[33]

Having closed the books on one fundraising campaign, Conn immediately began another. The Open Door campaign set an ambitious $10 million-dollar goal to fund another series of renovations, buildings, and infrastructure projects. Knowing that some questioned his commitment to construction over growing the endowment, employee benefits, and other "softer" improvements, Conn argued that he had no choice. Enrollment continued growing at an impressive rate, doubling from 1,200 when Conn took office in 1986 to over 2,400 in 1995. In that time Lee had been busy with construction projects, but it had added only a pair of new dormitories and renovated a single building for classroom use. The Dixon Center had limited classroom space, but the new recreation center, external programs building, and tennis courts did not add desks or beds to meet the new demand. The capital campaign sought to remedy that problem by adding living space, separate buildings to house the music and education programs, a student center, a new dining hall, a new east-west pedestrian mall, and extensive renovations to several buildings.[34]

An unexpected source, the 1996 Olympics, added another impetus for growth. When Atlanta won the opportunity to host the summer games, the Tennessee Ocoee Development Agency successfully lobbied to make the Ocoee River the site for the kayak and canoe events. The venue, located in nearby Polk County, would feature an engineered course within the natural setting of the river, and Cleveland was the nearest city. After months of negotiations, Conn signed an agreement to turn much of Lee's campus into an Olympic Village to house athletes from twenty-six countries. Although not part of the contract, Conn used the opportunity to push a new dining hall to the front of the construction queue, completing it and dorm renovations just in time for the games. When the athletes arrived, they lived in a village demarcated by ten-foot security fences, in an environment well-removed from the normal rules and life of Lee students. The school converted the recreation center into a social club, complete with a dance floor and alcoholic drinks. Sleeping arrangements in the dorms were not monitored, and the new cafeteria never served better, more varied food than in those weeks. Traditionalists in the church balked at life in the village, but for the college, the opportunity for students to participate in the event and the exposure generated for the school made the village worthwhile. Additionally, the generous profit margins on the Olympic contracts generated revenue that Conn reinvested to re-start the baseball program and develop its new field.[35]

As the Olympics closed, the college debated a move to university status. On one hand, the change in name carried a certain cachet that required little of the school other than a reorganization into colleges. It suggested that Lee had larger long-term goals that included graduate programs and a broader identity in the academic world. The admissions office favored the change, which they welcomed as another marketing tool. On the other hand, some faculty were concerned on two counts. They feared the change signaled a shift away from quality undergraduate teaching. Perhaps more troubling, the faculty lacked the resources and time necessary to undertake the research agenda often associated with university work. In his Celebration 1996 address, Conn made clear his preference. "It's easy to say, 'Well, let's just try to be a good little college,' rather than accept the challenge of measuring up to the standard of a university worthy of the name.... to declare such things as beyond our reach and settle back into a comfortable rut that doesn't stretch or challenge us. Instead, perhaps now is the time for Lee College to 'toss our caps' over the wall so that we have no choice but to follow."[36] Throughout 1996 the university studied the issue through the time-honored, but rarely influential, means of a task force, but by the time the board met in December to make a final decision, a positive outcome seemed certain. The announcement soon came that the school would make the transition on August 1, 1997.

If some questioned the move to university status, supporters could point to a series of academic successes that suggested that the move was timely. To start, the school's music program was undergoing a renaissance. When the Dixon Center opened in 1991, Conn invited outstanding national talents to kick off an annual presidential concert series. In 1994 the Curtsinger Music Building opened. The next year, music offered Lee's first graduate degree, the Master's of Church Music. For Conn, this was the logical place to start graduate studies. "There were basically two criteria to be met. There had to be an adequate demand for the program, and our faculty had to demonstrate that there was something that we could do better than anyone else. We want to offer programs that are unique; programs that we can claim as our niche."[37] The graduate degrees, like accreditation, brought more academic rigor to a music program whose ensembles had long been a hallmark of Lee. Established groups like Lee Singers, Campus Choir, Ladies of Lee, and Evangelistic Singers had traveled extensively through the years and become the best-known school brands. In the 1990s, they were joined by new groups. Voices of Lee, an acapella group under the leadership of Danny Murray, debuted at Celebration 1994 and soon challenged Singers as the school's top traveling ensemble. To serve the performance needs of music majors, the school organized Lee Chorale (1998), Wind Ensemble (1999), and Chamber Orchestra (1996). The growth and improvements in the music program culminated in accreditation by the National Association of Schools of Music in 1998.

Progress also was made on several other academic fronts. In 1990 the education program earned accreditation by the National Council for Accreditation of Teacher Education, and four years later SACS reaffirmed the school's accreditation for another full, ten-year period. Lee continued rolling out new academic programs, including master's degrees in counseling, liberal arts, and classroom teaching.[38] Then in 1998, Lee revised its thirty-year-old general education core. The new version retained the religion minor, adjusted some core classes, added a twelve-hour western humanities sequence, and introduced a cross-cultural requirement.[39] Study abroad opportunities grew at a steady rate, with trips to Germany, Ukraine, China, South Africa, and Honduras joining the Semester in Europe program. Lee also created the office of first year programs, which revised and improved the university's Gateway program—classes that helped first-year students and transfers adjust to university life in general, as well as to Lee's particular culture.

As the school evolved, so too did its administrative structure. Like all presidents before him, Conn recruited administrators who understood both campus and church culture. He did not seek people with experience in higher education, nor did he send out Lee's own to gain experience at other institutions before bringing them back to Cleveland. In his early years as president, he promoted from within or hired administrators from the church. He especially recruited from Mount Paran Church of God, where Conn's long-time friend and supporter Paul L. Walker was pastor. The progressive Walker not only held the pulpit and served on Lee's board but also founded a school from which Conn hired personnel, including two men who became top administrators—David Tilley and Gary Ray. As time passed, Conn grew administrators from inside Lee, mentoring promising undergraduates, hiring them as staff, and then promoting them to administrative posts. This practice helped produce an administrative team that was fully in line with Conn's vision and had little turnover, but also brought no outside experience or context to their jobs.

In 1989, Conn reorganized his administrative team. He created a cabinet consisting of Vice President and Dean of the College Ollie Lee, Vice President for Business and Finance David Painter, Vice President for Institutional Advancement Dale Goff, Vice President for Student Life Henry Smith, and Vice President and Executive Assistant to the President David Tilley. In 1997, the newly formed university organized into colleges, the largest of which was the College of Arts and Sciences, led by Carolyn Dirksen. Dirksen, who succeeded Lee as the vice president for academic affairs in 1999, was the first woman to hold a top administrative position since Mary Harrison Green led the high school in the 1940s. Although contemporaries, Lee and Dirksen represented two different generations of academic leadership. Ollie Lee was one of the Church of God's early pioneers in the field of higher education. He graduated from Lee's junior college in 1958, then, instead of pursuing the ministry, he took a bachelor's degree from Berea College. He earned a doctorate in sociology from the University of Pittsburg before joining the Lee faculty in 1967. One of the few church members to hold a terminal degree outside of theology, Lee rapidly rose from department head to dean to vice president, where he was a central figure in the school's efforts to move faculty standards, resources, and benefits closer to best practices.[40]

Dirksen grew up in a Church of God household in the small border town of Bisbee, Arizona. Like Lee, she was raised in modest circumstances, and like Lee she aspired to something more. She attended Cochise College before earning her bachelor's and master's degree in English from Northern Arizona. In 1968, at the age of twenty-one, Dirksen applied to serve in the field as a missionary. Her life in traditional missions, however, was never realized. The head of the Church of God's World Missions, knowing Lee's need for qualified teachers, instead sent her name to the college. Ultimately, Dirksen received an offer for a job to which she never applied. Surprised by the invitation, she accepted a one-year position—and stayed for five decades. While at Lee she earned her doctorate in linguistics from the University of Arizona. Murl Dirksen, an anthropology student she met at Northern Arizona, followed her to Lee. The two married, and he also joined the faculty. As a woman working in the church's very patriarchal structures, Dirksen quickly distinguished herself as an outstanding instructor. She won the school's first Excellence in Teaching Award in 1974 and the church's Distinguished Educator award in 1998. A capable administrator, she became a department chair in 1983, associate dean, and then Dean of Arts and Sciences. Dirksen stretched the cultural boundaries of the Lee community by promoting cross-cultural experiences (she spent a year teaching in China) and advocating for minority and foreign students. She also became one of Conn's friends and allies, serving as vice president for thirteen years.[41]

The mid-1990s marked an important turning point in Conn's ongoing conflict with Church of God traditionalists, led by the still-formidable Ray Hughes. In 1990 Hughes appeared poised to be elected for a third time as the denomination's general overseer. It was well-known that, if elected, Hughes would focus on the lack of Pentecostal identity at Lee, while Paul Conn was "ready to hunker down and get blown away."[42] Instead, the General Assembly elected Lamar Vest, Conn's ally, to the top spot. Hughes returned to the committee in 1992 and by 1996 had positioned himself for another run at the overseer's seat. He was again frustrated as Paul L. Walker, Conn's friend and mentor, won the election on the nominating ballot. For Conn, Walker's election meant he had won his fight for a new, evangelical Lee. But the battle was not quite over. Some traditionalists remained, and they openly criticized Lee's more progressive identity. Conn's last skirmish with the Executive Committee took place after he removed the words "A Church of God Institution" from the college seal. In a confrontational meeting, church leadership demanded the language be restored. Conn persisted, noting that his new design matched the seal used before 1965. It was a small, but highly symbolic victory for the president, who no longer had to look over his shoulder to see if his old antagonists could muster the strength to challenge his vision.[43]

By 2000, Conn and the Lee community reached the point at which physical and numerical growth was not only expected but had become necessary markers of success. Each semester the university trumpeted the latest enrollment record and each biennial Celebration event opened new buildings. Where once administrators had considered slowing growth, they now argued that the question of limits was an issue of commitment, not capacity. Conn said, "I bring a mental block to the concept that we might somehow have too many ... students. I look out over our students, eager, hard-working young men and women and I ask myself, which one of these is too many? Which one is the one we would reject and turn away for fear that we might exceed the mythical threshold of 'too many'?"[44] This perspective meant that Lee would also remain committed to an admissions policy with low entrance standards and high numbers of provisionally admitted students, even as its scholarships attracted more highly qualified applicants. The result was a growing student body in which

Centennial scholars studied alongside students who did not have a C average or a 17 on the ACT. While this might suggest a quantity over quality strategy, it reaffirmed Lee's tradition of accepting students from marginalized populations and giving them an opportunity to succeed.

As the student body expanded, Conn continued to focus fundraising on improving the physical campus. The endowment grew from $2.6 to $4.6 million in his first ten years, despite never being a priority for Conn.[45] To those who argued that he focused too much on bricks and mortar, he had several rebuttals at hand. There was the obvious need to keep pace with rising enrollment, but Conn also knew that the built environment of a campus was critical to its identity. When on faculty, he drove a friend through campus, who told him, "Paul, this is a slum."[46] The comment shocked Conn, but it made him realize that some visitors found the campus's tired, worn appearance off-putting. As president, Conn not only added new buildings, but did so in a way that created an aesthetic. Neo-Georgian architecture, immaculate grounds, buried utilities, and pedestrian malls were not cheap, but they created an environment that suggested quality and confidence. To those who argued that the endowment, research, and teaching were what really mattered, he argued, "Buildings aren't important. They are important only if you don't have them. . . . Lots of nice new buildings never educated anybody. But if you don't have a dorm for a kid to sleep in, then it's important. And if you don't have a classroom for a teacher to teach in, then nothing gets taught. Well, for years, Lee College has been defined too many times, by what it did not have. Because of what we did not have, students stayed away by the thousands, and it never mattered much what we did have, at least not to them."[47]

And so Lee continued to grow. Enrollment rose from 1,827 in 1991 to 2,477 in 1995. By 1996 it had the second-largest enrollment of any private college or university in Tennessee—surpassed only by Vanderbilt. By 2000 Conn had doubled the size of the campus to over forty acres and razed almost one hundred structures to make room for new building projects. Four new dorms, Livingston Hall (1995), Hicks Hall (1996), Keeble Hall (1999), and Storms Hall (2000) added 440 new beds, but even so the school never quite caught up with student demand for on-campus housing. The new Deacon Jones Dining Hall opened in 1996, and two years later the campus rebuilt the last surviving structure from Centenary College—the East Wing—into administrative offices. The $20 million Open Door campaign paid for a series of renovations and two new academic buildings, the Curtsinger Music Building (1995), and DeVos Education Building (1998). The dedication of the Paul Conn Student Center in 2000 finished the construction schedule.[48]

In his first sixteen years as president, Conn transformed Lee. When he joined the administration in 1984, he faced two major challenges. First, he sought to break the school out of the separatist, sectarian identity so prized by the traditionalists. Here he made quick progress. The failures of the second Hughes administration and progressive trends in the denomination created an opening that Conn broadened by growing the school. Second, he needed to create a new campus ethos that overcame the inertia of the early 1980s and looked past the school's limits. The habit of thinking defensively was not easy to reverse and no single initiative or moment turned the tide, but Conn consistently looked forward, not backward. As a result, his commitment, energy, and vision slowly took root. Small, tentative steps (his first new building was, after all, a maintenance shed) turned into a string of construction projects that transformed the physical campus. Likewise, small gains in the number of students on campus turned into a litany of new enrollment records. As Lee entered the twenty-first century, Conn had created an environment in which students, faculty, and staff asked, "What's next?"

Chapter 9

THE LEE EXPERIENCE

The University Enters
the Twenty-First Century

Lee University enjoyed unprecedented prosperity in the first decade of the twenty-first century, and the Lee community readily accepted the principle that success and growth were synonymous. Students poured into campus, and every fall the administration trumpeted a new record enrollment. Not only did tuition dollars fatten budgets, but money also rolled in from foundations, benefactors, and government grants. Paul Conn often quipped, "God doesn't like an idle backhoe," and the pace at which he transformed the physical campus was remarkable. New dormitories, apartments, and academic buildings appeared almost every year. Extracurricular activities and new academic programs multiplied as the faculty and staff embraced a culture in which things entrepreneurial, new, fresh, and innovative became the standard of success. This growth model reduced the emphasis on holiness and religious zeal and overshadowed endowment growth, scholarly output, and other measures that institutions of higher education use to measure success.

Year after year, Vice President for Enrollment Management Gary Ray (1999–2010) hoped for "one more" student than last term, and his admissions team consistently delivered. Total enrollment moved past three thousand in 1998 and broke four thousand just eight years later.[1] Students arriving at Lee discovered a school that not only offered a steadily increasing variety of academic programs, but also provided a dizzying array of extracurricular opportunities, all in a package that served their spiritual needs. In combination, these student-centered elements made up what became known on campus as the "Lee experience."

Many students began their Lee experience with the university's Summer Honors program. Developed as a recruiting tool to attract academically promising students, Summer Honors served (and continues to serve) as a microcosm of campus culture. It distilled the Lee experience into an intense, twelve-day program. Summer Honors highlighted social events, made spiritual development a priority, and offered a generous six academic credit hours for a pair of courses. The classes met twice a day and were taught by some of Lee's most personable professors. Meant to entice students, they featured topics such as "Doing Business with Sharks," "Hitler vs. Bonhoeffer," and "Keeping Secrets Secret." The coursework was not challenging, but finding the time and energy to invest in academics could be difficult—particularly with the program's busy social calendar. Summer Honors students traveled to Atlanta for a Braves baseball game and attended a pair of evening socials. They went to concerts in Chattanooga and enjoyed a movie night. Students participated in their own Olympics and braved white water rafting on the Ocoee River. The message was clear: college was full of people, events, and fun. Beyond this, the program was meant to have spiritual value as well. Devotionals and small groups started and ended each day, and students spent a morning participating in a service project. Summer Honors delivered a dynamic, socially engaging, spiritually underpinned academic summer camp that promised a similar experience for full-time students.

Like Summer Honors, Lee Day offers insight into university culture. An annual spring event for prospective students and their families, Lee

The Lee Experience: Lee Day block party, 2018.

Day attracted thousands of guests for whom the admissions team showcased the Lee Experience. Students toured campus, sat in on a class, and had the opportunity to register for the fall semester. And while there were sessions on financial aid and student success, Lee wanted to create "a jam-packed two days of information, fun, and excitement" to balance the academic side of college life. These included a musically themed "Lee U Spotlight," a Greek club-sponsored block party, drawings for scholarships, a cookout, and a stage show that promised a "lighthearted look at Lee." Education required time in the classroom, but Lee Day promoted music, competition, and high energy social gatherings as central to college life.[2]

Once enrolled as undergraduates students could choose from a wide variety of extracurricular opportunities on campus. The student life team, led by vice presidents Walt Mauldin (2001–2010) and Mike Hayes (2010–2022) wanted students to find their place at Lee—a smaller group within the larger Lee community where they could make friends who shared interests. Those interest groups connected students to their peers and the school. Athletic teams, choirs, ensembles, fraternities, and sororities were ready-made communities that enjoyed strong backing by the school administration. Characterized by social events best suited to outgoing, extroverted students, the dominant campus culture reflected the experiences of administrators and staff who had enjoyed similar opportunities while undergraduates at Lee.

Other yearly events, such as Dorm Wars and Pack and Stack, also typified the university's extroverted approach to student life. Dorm Wars brought together teams from the various dorms to compete in front of a thousand raucous students in Walker Arena. Played out in an environment akin to a professional wrestling event, the frenetic competitions became highlights of the year for the student life staff and half the students living on campus. The school also embraced Operation Christmas Child, a charity drive sponsored by Samaritan's Purse, a Christian non-profit that delivers gift-filled boxes to children in need. The school required first-year students in Gateway classes to collect items for gift boxes, then participate in a semester-ending Pack and Stack event. Held in Walker Arena, classes competed to complete the most gift boxes, took group pictures with Santa Claus, and participated in contests to win acclaim for the best (or worst) Christmas costumes. The loud, competitive gatherings were not for the faint of heart, but they perfectly captured the Lee ethos.[3]

An important part of this approach to campus life was the administration's promotion of Greek clubs. Student Life leaders made these local clubs the centerpiece of campus activities: subsidizing their activities,

The Lee Experience: Operation Christmas Child, 2016.

spotlighting them in promotional material, guaranteeing them a place in student publications, and securing them spots at high-profile university events like Lee Day and the commissioning service. While only about one in twenty students joined Lee's clubs, the casual observer could be forgiven for thinking that Greek block parties, Greek Olympics, Greek-letter intramural teams, and pledge classes dominated the campus. The administration purposed to expand the number of clubs to ensure places for students who wanted to experience Greek life. Some club traditions, including hazing, were out of place on a Christian campus that emphasized love for one's neighbor. "Tap night," during which clubs publicly accepted or rejected prospective members persisted for years before being reformed to protect the men and women the clubs did not select. For those who participated in Lee's Greek clubs, as had almost all senior administrators, it was natural to assume that they represented the most important student groups on campus.

Like the Greek clubs, vocal ensembles also held a prized position in

Lee culture. Voices of Lee, Lee Singers, Chorale, Ladies of Lee, Evangelistic Singers, Choral Union, and Campus Choir, which collectively attracted over three hundred participants, were vital parts of the music school. They served as a critical element of Lee's public outreach, crisscrossing the nation to perform in venues ranging from the presidential inauguration to the small sanctuaries of rural Church of God congregations. Any given weekend, the groups would leave for long road trips, sometimes returning to campus just in time for Monday morning classes. Lee's ensembles, not its sports teams, were the most recognized face of the university. Audiences saw young people who performed at a high level, witnessed for their faith, and loved their university. Most of the performers were not music majors, but the long hours in practice and on the road bound students together. For them, the ensembles became their social clubs. As such, these groups adopted many traditions usually associated with fraternities and sororities. Members went through inductions, received jerseys, and were assigned big brothers and sisters. They rivaled the Greek clubs in their numbers, influence, and shaping of Lee's identity.

The influence of vocal music hit new heights with the rise of popular television series that featured singing competitions. Individual Lee students auditioned for the shows, and in 2007 Phil Stacey broke through to the final rounds of *American Idol*. A vocal major and Lee Singer, Stacey shared some of his spotlight with Lee, which gladly promoted his success. Eight years later, history major Clark Beckham finished as the *American Idol* runner-up with his soulful voice and Motown-influenced sound. Later that same year, Jordan Smith won *The Voice*. Following in Smith's footsteps, in 2017 Campus Choir alumna Brooke Simpson finished third on *The Voice*. In sum, these four performers did more than promote their own careers. They brought welcome attention to Lee, which trumpeted their success in promotional and alumni publications.[4] If Lee's vocalists had not already earned top billing on campus, their feats on the nation's biggest stages solidified music's prominent place at the university.

Of course, most Lee students did not appear on *American Idol*, travel with Voices of Lee, play a varsity sport, or participate in Greek Life. They found their own peer groups in a host of formal and informal networks, many of which the university supported, and some it did not. And while it is not practical to detail the entire social landscape at Lee, a sampling of campus groups suggests the breadth of student interests, affiliations, and identities. Lee's students discovered their place in the usual sorts of college groups. However, some activities associated with college culture were less common, less celebrated, and never openly acknowledged. That is, while some students bought alcohol, threw parties, experimented with drugs, and identified as LGBTQ+, these activities fell outside the campus's evangelical Christian culture. As a result, they remained underground.

Instead, a host of religious activities defined much of Lee's public face. The most prominent were the most institutionalized—mandatory chapel and residence life small groups. By this time, Lee's chapel services had diversified considerably from previous generations' hymn and sermon model. Most students attended chapel in the 1,500-seat Conn Center on Tuesday and Thursday mornings. Student musicians of the chapel worship teams led students in praise and worship before giving way to a traditional sermon, although some chapels featured a concert, missionaries, or other special programming. Alternative chapels, held in the Dixon Center, featured topical sermon series, roundtables, and a more reserved worship experience. In contrast, the Stone Chapel hosted liturgical chapels that invited students to experience a version of high church worship. Begun in 2012 by pastor Heidi Johnson, the services featured organ music, responsive readings, communion, and a homily. And, once a semester, the university hosted convocation, a four-day event that echoed traditional Pentecostal revivals with nightly services. Students also invested in religious clubs such as Crossover, Backyard, and Campus Crusade.

The Lee Experience: Chapel, 2018.

They attended a wide variety of local congregations on Sunday (North Cleveland Church of God, First Baptist Cleveland, Public Church, and The Chapel were among their favorites), and met for informal Bible studies, some of which were hosted in professors' homes.

Additionally, students found their place in other formal and informal communities. Residence life staffs (resident directors, resident assistants, and resident chaplains), student media (*Vindagua* and the *Clarion* newspaper), and Student Leadership Council (which coordinated events on campus) not only provided essential services to students, but also created strong identity groups. The Diversity Council, Black Student Union, Asian Council, and like organizations provided voices and communities for Lee's minority and international students. Others engaged in intramurals or club sports like rugby or ultimate frisbee. Informal friend groups formed around other interests, like gaming, backpacking, road tripping, rock climbing, or spending time in local coffee shops. Lee's academically minded organizations gave many students a home, whether in the Kairos honors program, as McNair scholars, on the mock trial team, or in one of a growing number of discipline-specific organizations.

Many characteristics of the student body would have been familiar to generations of Lee faculty and staff. The university continued to welcome a large population of students who came from the bottom half of their high school class, with 31 and 22 percent of students coming from that demographic in 2000 and 2020, respectively. The campus also continued to lack racial diversity, a problem that the university did not effectively address. Admissions successfully delivered students to campus, but did not make the recruitment of minority populations a priority. In 2000, 89 percent of the student population was white and over the next twenty years the campus became only slightly more diverse, remaining 74 percent white; only 5 percent of students were African American and 3 percent Hispanic.[5] The Lee experience may have welcomed all comers, but the university made little effort to invite more diverse audiences to campus.

In contrast, under the oversight of Vice President for Academic Affairs Carolyn Dirksen (1999–2013), Lee's academic program steadily improved its reputation and offerings. From 2000 to 2015, the number of undergraduate majors increased from seventy-four to one hundred. In the same period, the school moved from six to fifteen graduate degrees.[6] Quantity does not necessarily mean quality, but outside observers began to confirm a change in the perceived value of Lee's program. Starting in 1983, *U.S. News and World Report* published a special edition that ranked

American universities. While many college administrators dismissed the rankings as superficial, almost all valued the public relations boost gained by a high spot on the ladder. Scores were based on measures such as reputation, standardized test scores, graduation and retention rates, and faculty. To ensure schools competed against like institutions, the magazine divided the higher education landscape into national universities, national liberal arts colleges, regional universities, and regional colleges. Lee first entered the *U.S. News* rankings in 2001 in the second tier of the Southern Liberal Arts division. Eight years later, Lee leapfrogged neighboring Middle Tennessee State and the University of Tennessee at Chattanooga in the rankings. By 2014 Lee was considered a top-tier regional university in the south. The university won other recognitions from *U.S. News*, including identification as an up-and-coming institution with outstanding study abroad programs. The university's position in the popular rankings may not have perfectly captured its place in the landscape of higher education, but Lee's climb demonstrated a rapid improvement in reputation and was a regular bragging point in school publications.[7]

As the university grew its academic program and reputation, it held fast to a student-centered campus, a central tenet of the Lee experience. Lee's faculty played a critical role in maintaining that focus. Most universities hire faculty to win grants, research, and publish, thereby adding to the school's prestige. Graduate training focuses almost exclusively on research, and interviews for new faculty normally concentrate on their research agenda. Tenure and promotion decisions rest almost exclusively on the faculty member's publication record. Logically, faculty prioritize their research agendas, which allow them to move to more prestigious research universities, where they train graduate students to form similar priorities.

Lee took a different path. From its earliest days as the Bible Training School, Lee sought faculty with advanced degrees, but emphasized teaching as ministry, not teaching as distraction from research. As BTS grew into Lee College and then Lee University, the quality of the faculty improved, but the principle of ministry over research did not change. For many years, administrators hired the most qualified Church of God members available. In the late 1960s, the college's pursuit of accreditation caused administrators to seek out and recruit the handful of church members who held graduate degrees. That first generation of faculty with doctorates taught at Lee because they felt called by God to do so. The salary was anemic, the facilities minimal, the students often underprepared for college work, and the workload was heavy—five to six courses a semester. Yet the professors stayed at the college and invested in the academic and spiritual lives of their students. They were called to teach, and their product was their students, not research and publication.

Paul Conn went to Lee College and understood the importance of teaching to the university. Even as he expanded and diversified the faculty, added graduate programs, and improved Lee's reputation among its peers, Conn kept the undergraduate classroom at the center of the Lee experience. In hiring new faculty, the university sought Christians who showed promise in the classroom. Practicing the faith was mandatory, but candidates were told that research would not be their priority. Instead, Lee based tenure and promotion decisions on teaching effectiveness and university service. In a radical departure from the programs in which they had trained, candidates learned that publications were valued but not necessary for advancement. Instead, teaching assessments made by undergraduates at the end of each semester played a central role in evaluating faculty for tenure and promotion. It should come as no surprise, then, Lee's top faculty award is for excellence in teaching, followed by awards for advising and scholarship.

While some faculty left Lee to pursue more traditional academic careers, many chose to invest in a school that valued their faith and their students. Lee regularly welcomed its own alumni onto the faculty. For some, like psychology professor Susan Ashcraft, Lee had always been part of their lives. Ashcraft's father was Delton Alford, the founder of Lee Singers. For her, Lee was always home. She played on its campus as a child and embraced the campus experience as an undergraduate. When she received a call about an open position on the faculty, she wrote, "At that moment, I realized God had brought me full circle. I would now return to my home, the place that was literally sewn into my DNA—the place where I had always wanted to teach and fulfill my vocation."[8] Others fell in love with Lee as undergraduates and returned as faculty or administrators, where they reengaged the Lee experience.

As Conn grew the faculty, increasing numbers of professors came to Lee with no previous history with the school. Rather, they held terminal degrees in their fields and desired to teach at an intentionally Christian university. One of these was Ben Christmann, who held a doctorate in biochemistry and molecular biology. A Presbyterian from Missouri, he attended nearby Covenant College before earning his PhD from St. Louis University. He started his career in the research lab, working for the Centers for Disease Control and Prevention before considering a career in academia. His decision to join the Lee faculty had nothing to do with

Pentecostalism or family history, but rather a belief that God called him to Lee. In fact, when Christmann interviewed with science faculty, he had already decided to take a commission in the US Navy. However, during his time on campus, he found a "clear sense of purpose and placement" in Christian higher education, turned down his commission, and dedicated his talents to Lee.[9]

As hiring accelerated to meet increasing enrollment, the administration found it more difficult (or possibly less desirable) to perpetuate the older, more religiously conservative, student-centered teaching model. That is, the new faculty bent less to Lee's culture and instead began to influence and shape that culture in new ways. One was an increasing emphasis on scholarship over teaching—a model that virtually every doctoral program embraced in order to prepare graduate students for the publish-or-perish world of academia. Another was a result of the growing religious diversity among faculty. Whereas Conn once had to defend hiring a Baptist soccer coach, Lee's full-time faculty came to include almost every Christian denomination. Professors were hired out of traditions far removed from Pentecostalism—Roman Catholic, Presbyterian, and Orthodox. Other faculty hailed from denominations and congregations that were liberal and progressive in their faith and practice. Furthermore, the university hired artists-in-residence and adjunct faculty from outside the Christian faith. While few in number, these faculty members represented a significant break from Lee's hiring practices and breached a firewall that maintained orthodoxy on campus.

The academic program in which faculty worked grew and evolved over time. Among the many changes that took place, three merit special consideration. The first was the growth of the global perspectives program. As one of President Conn's early initiatives, Lee began offering students the opportunity to study abroad for a semester in the United Kingdom. In 1998 the university made a cross-cultural experience a requirement for graduation. All students took courses preparing them for an encounter with another culture, preferably one outside of the United States. Few would argue that travel abroad did not enrich students' lives. Fulfilling the requirement, however, was not always an easy task. The mandate required significant institutional support for students, many of whom had neither the means nor the experience for foreign travel. Lee established a global perspectives office and backed its commitment to the program by pouring financial support into it. Rather than paying third parties to organize the trips, Lee relied on faculty volunteers to create courses and itineraries, recruit students, and both teach and chaperone

Students participating in Lee's Global Perspectives program pose outside Durham Cathedral in England, 2007.

students abroad. To ensure equity, the university sharply discounted tuition for classes, making trips an amazing value that combined experience with academic credit.

The global perspectives program had immediate and lasting success as faculty created trips that took students all over the world. Some trips, such as Professor Bob Barnett's trip to England and Scotland, grew into campus legends. Barnett, named a distinguished professor in 2012, was known for his willingness to invest in students outside the classroom. His seventeen-day trip became so popular that students camped out for two nights to secure their place on a trip that left seven months later. The experience was made all the more meaningful thanks to the assistance of Englishman Andy Sinclair, who Lee later awarded an honorary degree for his work with several Global Perspectives trips. Together, they took students to visit Iona, Edinburgh, Hadrian's Wall, the Lake District, and London. While abroad, Barnett challenged students to think about their lives in a global context, encouraged them to step outside their comfort zone, and taught them history on the ground where it took place. In doing so, Barnett joined dozens of professors and thousands of students in making travel an important part of the Lee experience.[10]

Another major innovation in the curriculum was the 2003 addition of a service requirement. Jump-started by a $4 million grant from the Lazarus Foundation and a $2 million grant from the Lilly Foundation, Lee took a new interest in the relationship between career, calling, and service. The new initiative took two related paths. The Poiema Project explored the relationship between Christian calling and career. It established new scholarships, a residence hall chaplain program, and an office of calling and career. It also included a theological exploration of calling. This investigation resulted in Professor Terry Cross's book *Answering the Call in the Spirit*, which asserted that Pentecostals had too narrowly defined God's calling to ministry. Cross argued that Christians should find a call that offers salvation and a relationship with God, then gives people a life that responds to that first call in whatever particular walk of life God calls them.[11]

The new initiative also required students to complete a course entitled "Biblical and Theological Foundations of Benevolence" and undertake eighty service hours. With this requirement, Lee put into action the idea that Christians should not only love God with all their heart, soul, mind, and strength, but should also love their neighbor as they loved themselves. Incoming students were introduced to service during new student orientation. On the Sunday before classes started, they participated in Deke Day, a requirement for the freshman Gateway class. Named for the Greek word for service, *diakonos*, Deke Day opened with a chapel service, after which hundreds of first-year and transfer students were sent to serve in local nursing and care homes.[12]

Under the leadership of William Lamb and the staff of the Leonard Center, the new program built upon a community service commitment initiated under President Conn. Lee already welcomed local residents to campus through a number of initiatives. By far the largest group of visitors were high school students attending summer camps. By 2015, over ten thousand had sampled Lee's hospitality at sports, church, and academic camps. Launched in 1991, the Presidential Concert Series invited talented musicians to perform at Lee in front of a mixed college and community audience. A typical year, such as 2004, included the Mendelssohn String Quartet, pianists Ning An and Gloria Chien, the St. Olaf Choir, and the Chamber Orchestra Kremlin. In 2007, the university added Encore classes for senior citizens. The program opened all undergraduate classes and special seminars to older citizens for a nominal fee. Encore was a huge success, with 350 people enrolled in 2019. And in cooperation with the local school system, Lee hosted the Lee University Developmental Inclusion Classroom, which utilized Lee students to help educate autistic children at a campus facility. The new service requirement sent students off campus and radically expanded Lee's footprint in the community. Lee students committed thousands of hours of required service and thousands more in voluntary service. Students also fulfilled some service hours as part of classes, such as tutoring in local schools. Many more hours were spent volunteering in a wide range of ways in the local community.[13]

Crossover, a student-led ministry to low-income communities in East Cleveland, was typical of students' outreach. Started by Lee student Aaron Skaggs in 2006, it grew from a small group of students making a single route through town to scores of students making more than a dozen trips. Every Saturday morning, while most of their friends slept in, a handful of students left Lee to pick up food from local contributors before returning to the Leonard Center. There they joined other students to fill food baskets, pray, and join teams heading into the community. At the core of each team were leaders who delivered food to the same families every week. As one student put it, "We take food, and . . . it gets our foot in the door, but the main reason we're there is just to love on people, to share Jesus with them, and be a constant source of love and encouragement." Through Crossover, students formed relationships and discovered that real service could be both joy filled and taxing, a gift to both the giver and recipient, meeting both physical and spiritual needs.[14]

A third major development took place in 2014, when the university trimmed the credits required for degree completion from 130 to 120 hours. The reduction kept pace with broader trends in higher education in Tennessee, but ended a forty-six-year-old requirement that students complete a Bible minor. In the 1960s, the college had simultaneously pursued SACS accreditation for a liberal arts college and debated the future of its Bible college. In the end, it won accreditation and closed the Bible college. To appease conservatives who feared the school was abandoning its BTS roots, the administration promised that all students would complete an eighteen credit-hour religion minor. Over the years, generations of Lee students graduated with the minor, but in 1998 the university replaced three hours of religion with a capstone class in the student's major. Six years later, the school replaced a three-hour religion class with a one-hour benevolence class and two credit hours for community service. The 2014 revisions removed academic credit for service hours and capstone no longer counted for religion credit. Students still took twelve hours of Bible and theology classes, but the minor passed away almost unnoticed by the campus community.[15]

The retiring of the Bible minor suggests two less obvious threats to Lee's Christian mission. First, the university took for granted its distinctive Christian, Pentecostal identity. The Lee community rarely met to consider and discuss what it meant to practice, protect, and celebrate that identity. They lacked opportunities to meet and agree about what beliefs and practices should be maintained or replaced. In good Pentecostal form, members relied on tradition and on the testimonies of their people. Faculty, staff, administration, and students regularly told their faith stories, but the assumption was that the sum of those narratives created a common understanding of what it meant to be a Christian institution. However, the community did not enjoy the common identity shared by members of BTS's peculiar Pentecostal, sectarian campus. Those early generations needed no confession or creed to set the boundaries for their faith and practice. However, by 2012 people from a wide variety of traditions interpreted those stories without the benefit of clear institutional foundations.

Second, the curricular change was typical of the sort of erosion of distinctives that took place over time. In itself, dropping an already compromised minor did not threaten Lee's identity, but it joined other losses whose cumulative weight effected change. The weakening of any one standard, be it the hiring of adjunct faculty from outside the faith or the expansion of chapel exemptions for students, was justified as pragmatic and expedient. Sometimes a department needed an instructor on short notice for a specialty class—and a Christian candidate was not available. Similarly, limited chapel seats made it a reasonable accommodation to expand exemptions to ease crowding. Neither decision appeared to threaten Lee's Christian character, but, along with other practical changes to policy, the total effect of such changes subtly reshaped campus culture.

But of all the changes at Lee, none more symbolized Conn's presidency than the sound of construction. The university steadily bought and removed rental properties on the edges of campus. One of the biggest additions came in 2000, when Conn acquired a seventeen-acre tract of land on the north side of campus from the Paul Card family. In doing so, he faced fierce opposition from affluent local homeowners. These residents of Cleveland's historic district initially attempted to block construction on the new property. They relented when Conn promised to avoid growth west of Ocoee Street or in the adjoining historic district. Lee went on to make two other major acquisitions that provided much-needed space for growth. In 2007, Conn outbid the competition to acquire the city's Mayfield Elementary School and its three-acre site. Three years later, he negotiated the purchase of the adjoining 6.5-acre First Baptist Church property for $5 million, extending the campus southward to the edge of Cleveland's downtown district.[16]

The properties soon featured new green spaces and several neo-Georgian, red bricked buildings with columned porticos and limestone trim. Three of these were major new academic buildings. The Devos Center for the Humanities (2004), School of Religion building (2008), and Science and Math Complex (2010) provided needed classrooms, faculty offices, and space for student learning. To meet the need for student housing, the university added New Hughes Hall (2011) to replace a forty-year-old dormitory that was removed to make way for other construction. For upperclassmen, the school built the Brinsfield Row townhomes (2004–2008). Additionally, the Mackenzie Athletic Building (2003), Leonard Center (2007), and renovated Walker Arena (2005) provided new homes for athletics, the university's service program, and a health clinic. To help tie together the growing campus, the city council agreed to close several public streets. Additionally, they reconfigured Parker Street, a north-south thoroughfare though the center of campus into a gently winding boulevard, complete with new lighting and pedestrian crossings.

In 2008, economic recession threatened to end Lee's growth. Triggered by the collapse of housing prices and the prevalence of subprime mortgage lending, the Great Recession was the worst economic disaster in the United States since the Great Depression. Between 2007 and 2009,

Darlia and Paul Conn walk through campus during Celebration 2014.

the stock market's Dow Jones Industrial Average was cut in half from its all-time high of 14,000. Americans watched as the value of their investment and retirement accounts plummeted, and the value of their homes fell by an average of 30 percent. Foreclosures rose and unemployment climbed to 10 percent by October 2009. Universities also struggled, although enrollments were little effected. Many students chose college over a weak job market, but at the same time more students became eligible for need-based federal Pell grants. As a result, use of Pell grants rose by 32 percent between 2006 and 2009. The recession's greater threat was to university endowments, which heavily invested in the stock market, and to fundraising campaigns, which relied on donors' generosity. Nationwide, giving dropped 11.7 percent from 2007 and endowment returns fell by a staggering 23 percent. At Lee, Conn reassured the university community that Lee's small endowment was conservatively invested and stable. Despite this good news, Conn stated that the school had "no 'safety net,' no 'bailout plan,' no 'deep pockets'" to fall back upon in hard times. Instead, like most universities, Lee repeatedly raised tuition, which jumped 33 percent between 2007 and 2014—the national average was 30 percent.[17]

When the recession began, Lee was in the middle of the largest fundraising campaign in school history. Following the successful $10 million Parker Street Corridor campaign (2004), the $25 million Press Toward the Mark drive included funding for a math and science building, religion building, technology upgrades, and other projects. When the recession set in, administration did not moderate their goals. Instead, they expanded the campaign to include the acquisition of the Mayfield property from the city, a 150-bed townhouse project, a $2 million scholarship drive, and construction of a limestone chapel at the main entrance to campus. The campaign shattered its original goal by raising a total of $34 million.[18] In addressing the Celebration 2010 audience, Conn scarcely mentioned the recession; instead he focused on Lee's future. He said, "All the work, the sweat, the building of an infrastructure, the recruiting of a first-rate faculty, the gradual change in public perception, the creation of an army of alumni, all that hard work has just now put us in a position to reach a future we never ever dared to dream." He called on the audience to "help Lee become something great—not another commonplace university, but a truly great Christian campus where students understood that excellence is worth the price, that faith is the only worldview that makes sense, and that service to others is ultimately the only worthy goal of one's life."[19]

For students, Lee's "Community Covenant" set standards for defining behavior on a Christian campus. Student handbooks had long defined boundaries for student conduct, but the covenant created an overarching framework for those standards. (For the full text of the Community Covenant, see Appendix B.) The covenant affirmed the Bible as a reliable and authoritative guide to faith and practice, citing scripture to back its five principles of respecting the dignity and worth of each individual, participating in corporate worship, attitudes and behaviors condemned by Scripture, an affirmation that all actions should be performed to the glory of God, and a prohibition on the use of alcohol, illegal drugs, and tobacco.[20] Twenty pages of specific policies followed the one-page covenant. These covered topics ranging from hazing to pornography, writing bad checks to climbing buildings, and drug use to sexual morality. Should a student break the covenant, the process was laid out for disciplinary actions and appeals.

The university required incoming students to sign a document indicating their willingness to live by the Community Covenant's standards. Herein lies a difficult question to answer: To what extent were the formal rules and procedures of the handbook applied to student life? Access to students' disciplinary files is out of the question, but the institution's history, the Conn administration's progressive views, and anecdotal evidence suggest the rules—whether in 1936, 1966, or 2006—were almost always applied with a predisposition toward grace, especially for first-time offenders.[21] Students would make mistakes, but they were rarely condemned or expelled. Conn's administration gave them an opportunity to accept discipline, learn from the experience, and conform to the broader campus culture. Second chances often gave way to third chances, but intransigence or behaviors that publicly embarrassed the school resulted in suspension or expulsion. This system worked best on campus, where most students lived. Off-campus parties, sexual relationships, and other violations of the covenant proved far more difficult to manage.

One challenge to Lee's conservative evangelical worldview came from the LGBTQ+ movement. From its founding, the Church of God maintained the conservative stance that sex outside of a marriage between a man and woman was sinful, however by the 1970s the Gay Liberation movement began to openly challenge traditional values and assumptions on sexuality. Gay men and lesbians demanded that same-sex relationships be treated like any other, both under the law and in American society. Increasing numbers of homosexual persons began to openly express their preferences. Some organized to lobby, protest, and otherwise promote positions that protected and promoted their sexual identity. As their cause slowly gained momentum, it expanded to include bisexual, transgendered, and other queer persons. By 2004 the movement made significant strides, with 54 percent of Americans agreeing that homosexuality should be considered an acceptable lifestyle, compared to 34 percent in 1982. Same-sex marriage gained equal ground, with 42 percent agreeing that same-sex marriages should be recognized by the law as valid. That stance was held by only 27 percent of Americans in 1996.[22]

In 2006, a group of activists joined together to confront the restrictive stances on sexuality held by conservative Christian colleges. Thirty-five gay, lesbian, bisexual, and transgender activists and their straight allies from the group Soulforce planned an initiative called the Equality Ride. Their goal was to confront discriminatory behavior codes at sixteen institutions associated with the Council for Christian Colleges and Universities, as well as three other schools. At their first two stops, Jerry Falwell's Liberty University and Pat Robertson's Regent University, riders were arrested for trespassing when they tried to enter campus.[23]

Lee was the third stop on the Equality Ride tour, but Conn was determined to avoid the confrontations that marked the activists' first two visits. Working from a position of "no condemnation, no compromise," he held fast to conservative views on sexuality. At the same time, he refused to ban Soulforce from Lee's campus. According to Conn, such action "would have served their purposes, but not ours. Their goal was to stigmatize us as a bunch of fundamentalist bigots. . . . We weren't going to give them that opportunity."[24] Instead, Conn gave the group access to campus on his terms. When Soulforce requested the opportunity to make presentations in Lee's chapel, classrooms, and small groups, Conn invited them to attend, but not lead, chapel and class. He even encouraged them to join students in the dining hall. And when someone spray-painted offensive graffiti on the Soulforce bus at a nearby park, Lee students scrubbed off the offending words.[25] Lee's measured response set a new standard for other schools on the Equality Ride itinerary. Lee's plan was so well received, a writer for *Christianity Today* editorialized that the university modeled the "Power of Hospitality."[26]

Online learning, a new trend in higher education, posed a very different sort of challenge to the Lee experience. In the business world, networked computers began replacing classroom settings for employee training in the early 1980s. In 1991, World Wide Web servers began to appear. Soon after, the for-profit University of Phoenix began offering internet-based education. Colleges and universities experimented with the new mode of delivery, and by 1998 three major public university systems had created their own online schools. By 2002, over 1.6 million students were taking online courses—a number that tripled over the next six years. Seeing an opportunity to tap into a new revenue stream, many traditional brick-and-mortar schools jumped into online education. Some, like Liberty University, enjoyed enormous success. They used the new revenue to pay off their debt, grow their campus, and increase their academic and public stature. Faced with a fiercely competitive market, new teaching methods, and faculty who were skeptical of the new delivery system, most new online programs had more modest results.[27]

Lee University had a long history of non-traditional learning opportunities. Through the years, they offered correspondence courses, distance learning, degree completion programs, and satellite campuses. In 1976, the university began a new initiative with the Church of God. For two decades the Continuing Education Program, led by Ray Hughes, Jr., offered a correspondence course designed to train men and women who had bypassed college and gone straight into ministry. The program evolved over time, adding extension services. It reorganized as the Department of External Services and in 2005 as the Center for Adult and Professional Services. While the program had some online offerings, Lee was slow to enter the broader online market. At the time online classes became popular, Lee was growing its traditional, undergraduate campus at a remarkable rate. Lee's administration saw little reason to join the online gold rush that had no connection to the Lee experience's relational, on-campus approach to higher education.[28]

The Great Recession of 2008 might have caused Lee's administration to reconsider online learning, but the Church of God provided impetus for the move. In 2012, Conn received a call from Raymond Culpepper, the church's general overseer. According to Conn, Culpepper said the denomination needed Lee to provide a cheap, accredited, online program for ministerial training. Specifically, he wanted the college to take over the online degree program once supplied by Patten College, a small Church of God school in Oakland, California. When Conn hesitated, the church leader told him that it was an "urgent priority" for the denomination. He intimated that the church expected something in return for its continued financial support of Lee. As a result, Culpepper and the board had agreed to absorb the online education arm of Patten by merging it with Lee's existing CAPS program.[29]

Conn hired Lee graduate Josh Black, the associate dean of Indiana Wesleyan's online program, to head up the Department of Adult Learning (DAL). Some of Lee's faculty had doubts about the new venture. They were deeply invested in Lee's traditional campus experience, had not been involved in the decision-making process, and hesitated to endorse the new DAL offerings. As the new program took shape, few on-campus faculty were willing participants in an online experiment that they believed would undermine the Lee experience. Despite their opposition, the program, which focused on educating non-traditional students, moved forward. Administrators developed a separate curriculum, staff, and culture that paralleled and rarely intersected the physical campus. DAL did not experience the success some universities enjoyed. It did, however, fill the long-time role of Lee's distance learning programs by helping non-traditional students complete their degrees. Prior to DAL, the CAPS program had 104 students in 2010, most of whom took classes at its Charlotte, North Carolina, site. DAL moved the programs online and averaged 752 students a year between 2015 and 2020. In 2018, 65 percent of DAL students were between the ages of 25 and 54. More than 90 percent were engaged in ministerial training.[30]

Following Vice President for Administration Gary Ray's 2010 departure, Conn restructured his cabinet, creating four new vice presidents. As had been his habit, he eschewed a broad search and promoted trusted, long-time employees from within the administration. He promoted Jayson VanHook to vice president for information services and Jerome Hammond to vice president for university relations. Phil Cook became the vice president for enrollment and Mike Hayes was promoted to head student development. Chris Conine, Carolyn Dirksen, and Walt Mauldin continued in financial, academic, and administrative roles. Debbie Murray replaced Dirksen in 2014 as the vice president for academic affairs, and Mauldin's position was eliminated after he left the university in 2014.

The new cabinet faced a challenge long forgotten by most of the Lee community: enrollment. Lee's long era of consistent growth in traditional undergraduate enrollment had ended. But to the casual observer, the end of record enrollments would have been easily missed. The university's graduate programs, Encore program, dual enrollment populations, and online students allowed Lee to grow in total headcount. All the while, the full-time undergraduate and graduate population plateaued and then began to slowly contract. So, the university could continue to advertise growth by combining all students into a total headcount, but the Encore and dual enrollment populations brought little revenue to the university, and two key enrollment sectors had begun to decline. Between 2011 and 2020, full-time undergraduates dropped by 10 percent (3,636 to 3,261), closely followed by a 12 percent decrease in graduate enrollment (390 to 342).[31]

Soft enrollment numbers may have led the administration to shift

Lee's emphasis from liberal arts to professional studies. Always entrepreneurial, the school never fully embraced the liberal arts model. The Bible Training School began with ministerial training, and its two-year liberal arts program combined business classes and a high school on the same campus. The four-year Lee College had a liberal arts flavor, but ministerial and education training were the school's defining features. Lee flirted with a nursing program in the 1980s, and in 1997 a new School of Education accompanied the move to university status, but Conn resisted new professional programs. In 2013, Conn changed his stance, announcing that Lee would start a nursing program. The startup process was not simple. Lee first had to earn approval from professional boards and agencies. Even hiring a new director required a forty-page letter of intent. The administration also had to find the means to construct a building to house the new School of Nursing and fund the resource-intensive program.

Nursing was still undergoing the accreditation process from the Commission on Collegiate Nursing Education when the first students enrolled in fall 2013. Under the leadership of Dean Sara Campbell, the new program won full accreditation in May 2016. That same year, nursing moved into its $10 million home on the south side of campus. The program was immediately successful, enrolling four hundred students by the start of the 2020 school year. In doing so, the school established a separate identity from the rest of campus. The nursing program dictated students' class schedules, locked their building to the general student population, sought modifications in the general education core, and held separate commencement exercises. Nursing, like many professional schools, ran as a semi-autonomous operation on Lee's campus.[32]

Four other initiatives continued Lee's expansion into the professions. The communication arts department moved to the southern tip of the campus and into a new $10 million building in 2014. In 2016 Lee cooperated with Tennessee Technical University to offer an engineering degree. The following year, the business faculty, who had long petitioned for a separate school, finally won their independence from the School of Arts and Sciences. The new School of Business found a home in the repurposed education wing of the former First Baptist Church. Surrounding a new lacrosse field and anchored by a 130-foot-tall bell tower, the new buildings created a distinct south campus quad whose geographic separation from the rest of campus suggested its different educational purpose.

As Lee changed its academic profile, the administration raised the status of its athletic program. After a thirty-seven-year affiliation with the National Association of Intercollegiate Athletics, in 2012 Lee announced that it was seeking membership in the more prestigious National Collegiate Athletic Association's Division II (NCAA, DII). Situated between big-budget Division I programs and Division III schools (which do not offer athletic scholarships), Division II balanced budgeting and the student-athletes' broader college experience. The move was not for a lack of success in the NAIA, where Lee consistently ranked within the association's top twenty athletic programs. In 2012 the college was again named the Southern States Athletic Conference's best overall program—the sixth time in seven years. Instead, the move to the NCAA was part of the university's long-term effort to raise its public profile. As Conn put it, "It's more than just athletics, really. It's a symbol of a larger move for the university as a whole."[33]

The change in associations was not without its challenges. Lee needed to impress the NCAA in order to become one of only eight schools allowed into Division II in 2012. It also needed a new conference home. The problems were intertwined in something akin to a catch-22. The NCAA valued schools with conference affiliations, and NCAA conferences could not admit members without DII membership. Lee found a potential home in the Gulf South Conference (GSC), won conditional membership in the NCAA, and began a three-year transitional period in fall 2012. In that time, Lee competed one final season in its old conference and association, then moved to GSC play. There, they met another obstacle. The college was not eligible to compete for NCAA championships until fall 2015. To fill the championship gap, Lee returned to the National Christian College Athletic Association and won five national championships in two years.

Once Lee's teams left behind their provisional status, they quickly demonstrated their ability to compete in the new division and conference. Over their first five seasons, Lee squads won sixteen conference championships and participated in NCAA national tournaments twenty-seven times. Additionally, they won the NCAA Award of Excellence in their first year as full members of the association.[34] Lee's new conference featured football as its premier sport, and the GSC strongly recommended that Lee start the sport. Conn never considered football a good fit for Lee, but he agreed to put the question on the table. Although expensive, the sport promised to bring around one hundred male students to campus and would bring another boost to the school's public profile. Some board members, most notably future president Mark Walker, supported the sport, but Conn and Athletic Director Larry Carpenter shelved the idea. For another few years, Lee's students could continue to say that the Flames remained undefeated on the gridiron.[35]

In 2018 Lee entered its centennial year, and the university community had much to celebrate. The campus spent the year remembering its origins, trials, successes, and the people who had played central roles in shaping the Lee experience. Celebrations embraced a wide range of activities: a speaker series, special chapel services, stories in the alumni magazine, historical reenactors on campus during homecoming, and countless other reminders of the school's past. Hazel Edwards Ivy returned to discuss her experience desegregating the campus. Delton Alford recalled the struggle to win accreditation. Other voices told of their unique Lee experiences. The centennial also produced two more lasting artifacts—a documentary film entitled *Hundred Year Journey* and a tabletop book entitled *Lift High the Flame*.[36] And, of course, the centennial recognized and celebrated President Conn's role in transforming Lee from a small, struggling denominational college into a strong, evangelical university that boasted a modern campus and over five thousand students. However, major changes and challenges lay on the horizon.

Chapter 10

TRANSITIONS

In November 2019, Paul Conn announced he would step down from the president's office at the start of the fall 2020 semester. He had considered resigning in 2006 after celebrating his twentieth anniversary as president but decided to stay on another five years to complete the $34 million Press Toward the Mark capital campaign. When Lee acquired the First Baptist property, Conn found another set of opportunities and challenges. So, he remained at the helm to shape the south campus. When Conn reached his twenty-fifth anniversary, the project was not yet complete. He told his wife, Darlia, that he would retire in 2016, but when 2016 arrived, there was still work to be done. Conn asked, and Darlia agreed, that he would extend his tenure two more years—in 2016 and again in 2018. At that point, Conn felt the time was finally right. He had completed the south campus expansion, and no new project whetted his appetite to stay in office. He was ready to put an end to the early mornings and late evenings, the trips to address the denomination's state councils, the perpetual fundraising, and the day-to-day grind of managing the university. For the seventy-three-year-old Conn, retirement promised the opportunity to travel, enjoy grandchildren, and reflect on his career.[1]

During his tenure, Conn transformed Lee from a small, struggling, denominationally specific college into a strong, evangelical, regional university. By almost any measure, he had achieved remarkable success. And here, the numbers can start to measure his impact. Total enrollment grew from 986 to 5,189 and those students were not only more numerous but were stronger academically, with the average ACT score for incoming students rising from 17 to 25 during Conn's tenure. In 1986, 160 faculty and staff delivered twenty-two majors in fifteen buildings on Lee's twenty-two-acre campus. By 2020, almost 160 faculty and 650 staff delivered 156 academic programs, including fifteen master's and three doctoral degrees. Conn built a campus that became a centerpiece of the Cleveland community. Its sixty-five buildings sat on a manicured 145-acre campus that was far removed from the tired set of buildings Conn inherited. The budget jumped from $6 to $102 million, and the endowment grew from $2 to $25 million. Lee's academic reputation had also grown. The school did not merit a ranking by *U. S. News* until 2001, when it was recognized as a second-tier regional liberal arts school. By 2020 the magazine ranked Lee as 34th of 132 universities in the south region. The ranking pitted Lee against peers including James Madison, Berry, Appalachian State, Western Carolina, and the College of Charleston.

Those numbers, while impressive, do not measure Conn's transformation of campus culture. When Conn joined the administration in 1985 as a vice president, the faculty and staff were as tired as the physical campus. Lee was not simply struggling, it was trapped in a downward spiral of falling enrollments, budget cuts, and layoffs. A mere five years

Paul Conn addresses the audience at Celebration 2016.

later, Conn reversed those trends. In the process, he helped faculty, students, staff, alumni, donors, and community members believe the school could achieve great things. Guarded optimism turned to belief, belief into enthusiasm, and enthusiasm into a certainty that Conn could take Lee from success to success. Granted, that confidence was not shared by every member of the community—certainly not by the traditionalists in the church, but despite the initial misgivings of some, Conn's leadership earned him a wealth of trust and goodwill. As Carolyn Dirksen put it, "The success of Lee under his leadership rests on his willingness and ability to dream big dreams and to recruit others to believe in them and to work for them. He completely re-envisioned what Lee was capable of academically and boldly led the institution to a level we barely dared to imagine."[2]

Conn's successor faced daunting challenges. New university presidents must build trust, connect with the community, raise money, and navigate institutional politics. They must also manage a range of budgetary, academic, and personnel issues. However, Conn was far more than Lee's chief executive; in many ways he was the founder of the modern university. For thirty-four years he shaped Lee's path, and only a handful of senior faculty and staff had known any other president. They had come to embrace his dreams, trust his judgment, and, almost without question, follow his lead. His success in growing the college gave Conn almost complete control of the school. His hands-on managerial style guaranteed he understood and had input in almost every aspect of university life, from class sizes to budget line items to public relations campaigns to control over faculty hiring, promotion, and tenure decisions. Businesses often struggle to find sound footing after a founder retires, taking with them the vision, energy, and commitment that made them successful. Following Conn posed all those challenges and more.

As Conn prepared to leave the president's office, the board created two new positions: chancellor and provost. Conn would become the school's first chancellor. In his new role he retained a seat on the cabinet and would manage special projects, including fundraising and community relations. More importantly, he hoped to serve as a sounding board and advisor for the next president, sharing with him wisdom, professional connections, and experience from thirty-four years in the president's office. This new position also allowed Conn to ensure a smooth transition for the new administration.

In choosing Conn's successor, Lee's board of directors worked with a small pool of candidates. They soon narrowed their list to three finalists:

Alisa White, Debbie Murray, and Mark Walker. From many points of view, White had the strongest resume. A graduate of Lee, she earned a PhD in mass communication from the University of Tennessee and served in top academic posts at several schools. She was vice president for academic affairs at the University of Texas at Tyler and Midwestern State University, then president of Austin Peay State University. Her father, Robert White, had been general overseer of the Church of God, and while she no longer was in the denomination, she understood the culture. At the same time, she was an outsider who had her own style, interests, methods, and goals. Her experience might bring fresh perspectives to Lee's traditions, but she likely would move the university in new directions.[3]

Several of Lee's vice presidents were also candidates. Vice President for Academic Affairs Debbie Murray emerged as a finalist. Murray's strengths lay in her connections to the Church of God and her history at Lee. A graduate of Lee (where her father, Jim Bilbo, taught on the faculty), Murray held an EdD from the University of Tennessee. She joined the Lee faculty in 1980 and served as a department chair and then dean of the College of Education before joining the cabinet in 2013. Murray had no professional experience outside Lee, but she had a deep understanding of school and church culture. She was at Lee during the lean years of the early eighties, had participated in the school's transformation, and was deeply committed to existing structures and traditions.

Ultimately, on January 31, 2020, the board chose Mark L. Walker as the new president of Lee University and named Murray as the university's first provost. Walker had longstanding ties to Lee, but his resume looked more like that of Ray Hughes than Paul Conn. Walker was not a Lee alumnus. He earned his undergraduate degree and a master's degree in counseling from Georgia State University in 1988. His PhD in organizational leadership was earned at Regent University in 2005. After a brief stint in the software industry, he followed his father, Paul L. Walker, into ministry in the Church of God. For twenty years, Walker served as senior pastor at Mount Paran North Church of God in Marietta, Georgia. Like his father, he served in denominational leadership, rising to the church's Council of Eighteen and serving as the chair of the Benefits Board. For seven years, he was a member of Lee's board of directors before accepting an offer from Conn to join the Lee administration in 2017. When hired, he was named a full professor, chair of the Christian Ministries Department, and Vice President for Ministerial Development. Though his resume lacked significant academic experience, Walker could claim a decade of service to the university and deep family ties to Lee. His father served on Lee's board for ten years and his wife, Udella, and two children were Lee graduates. Moreover, his connections to the denomination and commitment to Lee's Christ-centered mission recommended him for the job.

Before Walker could take office, the regular rhythms of university life were interrupted by an emerging threat that impacted every aspect of life in every corner of the globe. In the first months of 2020, the virus COVID-19 spread to the United States. Federal and state authorities were slow to recognize the severity of the new virus, which commonly caused respiratory symptoms resembling the common cold or flu. Moreover, COVID-19 was an airborne virus that spread easily and proved dangerous to the elderly and those with underlying health conditions. By March, early hot spots such as New York City were suffering from the growing pandemic. With few controls in place, hospitals were soon overwhelmed as researchers worked to find treatments for the disease. By the end of March 2020, the nation had more than 250,000 confirmed cases and the virus had claimed more than 7,000 lives. But the pandemic was just starting to take hold. State and local governments limited gatherings, and businesses began to close. Ten million Americans lost their jobs, with 6.6 million applying for unemployment benefits in the last week of March alone.[4]

The disease rapidly undermined the basic operating models for the nation's colleges and universities, which scrambled to adapt. Lee's administration responded cautiously to the threat, following the lead of other schools in extending spring break for an extra week. The twelve-day break helped faculty and staff make the emergency transition to online teaching and advising for the remainder of the semester. The transition was difficult, but Conn reported, "Our faculty stepped into the challenge; our staff performed superbly; and our students were responsive and cheerful about disruptions. So I believe we are going to serve our students well."[5] Even as classes continued, other parts of campus systematically shut down. Lee's health clinic began COVID-19 testing and quarantine procedures, but the dorms emptied, auxiliary services closed, and Lee Day went online. As the virus continued to wreak havoc, the administration canceled international trips planned for the summer, as well as spring commencement.[6]

Despite the virus, summer enrollment was strong, and Lee provided online and hybrid (rotating online and in-person) classes. Rising rates of coronavirus infection forced the administration to cancel plans for an August graduation. Conn wrote graduates, "I am heartbroken to disappoint you in this way. *I realize you have worked so hard to earn your degree* [his emphasis], and you have paid a big price for this pandemic already. . . . It's sad to me for another, quite selfish reason: as you know, August 1 will be my last day as president. For months, I have imagined spending that day with all of you. . . . So I realize this announcement brings a sense of loss for you, and I am right there with you."[7] The cancellation was disappointing in another way. It signaled that campus life was nowhere near returning to any semblance of normal—and the fall semester was about to begin.

On August 1, 2020 Walker formally took office as Lee's seventeenth president, and Conn began his new position as the school's first chancellor. Neither enjoyed the pomp and circumstance usually associated with such transitions. Instead, the focus remained on Lee's attempt to reopen campus in the face of the pandemic. Students returned to a host of new rules and procedures. Face masks, social distancing, temperature checks, and quarantines were mandatory. On campus, the new rules provided a reasonably safe space that might have limited the spread of the disease, but off-campus and informal gatherings likely nullified the school's official efforts to follow Centers for Disease Control and Prevention guidelines. Despite efforts to contain the pandemic, in December, a third commencement was canceled, as were almost all global perspectives trips. With the development of three vaccines conditions began to improve in the spring 2021 semester, and the university began to envision a return to normalcy.

By the summer of 2021, the administration had relaxed most campus restrictions. Students, faculty, and staff looked forward to the fall semester with a new sense of hope, but serious challenges were looming. First, Lee needed to once again fill the campus with the traditional undergraduate students that had always been the school's primary mission and lifeblood. Total enrollment fell from 5,189 in 2019 to 4,505 in 2021, and the critical traditional full-time undergraduate population dropped from 3,677 to 3,041.[8] Federal aid cushioned the immediate financial losses from slumping enrollment, but that aid would not last. Second, Lee's culture faced challenges from both the broader secular culture and from within the church, where traditionalists almost immediately tested Walker's commitment to denominational orthodoxy.

Problems began after a visiting pastor spoke in chapel about Christ as the embodiment of grace and truth. Conservatives found the message too accommodating to LGBTQ+ progressives and demanded that Walker remove video of the chapel service from the university website. Walker acquiesced and then addressed the controversy from the chapel pulpit. There he explained that Lee would continue to hold to traditional Christian, evangelical teachings on sexuality. This position set Walker firmly on the side of the Church of God's teaching that the only acceptable sexual activity was between a married man and woman. Walker went on to stress the need to love all people as neighbors, and loving neighbors in same-sex relationships meant calling them to repentance by the grace of God. The message reassured conservatives who feared that any opening to the LGBTQ+ community put the school on the slippery slope to liberalism. The message did not endear him with progressive elements on campus and resulted in the departure of a handful of faculty who had hoped that Lee would move to a welcoming and affirming stance on gender and sexuality.[9]

Lee's stance on sexuality clearly put it at odds with the dominant culture, and legislation threatened the school's protection under the law. For five decades Lee had operated under a religious exception to Title IX of the Education Amendments Act of 1972, which prohibits discrimination on the basis of sex in educational programs. Lee's religious exemption was at risk in 2021 when the House of Representatives passed the Equality Act for a second time.[10] The legislation proposed a revision to Title IX. In addition to sex, students could not be discriminated against based upon their sexual orientation or gender identity. To do so would be a violation of federal civil rights law. To ensure maximum compliance, the bill precluded institutions like Lee from claiming any exemption to the law. While the proposal died in committee, it reflected a growing consensus that LGBTQ+ people be welcomed in society. And that belief was also growing inside America's churches. By 2021, 36 percent of evangelicals believed homosexuality should be accepted, not discouraged. From 2004 to 2018, support for same-sex marriage among Americans rose from 31 to 61 percent. Among evangelicals, support grew from 11 to 29 percent in the same period.[11]

Walker maintained the denomination's longstanding teaching, but holding the line would not be easy. In the decade leading to 2021, the number of Americans who self-described as Christians dropped 12 percentage points to 63 percent of the population. At the same time, those describing themselves as atheist, agnostic, or nothing rose to 26 percent. Among Christians, only 44 percent reported that they attended weekly religious services. The school's longstanding identification as an evangelical institution also became more complicated as the meaning of the term changed over time. Whereas evangelicals once were identified by their views on Scripture, Christ, and conversion, "evangelical" had come adrift from those theological moorings. Instead, the label became a "theo-political brand." In common usage it became associated with an ideology that is an "amalgam of theological views, partisan political debates, regional power blocks, populist visions, racial biases, and cultural anxieties, all mixed in an ethos of fear." In short, the term took on a cultural value that many Americans identify with right wing, populist politics—not a traditional evangelical understanding of the Christian faith.[12]

Cultural pressures, the challenges of the pandemic, and steady drops in enrollment created conditions that might lead Lee down the path taken by many other faith-based institutions which have drifted from their historical roots. This study began by introducing the path taken by almost all sectarian educational institutions. Historians, especially James Burtchaell in *The Dying of the Light*, have traced similar patterns at dozens of other schools. These schools drifted away from their denominations—and from faith as the defining aspect of the education they provided. That change can take place at a slow, steady rate across decades, but is more often characterized by periods of rapid transformation. However, whether the change is slow or abrupt, sectarian schools eventually open their doors to the broader Christian community and assume an evangelical stance. In time, those intentionally Christian schools welcome more students, scholars, and staff who are sympathetic to the school's broad moral positions, if not the Christian faith. The school gradually distances itself from its denomination but justifies its faith-based status by employing the language of "critical mass"—it is Christian enough. At this point, a sufficient number of students, faculty, board members, and staff accept the school mission and practice the Christian faith, but that number drops over time.

Eventually, school leadership questions why the school clings to outdated language and traditions. They transition the school's faith traditions to "historical" status, where the founder's faith is relegated to a subpage three or four clicks deep on the school's website. There the reader can discover how the school once had a peculiar faith identity, and those beliefs are now part of the university's heritage.

For Burtchaell, the strongest proponent of this declensionist model, the causes of a school's move away from faith are many.

> The elements of the slow but apparently irrevocable cleavage of colleges from church were many. The church was replaced as a financial patron by alumni, foundations, philanthropists, and the government. The regional accrediting associations, the alumni, and the government replaced the church as the primary authority to whom the college would give an accounting of its stewardship. The study of their faith became academically marginalized and the understanding

of religion was degraded by translation into reductive banalities for promotional use. Presidential hubris found fulfillment in cultivating the colleges to follow the academic pacesetters, which were selective state and independent universities. The faculty transferred their primary loyalties from their college to their disciplines and their guild, and were thereby antagonistic to any competing norms of professional excellence related to the church.[13]

Burtchaell's assessment is an uncompromising and thought-provoking critique of the process by which schools marginalize faith. As such, it provides a useful, if sometimes flawed, set of measures to reflect upon Lee's history and relationship with the Church of God.

There is no question that Lee no longer resembles the holiness culture that shaped the early Church of God. However, Lee's steady move away from a legalistic, Pentecostal holiness culture generally paralleled the denomination's move along similar lines. The Bible Training School in postwar Sevierville was far removed from Nora Chambers' first classes, but student life remained firmly in the center of Church of God culture. Similarly, Ray Hughes's 1965 Lee campus featured any number of compromises to the broader culture. He opposed worldly fraternities and sororities but allowed Greek-letter clubs that mimicked their secular cousins. He also loosened dating rules and introduced varsity sports. In creating these openings, Hughes did not challenge his church's culture. Rather, he made compromises to grow enrollment by attracting Pentecostal young people who expected more social opportunities at college. Even the shorter skirts and longer hair tolerated by Charles Conn reflected choices made by families sending their children to Lee. As Hughes put it, "There is one thing that you and all of those in the Church of God must remember, and that is that we did not raise these young people, nor did we set their standards of living. They are Church of God members who came to us from Church of God pastors and are typical of most Church of God young people."[14]

Likewise, Lee's academic ambitions did not cause the school to move its allegiance from the Church of God to accreditors and outside constituencies. The denomination sought the validation promised by accreditation while simultaneously moving to offer bachelor's degrees. Conforming to secular standards did alter Lee's culture by causing the school to consolidate its diverse educational enterprises. This triggered an internal debate among faculty about the school's mission, but the decision to close the Bible college did not indicate an effort by administrators to weaken Lee's mission or ties to the Church of God. Instead, the denomination used SACS standards to drive improvement across the campus while simultaneously renewing its commitment to conservative, evangelical, Pentecostal doctrines and its Church of God constituency.

In short, for seven decades Lee did not distance itself from the denomination; it followed the church toward a more mainstream, but still distinctly Pentecostal, culture. Lee also remained under the direct control of the Church of God. In those years, ten of the university's fifteen presidents served as general overseer. Only one was not a church official. The denomination controlled not only the board, but weighed in on hiring practices, student life policies, and building programs. The church fathers approved school budgets, and the denomination invested heavily in its college. When the civil rights movement forced racial integration on the church and school, the denomination again set the pace of change. Church leaders regularly called presidents to their chambers for consultation, correction, and censure. Lee College's bookstore was part of the Church of God bookstore, and the school and church shared computer systems, as well as a library and auditorium. So, while the 1982 version of Lee College no longer resembled BTS, the denomination still held it close and considered it an integral part of the church.

Paul Conn transformed Lee, moving it from a sectarian college to a broadly evangelical university. In doing so, he was not attempting to divorce the university from the denomination, but envisioned an evangelical Christian school rooted in Church of God faith and practice. He loosened, but did not cut, the ties binding school to denomination. Conn personified the type of leader Burtchaell finds most dangerous to a school's sectarian identity (which he equates with religious identity). "With very few exceptions, the presidents who have been the strategists of religious alienation have been large souled, attractive, and trusted. They typically felt that their institutions were somehow confined, stifled, or trivialized by their church or denomination or order, and at a critical moment they greatly enhanced the professionalism, resources, and clientele of their colleges."[15] Conn was the charismatic visionary whose leadership inspired faculty, staff, and students to pursue a bold course. He believed that Lee's sectarian character kept it small, marginalized, and unlikely to serve its students or the denomination well. And at a critical moment, he brought to the school new benefactors, new professionalism, and new initiatives that reversed the school's fortunes and kicked off almost three decades of continuous growth.

Conn made the school's budget independent of the denomination, which in 2018–2019 contributed $2.75 million. While that number is meaningful, it represented only 3.5 percent of the school's total revenues, compared to 27 percent in 1981.[16] Additionally, Conn's student enrollment team recruited students from a wide range of backgrounds. While the school's distinctive Christian environment attracted people of like faith, significant numbers of Lee students came to Lee for reasons other than its Christian qualities. Low tuition, competitive sports programs, and a good liberal arts education drew students who saw a school that was the best value for their money or that offered the best chance to compete. Consequently, the student body not only lost many of its Church of God distinctives, but also saw its evangelical identity leavened by those outside the faith. Conn also made the university president accountable to the Lee's board of directors, not the Church of God's executive committee. He diversified the board to include non-Church of God members, however the church retained one important mode of formal control: the executive committee continued to approve all new and returning board members.

Faculty members play a critical role in shaping Lee's mission and identity. At BTS, faculty committed to the school's Christian, Pentecostal identity and a life of ministry. The classroom was a place to educate, preach, pray, and let the Spirit work—the line between church and school was faint, if discernable at all. Pentecostal faculty came to Lee to serve the church and, though armed with the passion of their faith, brought few academic credentials. They worried little about the standards set by the academy. They had more important work to do in preparing students for the ministry, welcoming spontaneous revival, and modeling holiness living. In time, this would change. Goaded by the expectations of accrediting agencies and the aspirations of the denomination, Lee College expected faculty to earn better academic credentials and take more seriously the education of the student body. Those faculty remained committed to the mission of the college as an extension of the ministry of the Church of God, but recognized the importance of attending graduate school to acquire discipline-specific training.

Paul Conn expanded and improved the faculty by welcoming non-Pentecostal faculty with terminal degrees, usually a doctorate, to campus. Burtchaell warns that such faculty train in secular graduate programs and measure success by standards set by their academic disciplines. Those programs view colleges and universities as vehicles for research, publication, artistic creativity, and other academic rewards. Serious commitment to a religious school's mission and service to students only undermines research agendas. Many new faculty bring the values and attitudes Burtchaell fears to Lee. As Christians, they are sympathetic to the school's mission, but are less willing to sacrifice personal and professional goals for the good of the university.

Further complicating the question, Lee has long defined its mission in a student-centered way. To serve Christ means long hours mentoring, counseling, serving, and ministering to students outside of the classroom. An increasing number of new faculty argue that students are best served by professors with active research agendas and strong academic reputations. These faculty attempt to juggle the demands of the academy with the equally time-intensive demands of Lee's culture. A few understand the mission but accept a place on the faculty with no intention of sacrificing their research agenda. Burtchaell's concern is that, over time, faculty loyalty and identity move from the school's Christian mission to the norms of the academy. "At first they took the religious character of the college for granted, or even as a saving grace; but it became an aspect, like the food service which did not require their management."[17] He warns that faculty move from Christian educators committed to the school's faith mission to academics working at a school with a Christian mission.

At Lee, few faculty fully embrace the academic model promoted by tier-one research universities, but many new faculty try to balance that model with the student-centered one long held by Lee. That change might signal the ongoing shift in allegiance identified by Burtchaell. But maybe not. Perhaps faculty will find balance and redefine the relationship between academic interests and mission. More problematic, from a continuity of mission perspective, is the faculty's apparent departure from the school's evangelical belief system. Here, the evidence is anecdotal, not statistical. Lee has not polled faculty (or students) about their belief systems, but recent faculty seminars focused on mission reveal considerable diversity among faculty regarding both lifestyle commitments and theological questions. Far from the shared identity held by BTS and Lee College faculty, the current university maintains a broadly inclusive approach to faith and practice that tolerates a range of heterodox beliefs.

In 2021, Lee began a series of internal conversations about mission, faith, and Lee's place in the evangelical world. Burtchaell finds on most campuses that "Almost without exception a rhetoric of concern [regarding mission] began on these campuses just as the critical turn had been made."[18] Lee might be an exception to the rule. Burtchaell found that such discussions typically began long after schools abandon hiring practices that incorporate a faith standard and emphasize commitment to the university's mission. In contrast, Lee's mission statement is unapologetically clear. "A personal commitment to Jesus Christ as Savior is the controlling perspective from which the educational process is carried out."[19] The school backs up that rhetoric by requiring all full-time faculty to be professing, practicing Christians as a condition of employment. Therefore, while faculty may not self-identify as evangelical or Pentecostal, the Christian faith remains a constant within faculty ranks.

Walker, in returning to an older tradition of churchmen leading the school, arrested any immediate drift from the Church of God. His uncompromising rhetoric indicated that he wanted to strengthen denominational ties. In his welcome to students Walker wrote, "We are proud to be a Christ-centered liberal arts university where our highest priority is to engage all students in a transformational journey of integrating faith, values, and vocation."[20] However, he inherited a student body, staff, and faculty who have steadily moved away from the denomination. Reinforced by the broader culture, the momentum toward more progressive positions and away from evangelical, Pentecostal standards could continue. Lee could drift quickly to being a "critical mass" school that opens its doors not only to students from outside the faith, but to faculty, staff, and administrators who will move the school even further from its roots. The test will be whether the school can hold fast to its evangelical mission, maintain a healthy relationship with the denomination, and also succeed in the highly competitive world of higher education.

Looking forward, Lee faces a period that rivals other critical transitions in the institution's history. Conn's long tenure provided three decades of security and continuity, but today Lee faces significant challenges as it moves into a new era. Changes in leadership, declining enrollment, and the pressure of an increasingly post-Christian culture threaten to change Lee's identity. In these contexts, the university might choose to follow the broad, well-trodden path toward a more secular identity in which students and faculty focus on academics and not faith, and where denominational distinctives are sacrificed to maintain federal aid and create a broader pool of students from which to recruit. Then again, Lee might join the handful of schools that create a distinct Christian identity in the face of an indifferent and even hostile culture—a path that is difficult to discern and increasingly contested. If Lee finds a way to reinforce its evangelical distinctives, maintain a healthy relationship with the Church of God, and encourage intellectual exploration and academic development, it will perhaps create a model for other like-minded institutions.[21]

Appendix A

THE CHURCH OF GOD DECLARATION OF FAITH[1]

We Believe:

- In the verbal inspiration of the Bible.

- In one God eternally existing in three persons; namely, the Father, Son, and Holy Ghost.

- That Jesus Christ is the only begotten Son of the Father, conceived of the Holy Ghost, and born of the Virgin Mary. That Jesus was crucified, buried, and raised from the dead. That He ascended to heaven and is today at the right hand of the Father as the Intercessor.

- That all have sinned and come short of the glory of God and that repentance is commanded of God for all and necessary for forgiveness of sins.

- That justification, regeneration, and the new birth are wrought by faith in the blood of Jesus Christ.

- In sanctification subsequent to the new birth, through faith in the blood of Christ; through the Word, and by the Holy Ghost.

- Holiness to be God's standard of living for His people.

- In the baptism with the Holy Ghost subsequent to a clean heart.

- In speaking with other tongues as the Spirit gives utterance and that it is the initial evidence of the baptism of the Holy Ghost.

- In water baptism by immersion, and all who repent should be baptized in the name of the Father, and of the Son, and of the Holy Ghost.

- Divine healing is provided for all in the atonement.

- In the Lord's Supper and washing of the saints' feet.
- In the premillennial second coming of Jesus. First, to resurrect the righteous dead and to catch away the living saints to Him in the air. Second, to reign on the earth a thousand years.
- In the bodily resurrection; eternal life for the righteous, and eternal punishment for the wicked.

Appendix B

LEE UNIVERSITY COMMUNITY COVENANT[2]

Lee University is a Christ-centered community, dedicated to the highest standards of academic achievement, personal development, and spiritual growth. Together, the community seeks to honor Christ by integrating faith, learning, and living while its members' hearts and lives mature in relationship to Jesus Christ and each other. Faith in God's Word should lead to behavior displaying His authority in our lives. Scripture teaches that certain attributes such as love, joy, peace, patience, kindness, goodness, faithfulness, gentleness, and self-control are to be manifested by members of the Christ-centered community (Galatians 5:22-23).

With this purpose and spiritual foundation, students are expected to comply with these lifestyle standards:

- Community life at Lee University should be marked by personal stewardship of abilities and resources and sensitivity to the God-given worth and dignity of each individual. In consideration of each member of the university community having been created in God's image as male and female, the university expects all members of this community to treat each other with respect and dignity regardless of any differences of belief and does not condone harassment of others.

- Corporate worship aids in community building and support of the body of Christ. We gather as a community at special times for nurture and instruction in the truths of God's Word. These activities include required attendance at chapel and spiritual emphasis weeks. Personal devotions and local church involvement are encouraged.

- Scripture condemns such attitudes as greed, jealousy, pride, lust, needless anger, an unforgiving spirit, harassment, and prejudice. Furthermore, certain behaviors are expressly prohibited by scripture.

These include theft, lying, cheating, plagiarism, gossip, slander, profanity, vulgarity, sexual immorality (e.g., pornography, premarital and extramarital sexual behavior, adultery, same-sex sexual behavior), drunkenness, gluttony, immodesty, and occult practices.

- Scripture teaches that all our actions (work, study, play) should be performed to the glory of God. We endeavor, therefore, to be selective in our choices of clothes, entertainment, and recreation, promoting those which strengthen the body of Christ and avoiding those which would diminish sensitivity to Christian responsibility or promote sensual attitudes or conduct.

- Since the body of the Christian is the temple of the Holy Spirit, it deserves respect and preservation of its well-being. Therefore, the use of alcohol, illegal drugs, or tobacco in any form and the abuse of prescriptions and over-the-counter drugs violate our community standard.

Appendix C

BTS/LEE COLLEGE/LEE UNIVERSITY PRESIDENTS WITH SERVICE IN CHURCH OF GOD LEADERSHIP, 1909–2020[3]

	NAME	BTS/LEE PRESIDENT	GENERAL OVERSEER	ASSISTANT GENERAL OVERSEER	EXECUTIVE COMMITTEE	EXECUTIVE COUNCIL
1	A. J. Tomlinson	1918–22	1909–23		1922–23	1917–23
2	F. J. Lee	1922–23	1923–28		1922–28	1917–28
3	J. B. Ellis	1923–24			1923–24, 1926–32	1917–32
4	T. S. Payne	1924–30			1924–32	1917–41
5	J. H. Walker, Sr.	1930–35	1935–44		1935–44	1934–48, 1950–54, 1958–62
6	Zeno C. Tharp	1935–44	1952–56	1948–52	1937–44, 1948–56	1932–24, 1935–60
7	J. H. Walker, Sr.	1944–45	1935–44		1935–44	1934–48, 1950–54, 1958–62
8	E. L. Simmons	1945–48		1944–45	1939–42, 1944–45	1939–48, 1950–52
9	John C. Jernigan	1948	1944–48	1952–54	1944–48, 1952–54	1935–54

10	J. Stewart Brinsfield	1948–51					1946–50
11	John C. Jernigan	1951–52	1944–48	1952–54	1944–48 1952–54		1935–54
12	R. Leonard Carroll	1952–57	1970–72	1964–70	1964–72		1964–72
13	Rufus Platt	1957–60					
14	Ray H. Hughes	1960–66	1972–74, 1978–82, 1996	1966–72, 1976–78, 1986–90, 1992–96	1966–74, 1976–82		1956–60, 1962–82, 1986–80, 1992–96
15	James A. Cross	1966–70	1958–62	1954–58	1954–62		1952–66, 1968–72, 1974–78, 1980–84, 1986–90
16	Charles W. Conn	1970–82	1966–70	1962–66	1952–56, 1962–70		1952–60, 1962–74, 1976–80
17	Ray H. Hughes	1982–84	1972–74, 1978–82	1966–72, 1976–78, 1986–90, 1992–96	1966–74, 1976–82, 1986–80, 1992–96		1956–60, 1962–82, 1986–80, 1992–96
18	Lamar Vest	1984–86	1990–94, 2000–04	1986–90, 1996-2000	1986–94, 1996-2000		1986–94, 1996-2000
19	C. Paul Conn	1986–2020					
20	Mark L. Walker	2020–24					

Appendix D

ENROLLMENT, 1930–2020[4]

	TOTAL HEADCOUNT		TOTAL HEADCOUNT
1930–31	87	1961–62	515
1934–35	131	1962–63	625
1940–41	212	1963–64	667
1942–43	216	1964–65	769
1943–44	516	1965–66	854
1944–45	550	1966–67	1,074
1945–46	543	1967–68	1,113
1946–47	535	1968–69	1,127
1947–48	571	1969–70	1,006
1948–49	643	1970–71	1,111
1949–50	584	1971–72	1,093
1950–51	611	1972–73	1,155
1951–52	440	1973–74	1,069
1952–53	380	1974–75	1,139
1953–54	488	1975–76	1,185
1954–55	504	1976–77	1,197
1955–56	466	1977–78	1,288
1956–57	496	1978–79	1,313
1957–58	368	1979–80	1,342
1958–59	387	1980–81	1,231
1959–60	344	1981–82	1,164
1960–61	294	1982–83	1,134

	TOTAL HEADCOUNT		TOTAL HEADCOUNT
1983–84	1,059	2002–03	3,711
1984–85	1,154	2003–04	3,809
1985–86	1,204	2004–05	3,849
1986–87	1,214	2005–06	3,911
1987–88	1,332	2006–07	4,012
1988–89	1,534	2007–08	4,086
1989–90	1,642	2008–09	4,147
1990–91	1,739	2009–10	4,262
1991–92	1,827	2010–11	4,377
1992–93	1,922	2011–12	4,904
1993–94	2,011	2012–13	4,954
1994–95	2,165	2013–14	4,922
1995–96	2,477	2014–15	5,104
1996–97	2,657	2015–16	5,041
1997–98	2,857	2016–17	5,302
1998–99	3,081	2017–18	5,370
1999–00	3,259	2018–19	5,386
2000–01	3,361	2019–20	5,189
2001–02	3,511	2020–21	5,204

Notes

Introduction

1. Minutes of the Supreme Council, 4 March 1949, Hal Bernard Dixon Jr. Pentecostal Research Center, Cleveland, TN (hereafter cited as PRC); James M. Beaty, "How We Came to Have a Seminary, 2014," MTS (photocopy), PRC.
2. Minutes of the Supreme Council, 4 March 1949, PRC; Beaty, "How We Came to Have a Seminary."
3. George Marsden, *The Soul of the American University: From Protestant Establishment to Established Nonbelief* (New York: Oxford University Press, 1994), James Burtchaell, *The Dying of the Light: The Disengagement of Colleges and Universities from their Christian Churches* (Grand Rapids: W. B. Eerdmans, 1998), George Marsden and Bradley Longfield, eds., *The Secularization of the Academy* (New York: Oxford University Press, 1992), Philip Gleason, *Contending with Modernity: Catholic Higher Education in the Twentieth Century* (New York: Oxford University Press, 1996). See also topic, see also Julie A. Reuben, *The Making of the Modern University: Intellectual Transformation and the Marginalization of Morality* (Chicago: University of Chicago Press, 1996) and Douglas Sloan, *Faith and Knowledge: Mainline Protestantism and American Higher Education* (Louisville: Westminster John Know Press, 1994). For a more positive assessment of Christian higher education, see Robert Benne, *Quality with Soul: How Six Premier Colleges and Universities Keep Faith with Their Religious Traditions* (Grand Rapids: Eerdmans, 2001) and William C. Ringenberg, *The Christian College: A History of Protestant Higher Education in America*, 2nd ed. (Grand Rapids: Baker Academic, 2006).
4. Benne, *Quality with Soul*, 48–50.
5. The list of standards is recognized, if not accepted, by most observers, for a supporter of these measures, see Benne, *Quality with Soul*, 49. For a similar list from a critic, see Merrimon Cuninggim, *Uneasy Partners: The College and the Church* (Nashville: Abingdon Press, 1994), 43-45.

Chapter 1

1. For the history of the Church of God, see: Charles W. Conn, *Like a Mighty Army: A History of the Church of God,* definitive edition

(Cleveland, TN: Pathway Press, 1994). Conn, a former leader of the Church of God and President of Lee College gives a sympathetic view of the church. See also Mickey Crews, *The Church of God: A Social History* (Knoxville: University of Tennessee Press, 1990), E. L. Simmons, *History of the Church of God* (Cleveland, TN: Church of God Publishing House, 1938), Stephen Benson Vaughan, "The Influence of Music on the Development of the Church of God (Cleveland, Tennessee)," PhD Diss. (University of Birmingham), and David Roebuck, "Restorationism and a Vision for World Harvest: A Brief History of the Church of God," last modified 1999, accessed 30 November 2024, https://www.dixonprc.org/histories-of-the-church-of-god.html#/, and Louis F. Morgan, ed., Encyclopedia of Lee History, leehistory.com.

    This chapter benefited from a paper I presented before I ever conceived of this history, "Pro Ecclesia: The Historic Religious Roots of Lee University" (Conference Paper, 2014 Cedarville Spring Symposium: Historic Religious Roots and the Future of Higher Education, Cedarville University).

2. Roebuck, "Brief History," 8-9; Conn, *Mighty Army*, 82-85.
3. David Bebbington, *The Dominance of Evangelicalism: The Age of Spurgeon and Moody* (Downers Grove, IL: Intervarsity Press, 2005), 22-23.
4. As defined by a Presbyterian General Assembly in 1910. A more comprehensive set of twelve fundamentals was published in 1912. Barry Hankins, *American Evangelicals: A Contemporary History of a Mainstream Religious Movement* (New York: Rowman and Littlefield, 2009), 29.
5. "The Church of God," 15 August 1910, *The Evening Light and Evangel*, 3.
6. Acts 2:4 (ESV).
7. Arlene M. Sànchez-Walsh, *Pentecostals in America* (New York: Columbia University Press, 2018), xxii-xxiii.
8. Roebuck, "Brief History," 8-9. For the best biography of Tomlinson, see Roger Robins, *A. J. Tomlinson: Plainfolk Modernist* (New York: Oxford University Press, 2004); Randall J. Stephens, *The Fire Spreads: Holiness and Pentecostalism in the American South* (Cambridge: Harvard University Press, 2010).
9. Church of God, *Echoes from the General Assembly* [1912] (Cleveland, TN: n.p, n.d.), 31. (Hereafter, general assembly short citations will read, *General Assembly*, date.)
10. This three-part formula can be found in almost any early Church of God publication or sermon, including several references in an early edition of the church newsletter, *Evangel*, 15 September 1912, 2-5.
11. Church of God, *Echoes from the Ninth General Assembly* [1914] (Cleveland, TN: n.p, n.d.), 47.

12. Sam Perry, "Some Hindrances," *Church of God Evangel*, 14 November 1914, 6.
13. Crews, *Social History*, 38-42; Mrs. F. J. Lee, *Sketches and Sermons*, 197, cited in Crews, *Social History*, 39.
14. "What Shall We Do?" *Evangel*, 16 September 1916, 1.
15. Church of God, *Minutes of the Sixteenth Annual Assembly* [1921] (Cleveland, TN: n.p, n.d.), 73-95; Church of God, *Minutes of the 1940 Annual Assembly* (Cleveland, TN: Church of God Press, 1940), 61-110; Conn, *Like a Mighty Army*, 581.
16. Crews, *Social History*, 21-23.
17. Charles Conn, "Ministry of the Written Word," *Evangel*, 5 March 1956, 3-4; Joel Tramell, "Publishing the Gospel," *Church of God History and Heritage*, Winter 1998, 1-5, accessed 20 January 2020, http://www.cogheritage.org/images/uploads/1998-winter.pdf; "Our Publications," *Evangel*, 21 March 1914.
18. Church of God, *Minutes of the Sixth General Assembly* [1911] (Cleveland, TN: n.p., n.d.), 8.
19. "The Assembly," *Evangel*, 14 November 1914, 2.
20. Church of God, *Minutes of the Thirteenth Annual Assembly* [1917] (Cleveland, TN, n.p., n.d.), 20.
21. Church of God, *General Assembly*, 1917, 44.
22. Edward A. Purcell, Jr., *The Crisis of Democratic Theory: Scientific Naturalism and the Problem of Value* (Lexington: University Press of Kentucky, 1973), 7, cited in Robins, *Plainfolk Modernist*, 44.
23. R. E. Hamilton, Personal Correspondence, 1 May 1963, in Mauldin A. Ray, *A Study of the History of Lee College, Cleveland, TN* (Ed. D. diss., University of Houston, 1964), 37.
24. Jesse Lyman Hurlbut, *Hurlbut's Teacher-training Lessons for the Sunday School* (New York: Eaton and Mains, 1908).
25. *The Church of God Bible Training School Catalog*, 1929, 5-6.
26. Iris M. Tomlinson, "The Yesterdays of the Bible School," *Evangel*, 13 April 1918, 1.
27. J. B. Ellis, "The Bible Training School," *Evangel*, 13 April 1918, 2.
28. Tomlinson, "The Yesterdays of the Bible School," *Evangel*, 13 April 1918, 1.
29. Evangelistic License, Nora Chambers, 20 August 1910, Information Files, Nora Chambers File, PRC.
30. "Youth Interviews Experience," *The Lighted Pathway*, June 1949, 14. *The Lighted Pathway*, first published in 1929, was the monthly magazine published for families and the youth of the church.
31. Roebuck, "A Brief History," 17.

32. Iris M. Tomlinson, "The Yesterdays of the Bible School," *Evangel*, 13 April 1918, 1.
33. "Bible Training School Celebrates Silver Anniversary," *The Lighted Pathway*, April 1943, 10.
34. Terrell McBrayer, *Lee College: Pioneer in Pentecostal Education* (Cleveland, TN: Pathway Press, 1968), 21.
35. Tomlinson, "Yesterdays," *Evangel*, 13 April 1918, 2.
36. Tomlinson, "Yesterdays," *Evangel*, 13 April 1918, 1, 2.; J. B. Ellis, "The Bible Training School," *Evangel*, 13 April 1918, 2; Louis Morgan, "Laying the Foundation: The First Students at Bible Training School," *Evangel*, accessed 14 January 2020, https://www.evangelmagazine.com/2018.01/laying-the-foundation/.
37. A. J. Tomlinson, "The Awful World War," *Evangel*, 24 February 1917, 1; also see A. J. Tomlinson, "The Awful War Seems Near," *Evangel*, 31 March 1917, 1.
38. A. J. Tomlinson, Editorial, *Evangel*, 26 May 1917, 2; Tomlinson, Editorial, *Evangel*, 21 July 1917, 2; Tomlinson, "Days of Perplexity," *Evangel*, 26 January 1918, 1.
39. *General Assembly*, 1917, 65.
40. A. J. Tomlinson, Editorial, *Evangel*, 14 September 1918, 2. For a more full explanation of the church's response to World War One, see "Turn the other cheek," chapter six in Crews, *Social History*.
41. 1 Cor. 14:34, Joel 2:28 (KJV); Crews, *Social History*, 93.
42. Nora Chambers certificate is reproduced in Tatiana Gorbacheva, "Nora Chambers—Education Pioneer," Fall 1997 *Church of God History and Heritage*, 4.
43. David Roebuck, "Unraveling the Cords that Divide: Cultural Challenges and Race Relations in the Church of God (Cleveland, Tennessee)," paper presented at the 40th Meeting of the Society for Pentecostal Studies, 2011, 5-7; Crews, *Social History*, 162-165.
44. Crews, *Social History*, 165.
45. Julia Blackwelder, "Southern White Fundamentalists and the Civil Rights Movement," *Phylon* 40 (1979): 337.
46. Roebuck, "A Brief History," 11-12.
47. Centers for Disease Control and Prevention, "1918 Pandemic (HINI Virus)," accessed 22 January 2020, https://www.cdc.gov/flu/pandemic-resources/1918-pandemic-h1n1.html.
48. A. J. Tomlinson, "Healing and Health," *Evangel*, 12 January 1918, 1. For one so sure of the power of faith healing, Tomlinson appeared at a loss to argue against the closing of Sunday Schools, churches, and even the General Assembly of 1918 on account of the influenza pandemic.

49. Allen R. Coggins, "Influenza Epidemic of 1918-1919," *Tennessee Encyclopedia*, March 2018, https://tennesseeencyclopedia.net/entries/influenza-pandemic-of-1918-19/; "Death List," *Evangel*, 4 January 1919, 2.
50. R. E. Stockholm, "Education and the Church of God," *Evangel*, 21 April 1923, 4.
51. Iris M. Tomlinson, "The Bible School," *Evangel*, 12 April 1919, 8.
52. J. B. Ellis, "The Bible Training School," *Evangel*, 13 April 1918, 2.
53. Iris M. Tomlinson, "The Bible School," *Evangel*, 12 April 1919, 1, 8.
54. F. J. Lee, "Go Ye, But Wait," *Evangel*, 23 April 1921, 3.
55. It's difficult to perfectly calculate the value of a dollar over time, but $1 in 1918 would have around $18 purchasing power in 2020. A semester's tuition, then would have been around $252. U.S. Inflation Calculator, accessed 6 May 2020, https://www.usinflationcalculator.com.
56. Notices, 5 April 1919, 2; Iris Tomlinson, "The Bible School," *Evangel*, 12 April 1919, 1. The seminar's content was not specified, but likely was the same as a two-week seminar, identified with the school, that he conducted in Alabama in February 1919, "Bible School," 1 February 1919, 2; "Bible Training School," *Evangel*, 13 September 1919, 4; Iris Tomlinson, "Good in Studying the Bible," *Evangel*, 17 April 1920, 1, 3; Iris Tomlinson, "Good in Studying the Bible," *Evangel*, 17 April 1920, 1.
57. "Bible Training School Celebrates Silver Anniversary," *The Lighted Pathway*, 1 April 1943, 10.
58. Jesse Danehower, Personal Correspondence, 11 February 1963 in Ray, *History of Lee College*, 37.
59. Letter, *Evangel*, 30 April 1921, 2.
60. Letter, *Evangel*, 4 June 1921, 2.
61. A. J. Tomlinson, Letter to Prospective Students, 1921, Bible Training School Manuscript Documents, Box 190, PRC.
62. "Notice," *Evangel*, 10 December 1921, 1.
63. "Report of the Investigation: Proceedings of Elders Council and Correspondence," *Evangel*, 14 July 1923, 3, 4; Robert F. Martin, "Tomlinson, Ambrose Jessup," NCPedia, accessed 22 January 2020, https://www.ncpedia.org/biography/tomlinson-ambrose-jessup; Conn, *Mighty Army*, 210-218.
64. Conn, *Mighty Army*, 226-227.
65. "Bible Training School Celebrates Silver Anniversary," *The Lighted Pathway*, 1 April 1943, 10; Notices, *Evangel*, 5 June 1920, 2; Notices, *Evangel*, 19 June 1920, 2; "Youth Interviews Experience," 14.
66. R. E. Stockholm, "Education and the Church of God," *Evangel*, 21 April 1923, 4.

Chapter 2

1. J. B. Ellis, "Bible Training School," *Evangel*, 26 April 1924, 3.
2. *The Church of God Bible Training School Catalogue*, 1932-1933, 12.
3. *The Church of God Bible Training School Catalog*, 1935-1936, 12.
4. While one can see the prophetic emphasis in almost any issue of the *Evangel*, see for example: on communism, Louis Bauman, "When Russia's Bear Meets Judah's Lion," *Evangel*, 10 June 1933, 3, on dictators, E. C. Clark, "The Coming Crisis and the World Economic Order," *Evangel*, 22 July 1933, 8; on the NRA, S. W. Latimer, "Information Concerning the N.R.A.," *Evangel*, 9 September 1933, 15; on the threat of war, S. W. Latimer, "Troubles That Are Ahead of Us," *Evangel*, 22 April 1933, 3-4.
5. Expenses from *Bible Training School Catalog*, 1929, 7.
6. Pearl Auten, "Great Place for Christian Training," *Evangel*, 27 November 1926, 3.
7. Maggie Free, "The Closing of the Bible Training School," *Evangel*, 16 February 1924, 3.
8. J. B. Cole, "The Bible School is God's," *Evangel*, 4 July 1931, 3.
9. *Bible Training School Catalog*, 1929, 6.
10. W. Jackson, Letter, *Evangel*, 26 December 1925, 4.
11. William Auten, "To the Bible Training School," *Evangel*, 19 September 1925, 3.
12. *Bible Training School Catalogue*, 1931-1932, 12.
13. J. B. Ellis, "The Bible School," *Evangel*, 16 February 1924, 3.
14. *Bible Training School Catalog*, 1929, 13.
15. "Attend the Bible School," *Evangel*, 19 March 1927, 1.
16. "A Week in Bible School," *Evangel*, 2 January 1937, 7.
17. While these changes can be followed in church records, they are more easily followed in Stephens, *The Fire Spreads*, 48-52.
18. For Swiger's story, see Hollis Gause, "Lee's Lady of Missions," *Evangel*, 12 June 1972, 14.
19. Advertisement, *Evangel*, 29 November 1919, 3; Advertisement, *Evangel*, 7 June 1919, 4.
20. Church of God, *Minutes of the Fifteenth General Assembly* [1920] (Cleveland, TN: n.p., n.d.), 66.
21. Church of God, *Minutes of the Twenty-Fifth Annual Assembly of the Church of God* (Cleveland, TN: Church of God Publishing House, 1930), 41,42; Church of God, *Minutes of the Thirty-First General Assembly of the Church of God* (Cleveland, TN: Church of God Publishing House, 1936), 33-36, 151.

22. *The Church of God Bible Training School Catalogue*, 1931-1932, 23. Conn, *Mighty Army*, 271.
23. Bible Training School, *Echoes*, February 1932, Folder: Bible School Echoes, Fan-March 1932, Box 109a, PRC.
24. For recognition of B. C. Robinson as a vocal music teacher, Willie Goins, "Illinois Student," *Evangel*, 26 March 1927, 3, and the new department in *Bible Training School Catalogue*, 1931-1932, 23; for information on the music faculty, classes, and students, see the *Bible Training School Catalogue*, 1931-1932; for more on the Band Boys, see H. L. Carpenter, "On the Firing Line," *Evangel*, 21 June 1924, 1; for the Gleeful Five see *Evangel*, 11 March 1933, 12.
25. Charles Conn, "Music in the B.T.S.," *Evangel*, 2 December 1939, 9.
26. J. H. Walker, "Bible Training School Department," *Evangel*, 11 October 1930, 3, Henrietta Green, "Department of Secretarial Sciences," *Evangel*, 15 March 1941, 9, and the *Church of God Bible Training School Catalogue*, 1930-1931, 23.
27. *Bible Training School Catalogue*, 1932-1933, 13.
28. Walker in *Bible Training School Catalogue*, 1931-1932, 20-21; for the High School, see "The Church of God Bible Training School Echoes," *Evangel*, 24 September 1932, 3; for Greek classes, see Dixie Greenwood, "School," *Evangel*, 5 November 1932, 4 and *The Church of God Bible Training School Catalog, 1934-1935*, 13; Conn, *Mighty Army*, 258.
29. For the school's financial struggles, see reports in the general assembly minutes. For the example above, see Church of God, *Minutes of the Twenty-seventh General Assembly* (Cleveland, TN: Church of God Publishing House, 1932), 45. Church of God, *Minutes of the Twenty-Ninth General Assembly of the Church of God* (Cleveland, TN: Church of God Publishing House, 1934), 49; Advertisement, "Northwest Bible School," *Evangel*, 9 November 1935, 16; First Year, "Northwest Bible and Music Academy to Open November 23," *Evangel*, 12 September 1936, 6.
30. George Poteet, "Hurrah for Our Bible School," *The Lighted Pathway*, July 1938, 10.
31. J. H. Walker, "Our New Home for the Bible Training School," *Evangel*, 24 September 1938, 7.
32. J. H. Walker, "Our New Home for the Bible Training School," *Evangel*, 24 September 1938, 7.
33. "Amounts Paid on Bible School, *Evangel*, 5 November 1938; "Our Bible School," *Evangel*, 14 January 1939, 9.
34. Transcript of BTS Chapel Service, 3 February 1944, Box 109a, Folder: Untitled, PRC, Lee College Archives (hereafter LCA).

35. Minutes of the Council of Twelve, 26 August 1942, PRC.
36. Church of God, *Minutes of the Thirty-Seventh General Assembly of the Church of God* (Cleveland, TN: Church of God Publishing House, 1942), 38.
37. Conn, *Mighty Army*, 581-583.
38. John C. Jernigan, "Looking Forward," *Evangel*, 20 January 1945, 3.
39. John C. Jernigan, "Annual Address," Church of God, *Minutes of the Forty-First General Assembly of the Church of God* (Cleveland, TN: Church of God Publishing House, 1946), 18.
40. Church of God, *General Assembly*, 1940, 20-21.
41. George Ayers, "New Bible Training School," *The Lighted Pathway*, January 1939, 15; Charles Conn, "Sevierville and the B.T.S.," *Evangel*, 18 November 1939, 9; Charles Conn, "Bible School Closes," *Evangel*, 13 April 1940, 5.
42. *Vindagua*, 1942, 3.
43. *Bible Training School Catalogue*, 1932-1933, 21.
44. For a good representation of the sports played by students, see the photos of the Girls and the Boys Athletic Clubs, *Vindagua*, 1945, 76-80.
45. "The Difference Enjoyed," *The Lighted Pathway*, September 1942, 7.
46. "The Difference Enjoyed," *The Lighted Pathway*, September 1942, 7.
47. See the *Vindagua*, 1943, 48 and 1945, 87 for examples of socials. Evelyn Walker-Holcombe, who was at BTS from 1936 to 1942, tells her story on *Hundred Year Journey*, directed by Jeff Salyer, Rob Reid, and Chad Guyton (Cleveland, TN: Lee University Films, 2018), DVD.
48. Minutes of the Bishops' Council, 23 August 1943, PRC.
49. J. H. Walker, "Bible School Closing," *Evangel*, 4 February 1939, 6.
50. Benjamin DeLay, "A Day in B.T.S.," *Evangel* 10 January 1942, 7; Hoyet Bridges, "A Visit to the Bible School," *Evangel*, 4 January 1942, 13; Hoyet Bridges, "Our Work at the Prison Camp," *Evangel*, 22 February 1941, 11.
51. First notice of the radio show appears in a list of eight church radio shows in *Evangel*, 29 October 1938, 14; *Vindagua*, 1945, 50.
52. "On the Air," *Evangel*, 15 June 1940, 15.
53. Church of God, *General Assembly*, 1940, 31.
54. Zeno Tharp, "B.T.S. is Getting a Library," *Evangel*, 21 September 1940, 18.
55. Zeno Tharp, "Closing the 1941-42 Term," *Evangel*, 9 May 1942, 12.
56. Letter, J. Richardson to Mary Green, 31 December 1948, Box 75, Folder 10, PRC, LCA; News Release, 20 March 1951, Box 75, Folder 10, PRC, LCA.
57. *Vindagua*, 1943, 62.
58. "Every Week Around the B.T.S," *Evangel*, 10 October 1942, 5; Zeno Tharp, "Report from Church of God Bible School," *Evangel*, 29 November 1941, 6.
59. *Evangel*, 19 October 1946, 8.
60. Church of God, *General Assembly*, 1946, 177.

61. "B.T.S. and College Echoes," *Evangel*, 15 August 1942, 8.
62. "B.T.S. and College," *The Lighted Pathway*, September 1942, 25.
63. Barney Smith, "Bible Training School and College," *The Lighted Pathway*, February 1945, 13.
64. "Armistice Program at the B.T.S.," *Evangel*, 28 November 1942, 6, 7; *The Lighted Pathway*, February 1943, 12; *Evangel*, 6 February 1943, 10; *The Lighted Pathway*, July 1943, 14.
65. Claude Phillips, "Third Term in B.T.S.," *The Lighted Pathway*, November 1943, 9.
66. J. D. Bright, "The B.T.S. Grows Better," *Evangel*, 20 November 1943, 10.
67. Zeno Tharp, "A Record Enrollment," *Evangel*, 6 November 1943, 10.
68. J. D. Bright, "The B.T.S. Grows Better," *Evangel*, 20 November 1943, 10.
69. Zeno Tharp, "B.T.S. and College Closing," *Evangel*, 15 April 1944, 10.
70. Church of God, *General Assembly*, 1941, 14; Zeno Tharp, "Report from Church of God Bible School," *Evangel*, 29 November 1941, 6; J. D. Bright, "Bible Training School," *Evangel*, 13 June 1942, 6; *The Lighted Pathway*, September 1942, 6.
71. Zeno Tharp, "Bible Training School Looks at the Past and to the Future," *The Lighted Pathway,* August 1944, 7.
72. *Vindagua*, 1945, 10, 88.
73. The Church of God, *The Lighted Pathway*, August 1945, 4-5; Edward Woods, "News from the Bible Training School," February 1946, 21-22; *Lee College Catalog*, 1947-1948, 18.
74. Simmons, *History of the Church of God*.
75. Conn, *Mighty Army*, 252, 300, 301.
76. Raphael Stephens, "A History of Governance at Lee College," EdD Diss. (College of William and Mary, 1981), 80, 93; Church of God, *General Assembly*, 1946, 29.
77. Earl Tapley, *The Way it Was: A Family History and Personal Memoirs* (St. Petersburg, FL: Southern Heritage Press, 2000), 59-65.
78. Church of God, *General Assembly*, 1946, 29.
79. *Teachers Guide*, c. 1942, Box 109a, Folder: Untitled, PRC, LCA.
80. Always looking to improve appearances, the denomination claimed another three faculty, but these were staff and administrators (including the head of cafeteria operations), *The Lighted Pathway*, December 1942, 12; *Vindagua,*1943, 8-13; salaries from Church of God, *Minutes of the Thirty-Eight General Assembly* (Cleveland, TN: Church of God Publishing House, 1943), 44.
81. *Vindagua*, 1946, 11-16; Church of God, *General Assembly Minutes*, 1946, 50, 60.

82. *Evangel*, 2 November 1946, 15.
83. *Lee College Catalog*, 1947-1948, 37; "News from Bible Training School," *The Lighted Pathway*, March 1946, 15.
84. *Evangel*, 27 April 1946, 10.
85. Editor, "B.T.S. and College Closes Another Successful Term," *Evangel*, 7 June 1947, 4.

Chapter 3

1. Statistic from Kenneth A. Simon and W. Vance Grant, *Digest of Educational Statistics*, Office of Education, Bulleting 1965 (Washington, D.C.: U. S. Government Printing Office, 1965), 47.
2. E. L. Simmons, "Bible Training School and Its Mission," *The Lighted Pathway*, August 1946, 8.
3. The decision to move back to Cleveland was broadly welcomed, but not without its detractors. In an ill-considered move, the committee negotiating the purchase had contacted by mail the pastorate to solicit their opinions. The mixed messages that returned to the committee threatened to delay, and even undo, the deal, however Bob Jones, desperately wanting to sell the campus and short on interested buyers, patiently waited for the Church of God to agree to the purchase. Negotiations began in February 1946, with an agreement made in principle, but were not finalized until August 1946. See Minutes of the Council of Twelve, 26-27 February 1946, PRC; Minutes of the Council of Twelve, 27 April 1946, PRC; Minutes of the Supreme Council, 13 August 1946, PRC.
4. E. L. Simmons, "A Farewell," *The Lighted Pathway*, August 1948, 5.
5. "Lee College," *The Lighted Pathway*, September 1950, 20.
6. Tapley, *The Way it Was*, 159-160; J. Stewart Brinsfield, Interview by Charles W. Conn, 11 December 1991, PRC; Minutes of the Supreme Council, 9 September 1947, PRC; Minutes of the Bishop's Council, 26 August 1948, PRC.
7. Church of God, *General Assembly*, 1942, 127.
8. Roebuck, "Brief History," 13.
9. 1 John 3:9 KJV.
10. Church of God, *Minutes of the Forty-Second General Assembly* (Cleveland, TN: Church of God Publishing House, 1948), 31.
11. Church of God, *General Assembly*, 1948, 186-194; David Roebuck, "Declaration Prevents Church Division," *Church of God History and Heritage* (Summer 1998), 1-2, 5-6.
12. Alan Brinkley, *The Unfinished Nation: A Concise History of the American People*, 6th ed. (New York: McGraw-Hill, 2010), 726.

13. Crews, *Social History*, 138-139.
14. Iris M. Tomlinson, "The Yesterdays of the Bible School," *Evangel*, 13 April 1918, 1.
15. Evaluative Study of the Visiting Committee of the Accrediting Association of Bible Colleges, September 19-21, 1959, Box 1, Folder 00, PRC, LCA.
16. P. E. Day, "Repent and Get Back to God," *Evangel*, 22 February 1947, 3.
17. *Lee College Catalog*, 1948-1949, 7.
18. *Lee College Catalog*, 1948-1949, 10-12.
19. *The Lighted Pathway*, July 1949, 24; *Evangel*, 26 November 1949.
20. *Lee College Catalog*, 1950-1951, 13-14.
21. Joel A. Carpenter, *Revive us Again: The Reawakening of American Fundamentalism* (Cambridge: Oxford University Press, 1997).
22. Conn, *Mighty Army*, 313.
23. *Lee College Catalog*, 1950-1951, 12.
24. John Jernigan, "Report on Lee College," *Evangel*, 10 November 1951, 6.
25. Charles Conn, "Our Returning Students, *The Lighted Pathway*, June 1949, 3.
26. A. W. Ellington, "Does Lee College help or Hinder One Spiritually," and Guynelle Steedley, "How Lee College Helped Me Become a Christian," *The Lighted Pathway*, February 1950, 20.
27. Harold Chesser, "Is Lee Dead Spiritually?" *Evangel*, 26 January 1952, 9.
28. J. D. Bright, editorial, *Evangel*, 4 March 1950, 3; Charles Conn, "Spirituality at Lee College," *Evangel*, 25 February 1950, 11; Chesser, Brinsfield, and Tharp in "Lee College's Great Revival," *Evangel*, 4 March 1950, 9, 10.
29. *Lee College Catalog*, 1956-1958, 29.
30. Glenda Cleghorn, "Lee College Pioneers for Christ," *Evangel*, 18 January 1965, 9; *Vindagua*, 1956, 95; *Vindagua* 1960, 116. Regarding Beach, see Peggy Scarborough, *Power to Witness: The Story of Charles Beach* (Cleveland, TN: Pathway Press, 2002).
31. Dating story as told by Ollie Lee and Delton Alford in *Hundred Year Journey*.
32. Simmons, *History of the Church of God*; Conn, *Mighty Army*, 252, 300, 312-313.
33. Minutes of the Supreme Council, 24 August 1948, PRC.
34. E. M. Tapley, "Lee College is Having a Great New Year," *Evangel*, 16 October 1948, 6.
35. *Student Handbook*, 1949-1950, Unlabeled Storage Box, PRC.
36. Donald S. Aultman, *You Can Go Home Again: Journey of a Pentecostal* (Cleveland, TN: DSA Publications, 2010), 68-69.
37. J. Stewart Brinsfield. Interview by Charles W. Conn, 11 December 1991, PRC.

38. J. Stewart Brinsfield, Interview by Charles W. Conn, 11 December 1991, PRC; Minutes of the Supreme Council, 13 August 1952, PRC; Tapley, *The Way it Was*, 162-166, 170-171.
39. Tapley served as interim from January 24, 1951, to April 16, 1951. E. M. Tapley, "Revival Fires Burn Again at Lee College," *Evangel*, 24 February 1951, 6.
40. Conn, *Mighty Army*, 315, 334; John C. Jernigan, "A Church of God Institution," *Evangel*, 25 August 1951, 6.
41. John C. Jernigan, "Report on Lee College," *Evangel*, 10 November 1951, 6.
42. Tapley, *The Way it Was*, 168-172.
43. R. Leonard Carroll, "A Message from the President," *Evangel*, 21 May 1956, 3.
44. *Lee College Catalog*, 1953-1954, 17.
45. *Student Handbook*, c. 1953, Unlabeled Storage Box, PRC.
46. Meeting of Administrators, Head of Divisions, and Dormitory Supervisors," 5 November 1954, Box 29, Folder 8, PRC, LCA; Minutes, Meeting of Lee College Administration, 24 October 1955, Box 29, Folder 9, PRC, LCA.
47. *Student Handbook*, c. 1953; Tapley, *The Way it Was*, 172.
48. Conn, *Mighty Army*, 376.
49. Rufus L. Platt, "Why I Came to BTS," *Evangel*, 26 October 1946, 10.
50. Delton Alford and Evaline Echols, *Hundred Year Journey*.
51. *Bible Training School Catalog*, 1937-1938, 11-14; *Lee College Catalog*, 1948-1949, 12-14; *Lee College Catalogue*, 1958-1959.
52. *University of Chattanooga Catalog*, 1957-1958, 5-12; *Southern Missionary College Catalog*, 1957-1958; J. H. Walker, "Are Private Colleges Overcrowded?" *Evangel*, 29 August 1960, 3.
53. Preston Pendergrass, "Bob Jones College to become Lee College," 10 June 1947, Cleveland *Daily Banner*.
54. E. M. Tapley, "Lee College High School is Accepted into Southern Association of Colleges and Secondary School," *Evangel*, 12.
55. E. M. Tapley, "The Church of God and the Future of Pentecostal Education," *Evangel*, 14 January 1950, 7.
56. Ray Hughes, "The Transition of Church-Related Junior Colleges to Senior Colleges, with Implications for Lee College" (Ed. D. diss., University of Tennessee, 1966), 52.
57. Church of God, *General Assembly*, 1917, 44.
58. *Lee College Catalog*, 1954–1955, 74.
59. *Lee College Catalog*, 1954–1955, 101-111.
60. *Lee College Catalog*, 1956–1958, 96-106.

61. "Robert Humbertson, "Fall Registration at Lee College," *Evangel*, 21 January 1957, 13.
62. "Evaluative Study of the Visiting Committee of the Accrediting Association of Bible Colleges," September 19-21, 159, Box 1, Folder 00, PRC, LCA.
63. Rufus Platt, "Lee College Expands!" *The Lighted Pathway*, July 1956, 3.
64. Hughes, "Church-Related Junior Colleges," 24.
65. *Lee College Catalog*, 1949-1950, 8; *Lee College Catalog*, 1950-1951, 8; *Lee College Catalog*, 1953-1954, 12.
66. 1948 veterans estimated in "Here and There," *Evangel*, 6 November 1948, 4. 1949 from the *Lee College Catalog, 1950-1951*, 89; other data is drawn from internal reports: Enrollment Files, Box 91, Folder 5; Box 92, Folder 4; Box 92, Folder 10; Box 92, Folder 16; Box 92, Folder 22, PRC, LCA.
67. Ray, "A Study of the History of Lee College," 133-134; James Cross to O. Ray, 6 September 1968, Box 42, Folder 5, PRC, LCA.
68. U.S. Department of Veterans Affairs, "Education and Training: History and Timeline," accessed 24 March 2020, https://benefits.va.gov/gibill/history.asp.
69. "Lee College Echoes," *The Lighted Pathway*, January 1949, 19.
70. David M. Kennedy, *Freedom from Fear: The American People in Depression and War, 1929-1945* (New York: Oxford University Press, 1999), 710.
71. Church of God, *Minutes of the Forty-Seventh General Assembly Minutes* (Cleveland, TN: Church of God Publishing House, 1958), 32.
72. James Cross to O. Ray, 6 September 1968, PRC, Box 42, Folder 5, PRC, LCA.
73. See R. Leonard Carroll, Lee College Faculty Meeting, 24 February 1955, Box 84, Folder 12, PRC, LCA.
74. Inflation for the decade of the 1950s was a modest 2.05 percent, U.S. Inflation Calculator, accessed 24 March 2020, https://www.usinflationcalculator.com.inflation/historical-inflation-rates; *Lee College Catalog*, 1950-1951, 34; *Lee College Catalog*, 1960-1961, 41.
75. H. D. Williams, "Financing God's Work," *Evangel*, 10 March 1956, 11.
76. Another $500 was approved to cover the costs of a visiting SACS committee visiting Lee. Church of God, Supreme Council Meeting Minutes, 8 March 1960, PRC.
77. Minutes of the Supreme Council, 9 March 1960, PRC.
78. The best account of the civil rights movement in Tennessee is Bobby Lovett, *The Civil Rights Movement in Tennessee: A Narrative History* (Knoxville: The University of Tennessee Press, 2005).
79. Crews, *Social History*, 167. African American churches in states that did not practice legal, Jim Crow segregation had the option of being

administered by the Overseer of the Church of God Colored Work or to be part of the broader church organization. Black churches in the South did not have this option.

80. Minutes of Meeting of Lee College Administration, 27 September 1955, Box 29, Folder 29, PRC, LCA.
81. Minutes of Meeting of Lee College Administration, 8 February 1956, Box 29, Folder 10, PRC, LCA.

Chapter 4

1. Charles Paul Conn, the son of Charles W. Conn, normally went by the name of Paul and will be referred to as such.
2. To give measure to Hughes's popularity, he was almost elevated to the post of National Youth Director in 1948 but fell six votes shy (of 623 cast). Minutes of the Bishop's Council, 24-28 August 1948, PRC.
3. Doc Hughes, "Voice of a Legacy: Ray. H. Hughes, Sr.," *Evangel* (online), accessed 31 March 2020, https://www.evangelmagazine.com/2018/06/voice-of-a-legacy; MGM Ministries, "A Biography of Dr. Ray H. Hughes," accessed 24 February 2022, mgmministries.org/ray-hughes/. To hear Hughes, search online for his filmed revival messages, such as his message at a South Carolina Camp Meeting: Ray Hughes, "The Power of His Name," accessed 3 January 2024, https://youtube.com/DKlnoj21lqY.
4. Evaline Echols, *Hundred Year Journey*.
5. Conn, *Mighty Army*, 547-563. Note that until 1988, the general overseer also served as the president of the seminary.
6. Speech, Ray Hughes to the Lee Faculty, 4 February 1965, Box 84, Folder 14, PRC, LCA.
7. Letter, James Cross to V. Hargrave, 28 August 1967, Box 39, Folder 9, PRC, LCA.
8. Crews, *Social History*, 61-62.
9. Conn, *Mighty Army*, 388-389.
10. Church of God, *Minutes of the Fiftieth General Assembly of the Church of God* (Cleveland, TN: Church of God Publishing House, 1964), 11.
11. Letter, James Cross to R. Burroughs, 15 August 1968, Box 41, Folder 2, PRC, LCA.
12. Letter, Ray Hughes to J. L. Sullivent, 11 January 1962, Box 33, Folder 13, PRC, LCA.
13. Letter, Ray Hughes to Bedford Smith, 27 September 1965, Box 39, Folder 5, PRC, LCA.

14. Letter, Ray Hughes to Danny Drake, 7 January 1964, PRC, Box 34, Folder 10, PRC, LCA.
15. Ray Hughes, Speech to the Lee Faculty, 4 February 1965, Box 84, Folder 14, PRC, LCA.
16. National Center for Education Statistics, *120 Years of American Education: A Statistical Portrait* (Washington: National Center for Education Statistics, 1993), 76-77.
17. Conn, *Mighty Army*, 390-391.
18. Ray Hughes, "Lee College in Prospect," *Evangel*, 2 January 1961, 7.
19. Advertisement, *The Lighted Pathway*, July 1962, 28; Advertisement, *The Lighted Pathway*, December 1963, 28.
20. See, for example, a report of Louisiana Day, Floyd Carey, "Louisiana's Diamond Jubilee Car Caravan to Cleveland," *Evangel* 14 August 1961, 5.
21. "First College Day," *Evangel*, 6 April 1964, 11; "National College Day," *The Lighted Pathway*, June 1964, 14-15.
22. Conn, *Mighty Army*, 386.
23. *Lee College Catalog*, 1968-1969, 93.
24. Alford would also serve as Vice President for Academic Affairs from 1976 to 1980.
25. "Those Singing Singers," *Evangel*, 9 March 1970, 27.
26. Delton Alford, interview for *Hundred Year Journey* centennial project, 2018.
27. See *Evangel*, 2 October 1967, 4-9, 15, 20.
28. "The Evangelistic Singers' Story, Part 1," *Torch* Fall, 2017, 34-6; Ladies of Lee, "Ladies of Lee Ministry Manual," Fall 2016, author's private collection; Dirksen Centennial Interview.
29. In response to hazing incidents, Lee required sponsors to attend club initiations and restricted club activity to campus, Minutes of Lee Faculty Meeting, 17 August 1968, Box 84, Folder 14, PRC, LCA.
30. See, for example, Alan Walker, "Lee's Upsilon Xi Contributes to Mission School," *Evangel*, 25 July 1965, 15.
31. *Vindagua*, 1942, 52; *Vindagua*, 1947, 68-79; *Vindagua*, 1956, 100; *Vindagua*, 1957, 136-148.
32. For the Dragon mascot, see *Vindagua*, 1961, 129.
33. Hughes to James Wiley, 8 October 1964, Box 36, Folder 8, PRC, LCA.
34. Charles Conn to Cross, 6 March 1967, Box 39, Folder 4, PRC, LCA.
35. The conference included Lee, Atlanta Christian College, Bryan College, Covenant College, Emmanuel College (GA), Johnson Bible College, Tennessee Temple College, and Toccoa Falls Bible College; Letter, Charles Conn to James Cross, 21 April 1969, Box 43, Folder 4, PRC, LCA.

36. *Vindagua*, 1967, 138-139.
37. *Vindagua*, 1968, 138-145.
38. *Vindagua*, 1969, 103-111; *Vindagua*, 1970, 104-111.
39. Larry Carpenter, interview by author, 29 April 2020; Letter, Conn to Lee Roberson, 7 March 1974, Box 50, Folder 2, PRC, LCA.
40. Public Broadcasting System, "The First Violent Protest," The American Experience, accessed 4 May 2020, https://www.pbs.org/wgbh/american experience/features/two-days-in-october-student-antiwar-protests-and-backlash/.
41. E. M. Schrieber, "Opposition to the Vietnam War among American University Students and Faculty," *The British Journal of Sociology*, vol 24 number 3 (September 1973), 290.
42. For an example of such reporting, see Daniel Levy, "Behind the Anti-War Protests that Swept America in 1968" *Time*, accessed 4 May 2020, https://time.com/5106608/protest-1968/. In one paragraph he writes "Agitation spread to hundreds of schools," notes three-quarters of student supported the right to protest and highlights an act of arson to demonstrate radicalism. All of this is true, but in combination it incorrectly suggests widespread (and heavily supported) protests tinged with violence.
43. Schrieber, "Opposition," 290.
44. Joseph A. Fry, *The American South and the Vietnam War* (Lexington: University of Kentucky Press, 2015), 285. For broader studies of campus protest see Charles DeBenedetti and Charles Chatfield, *An American Ordeal: The Antiwar Movement of the Vietnam Era* (Syracuse: Syracuse University Press, 1990).
45. "Tribute to the Military," *Evangel*, 30 September 1968, 15.
46. Letter, Hughes to Mrs. Joe Walker, 23 August 1965, Box 36, Folder 9, PRC, LCA; Cross Address to Servicemen, 30 January 1968, Box 47, Folder 7, PRC, LCA. For a typical letter requesting deferral, see Letter, Cross to Selective Service Board, 10 July 1968, Box 39, Folder 10, PRC, LCA.
47. Donald Aultman, "The Future Looks Bright," *Evangel*, 4 November 1968, 15.

Chapter 5

1. This chapter is based on a pair of conference papers I wrote: "Staying the Course: Lee University's Changing Constituencies" (Conference Paper, 2014 Conference on Faith and History, Pepperdine University)

and "'I Took Them at Their Word': Integrating Lee College" (2016 Conference on Faith and History, Regent University).
2. Cited in Conn, *Mighty Army*, 391.
3. Minutes of the Lee College Board of Directors, 8 February 1966, Box 25, Folder 4, PRC, LCA; Special Called Meeting of the Lee College Board of Directors, 12 August 1963, Box 25, Folder 2, PRC, LCA.
4. Minutes of the Lee College Board of Directors, 8 February 1966, Box 25, Folder 4, PRC, LCA.
5. Minutes of the Lee College Board of Directors, 8 February 1966, Box 25, Folder 4, PRC, LCA.
6. Speech by Ray Hughes to the Faculty, Minutes of the Lee College Faculty meeting, 4 February 1965, Box 85, Folder 14, PRC, LCA.
7. Conn, *Mighty Army*, 385-386.
8. Letter, Charles Vail to James Cross, 8 December 1967, Box 75, Folder 12, PRC, LCA.
9. J. H. Walker, "Progress Report on Accreditation for Lee's Liberal Arts College," *Evangel*, 12 February 1968, 4.
10. Charles Conn, "The Church and Education," *Evangel*, 12 February 1968, 5.
11. Charles Conn, "Christian Education in Time of Crisis," *Evangel*, 12 February 1968, 22.
12. R. H. Gause, "A Profile of Lee's Bible College," *Evangel*, 12 January 1968, 9.
13. Accrediting Association of Bible Colleges, Report of Visit to Lee College, 12-13 February 1968, Box 75, Folder 21, PRC, LCA.
14. Letter, James Cross to J. Mostert, 19 September 1968, Box 42, Folder 2, PRC, LCA.
15. Southern Association of Colleges and Schools, A Report on Lee College, Cleveland, Tennessee, 1967, Box 75, Folder 13, PRC, LCA.
16. SACS, Report on Lee College, 1967, Box 75, Folder 13, PRC, LCA.
17. Letter, James Cross to Charles Conn, 24 October 1967, Box 39, Folder 4, PRC, LCA.
18. This position is clearly seen in a speech by Hughes to the faculty, 4 February 1965, Box 84, Folder 14, PRC, LCA.
19. SACS, Report on Lee College, 1967, 16, Box 75, Folder 13, PRC, LCA.
20. Lee College Faculty, Lee College Self-Study Report, 1966, 77, Box 75, Folder 12, PRC, LCA; Minutes, Lee College Faculty Meeting, 4 February 1965, Box 84, Folder 14, PRC, LCA.
21. Minutes of the Board of Directors, 12 March 1968, Box 25, Folder 6, PRC, LCA.

22. Lee College, *Institutional Self-Study Report of Lee College* (Cleveland, TN: Lee College, 1973). A decade later, in 1984, SACS reported faculty satisfaction with the school's academic freedom: "Faculty members of the College, nevertheless, report consistently that the College has respected academic freedom. The Church's commitment of faith is clear. Within the context of that commitment, there appears to be genuine academic freedom." "Report of the Visiting Committee (Reaffirmation Evaluation) for the Southern Association of Colleges and Schools," April 8-11, 1984, LC collection in process, no folder, PRC, LCA.
23. Minutes, Lee College Board of Directors, 21 May 1968, Box 25, Folder 16, PRC, LCA.
24. Letter, J. H. Warf to James Cross, 24 May 1968, Box 75, Folder 17, PRC, LCA.
25. Ollie Lee and Delton Alford, interviews for *Hundred Year Journey* centennial project, 2018.
26. Letter, James Cross to J. Browning, 16 July 1968, Box 41, Folder 2, PRC, LCA.
27. Aultman, *You Can Go Home Again*, 223-224; Delton Alford, *Hundred Year Journey*.
28. Carolyn Dirksen, interview for *Hundred Year Journey* centennial project, 2018; Aultman, *You Can Go Home Again*, 223-224.
29. Charles Padgett, "'Without Hysteria or Unnecessary Disturbance': Desegregation at Spring Hill College, Mobile, Alabama, 1948-1954," *History of Education Quarterly* 41 (Summer 2001), 171.
30. Melissa Kean, *Desegregating Private Higher Education in the South: Duke, Emory, Rice, Tulane, and Vanderbilt* (Baton Rouge: LSU Press, 2008), 1.
31. Minutes of Meeting of the Lee College Board of Directors, 12 August 1963, Box 25, Folder 2, PRC, LCA.
32. Minutes of Meeting of the Church of God Supreme Council, 13 August 1963, PRC.
33. Letter, Wade Horton [General Overseer, Church of God] to President Ray Hughes, 21 August 1963, Box 33, Folder 2, PRC, LCA.
34. Letter, Ray Hughes to O. C. McCane, 24 October 1961, Paul Conn's personal files.
35. Letter, Ray Hughes to A. E. Justice, 15 November 1961, Paul Conn's personal files.
36. Letter, Ray Hughes to Bill Watson, 25 September 1963, Box 34, Folder 3, PRC, LCA; Letter, Ray Hughes to O. H. Wolff, 23 January 1964, Paul Conn's personal files.
37. Letter, John Bush to Ray Hughes, 30 August 1963, Box 32, Folder 4, PRC, LCA.

38. Letter, Bill Watson to Ray Hughes, 11 September 1963, Box 34, Folder 3, PRC, LCA.
39. Letter, Ray Hughes to Bill Watson, 25 September 1963, Box 34, Folder 3, PRC, LCA.
40. Letter, Ray Hughes to John Bush, 12 September 1963, Box 32, Folder 4, PRC, LCA.
41. Letter, Ray Hughes to Bill Watson, 25 September 1963, Box 34, Folder 3, PRC, LCA.
42. Attached report to letter, Howard Rogerson to Ray Hughes, 25 November 1963, Box 33, Folder 11, PRC, LCA.
43. Minutes of the Supreme Council, 18 March 1964, PRC.
44. Minutes of the Supreme Council, 26 May 1964, PRC.
45. Joint Supreme Council-Lee Board of Directors Meeting, Minutes of the Supreme Council, 26 May 1964, PRC.
46. Minutes of the Supreme Council, 29 July 1964, PRC.
47. Minutes of the Supreme Council, 28 May 1964, PRC.
48. Minutes of the Supreme Council, 18 March 1964, PRC; Minutes of the Supreme Council, 26 May 1964, PRC; Minutes of the Executive Council, 1 March 1965, PRC.
49. U.S. Department of Education, Office of Civil Rights, "Education and Title IX," accessed 5 October 2016, http://www2.ed.gov/about/offices/list/ocr/docs/hq43e4.html.
50. Letter, President Ray Hughes to Wade Horton, General Overseer of the Church of God, 23 July 1964, Box 35, Folder 4, PRC, LCA.
51. Stanley Butler, "How to Enter Lee College" November 1967, *The Lighted Pathway*, 26.
52. Minutes of the Supreme Council, 29 July 1964, Supreme/Executive-General Councils, March 16-20, 1964-January 6, 1965, PRC; Minutes of the Executive Council, 1 March 1965, Minutes of the Executive Council, March 1-5, 1965 to July 25-30, 1966, PRC.
53. Some more conservative Church of God members feared that the aid would prohibit faculty from praying before their classes or would otherwise inhibit their religious freedom.
54. Minutes of the Lee College Board of Directors, 8 February 1966, Box 25, Folder 4, PRC, LCA.
55. Lee's Board of Directors seconded and carried the Church of God's resolution on the integration of Lee, but did so after the fact (and after the ultimatum on federal aid) on February 8; Minutes of the Lee College Board of Directors, 8 February 1966, Box 25, Folder 4, PRC, LCA.
56. Church of God, *Minutes of the Fifty-First General Assembly of the Church of God* (Cleveland, TN: Church of God Publishing House, 1966), 62.

57. For context, it was not until August 1965 that the state of Tennessee approved the desegregation plan proposed by Bradley County (in which Lee was located). Cleveland *Daily Banner*, 25 August 1965, 1.
58. The university records do not contain a record of any meetings or correspondence which suggest the school's strategy for recruiting and/or selecting Bacon or Cox.
59. Hazel Edwards Ivy, interview by author, 23 November 2015, 22 January 2016.
60. Letter, Ridley Usherwood, et. al., to James Cross, Feb. [day illegible] 1969, Box 44, Folder 4, PRC, LCA; James Cross to Ridley Usherwood, et. al., 20 February 1969, Box 44, Folder 4, PRC, LCA; Mike Linley, interview with author, 2 March 2016; Pauline Washington, interview by author, 27 February 2016.
61. Mike Linley, interview by author, 2 March 2016.
62. Lee College Progress Report, attachment to letter from Ray Hughes to Wade Horton, 26 April 1966, Box 38, Folder 7, PRC, LCA; Minutes, Lee College Faculty Meeting, 7 December 1966, Box 84, Folder 14, PRC, LCA; Lee College Progress Report, attachment to letter from James Cross to Charles Conn, 26 April 1966, Box 39, Folder 4, PRC, LCA.

Chapter 6

1. The vice president at the time, Don Aultman, claims that Cross and the board promised him the president's office, but suggests that a) some church fathers saw him as too liberal and b) Conn used his position in the church to secure the job. Aultman would stay another two years at Lee before resigning. Aultman, *You Can Go Home Again*, 227-230.
2. Paul Conn, interview, *Hundred Year Journey* centennial project, 2018.
3. Charles Conn, "Christian Education in Time of Crisis," *Evangel*, 12 February 1968, 22.
4. Brinkley, *The Unfinished Nation*, 787.
5. Charles Conn, Personal Journals, 10 October 1974, Paul Conn personal collection.
6. Executive Council, Statement on Modest Apparel, 1967, attached to letter James Cross to Charles Conn, 11 December 1967, Box 39, Folder 4, PRC, LCA.
7. James Cross to Charles Conn, 11 December 1967, Box 39, Folder 4, PRC, LCA.
8. *Lee College Bulletin*, 1969-1970, 8.
9. *Lee College Bulletin*, 1982-1983, 4.

10. Charles Conn, Address at the Symposium on the Church of God Declaration of Faith Article VII: Holiness, November 1975, accessed 3 January 2024, https://www.youtube.com/watch?v=X8_Fnb7FiiE.
11. Church of God, *Minutes of the Fifty-fifth General Assembly of the Church of God* (Cleveland, TN: Church of God Publishing House, 1974), 51.
12. *Lee College Catalog*, 1975-1976, 26.
13. See, Discipline Committee Minutes, Box 96g, Folder: Minutes-Conti, PRC, LCA, Long-Term Storage at the International Offices (hereafter LTS).
14. Evaline Echols, interview, *Hundred Year Journey* centennial project, 2018.
15. See the 1970, 1975, and 1980 issues of the *Vindagua*.
16. For examples of this type of letter, and presidential responses, see Letter, Charles Conn to Mrs. W. Osborne, 19 February 1971, Box 47, Folder 7, PRC, LCA; Letter G. Dunn to Ray Hughes, forwarded to Charles Conn, 4 January 1973, Box 49, Folder 7, PRC, LCA; Letter, Charles Conn to G. Dunn, 8 January 1973, Box 49, Folder 7, PRC, LCA; Letter, Wade Horton to Charles Conn, 18 March 1976, Box 52, Folder 11, PRC, LCA; Letter, Charles Conn to Wade Horton, 25 March 1976, Box 52, Folder 11, PRC, LCA; Letter, Russell Summer to Bill Henning, 22 March 1979, Box 58, Folder 11, PRC, LCA.
17. Letter, Charles Conn to Elmer Golden, 6 June 1974, Box 49, Folder 14, PRC, LCA; Hugh F. Pyle, *Skimpy Skirts and Hippie Hair* (Murfreesboro, TN: Sword of the Lord Publishing, 1972).
18. Letter, Charles Conn to G. Dunn, 8 January 1973, Box 49, Folder 7, PRC, LCA.
19. Letter, Wade Horton to Charles Conn, 18 March 1976, Box 52, Folder 11, PRC, LCA; Letter, Charles Conn to Wade Horton, 25 March 1976, Box 52, Folder 11, PRC, LCA.
20. Memorandum, Cecil Knight to Charles Conn, 29 September 1977, Box 54, Folder 10, PRC, LCA.
21. Charles Conn to G. Dunn, 8 January 1973, Box 49, Folder 7, PRC, LCA.
22. Guidance in Memorandum, Wade Horton to All Department Heads, 30 Sept 1974, Box 49, Folder 16, PRC, LCA; for an example of dress, see *Vindagua*, 1975, 4, 5.
23. Letter, Charles Conn to Leo Shores, 4 October 1979, Box 59, Folder 1, PRC, LCA.
24. Letter, Charles Conn to Donald Aultman, 28 June 1971, Box 46, Folder 14, PRC, LCA.
25. Letter, Wade Horton to Anonymous Lee Student, attached to letter, Wade Horton to Charles Conn, 9 October 1975, Box 50, Folder 17, PRC, LCA.

26. Letter, Charles Conn to B. Lawson, 10 December 1979, Box 58, Folder 7, PRC, LCA.
27. Letter, Charles Conn to E. Stewart, 24 July 1980, Box 60, Folder 11, PRC, LCA.
28. Lee College, *Self-Study*, 1973, 64-70, 150, 448.
29. Lee College, *Self-Study*, 1973, 465; Enrollment Data, no date, Box 13, Folder 24, PRC, LCA.
30. Letter, Raymond Spain to James Cross, 9 March 1970, Box 44, Folder 21, PRC, LCA; Letter, F. Timmerman to Charles Conn, 19 January 1979, Box 59, Folder 4, PRC, LCA.
31. Letter, Raymond Spain to James Cross, 9 March 1970, Box 44, Folder 21, PRC, LCA; *SACS Self-Study, 1973*, 150; Lee College, *Lee College Institutional Self-Study Report* (Cleveland, TN: Lee College, 1984), 208.
32. Letter, Charles Conn to W. Baldwin, 29 March 1976, Box 53, Folder 1, PRC, LCA; Letter, Charles Conn to Sam Colbert, 7 September 1976, Box, 52, Folder 4, PRC, LCA.
33. Financial Data Report, Attached to Minutes of Self Study Financial Resources Committee, 13 September 1983, Box 15a, Folder 4, PRC, LCA; Report of the Visiting Committee (Reaffirmation Evaluation) for the Southern Association of Colleges and Schools, 8-11 April 1984, LC Collection in Process, no folder, PRC, LCA.
34. Letter, Charles Conn to Gordon Sweet, 27 November 1973, Box 49, Folder 4, PRC, LCA.
35. U.S. Department of Education, Title III, Part A Programs—Strengthening Institutions, accessed 1 September 2024, https://www2.ed.gov/programs/iduestitle3a/index.html.
36. Ten Year History, Development Office, 1972-1982, 1983, Box 15a, Folder 16, PRC, LCA.
37. Ralph Waldo Lloyd, *Maryville College: A History of 150 Years, 1819-1969* (Maryville, TN: Maryville College Press, 1969), 242.
38. Report, Hughes to Lee Board of Directors, 8 February 1966, Box 24, Folder 1, PRC, LCA.
39. Letter, Charles Conn to P. J. Zondervan, 4 October 1972, Box 47, Folder 22, PRC, LCA.
40. Memorandum, F. W. Goff to Charles Conn, 2 September 1974, Box 49, Folder 14, PRC, LCA.
41. See, for example, Letter, Harmon Roberts to Wayne Chambers, 24 January 1974, Box 50, Folder 2, PRC, LCA.
42. Minutes of the Executive Council, 28 August 1970, PRC.
43. Letter, Wade Horton to Charles Conn, 23 April 1974, Box 49, Folder 16,

PRC, LCA; Charles Conn to Wade Horton, 15 May 1974, Box 4, Folder 16, PRC, LCA.
44. Minutes of the Feasibility Study Committee, 24 November 1972, Box 10g, Folder: Feasibility Study Committee, PRC, LCA, LTS.
45. Conn, *Mighty Army*, 459.
46. Conn, *Mighty Army*, 445.
47. James M. Beaty, "How We Came to Have a Seminary," unpublished manuscript, 2014, 5-7, PRC.
48. Conn, *Mighty Army*, 449-450; for more on Arrington, see *Torch*, Fall 2001, 6-7; *Torch*, Summer 2011, 24-25.
49. Letter, Joseph Brink to Charles Conn, with attached report, 18 May 1979, Box 10g, Folder: Southern Association Report, 1979, PRC, LCA, LTS.
50. Lee College, *Self-Study*, 1973, 191-192; Lee College, *Self-Study*, 1984, 274.
51. Report of the 1972 SACS Visiting Committee, 22 August 1973, Box 10, Folder 27, PRC, LCA; Lee College, *Self-Study*, 1973, 203-204, 219-225; Lee College, *Self-Study*, 1984, 28.

Chapter 7

1. National Center for Education Statistics, *120 Years of American Education*, 55.
2. Enrollment Data, no date, Box 13, Folder 24, PRC, LCA; Lee College, *Self-Study*, 1984, 118; Memorandum, David Painter to Jerry Howell, 25 February 1982, Box 62, Folder 11, PRC, LCA.
3. Ollie Lee, Presentation to the Faculty, Lee University, 28 October 2018.
4. President's Report to the Board of Directors, 12 November 1981, Box 36g, Folder: Board, 1981, PRC, LCA, LTS; Ollie Lee, Presentation to the Faculty, Lee University, 28 October 2018.
5. Transcript, ABC World News Tonight, 16 April 1981, Internet Archive, accessed 19 May 2020, https://archive.org/stream/ABCNews19781979/ABC%20News-1981-1982-A-b.txt.
6. U.S. Inflation Calculator.
7. Letter, Harmon Roberts to Wayne Chambers, 24 January 1974, Box 50, Folder 2, PRC, LCA; Letter, Charles Conn to F. W. Goff, 9 January 1974, Box 50, Folder 15, PRC, LCA.
8. Transcript, ABC World News Tonight, 16 April 1981.
9. Investment Projections, attached to the Minutes of the Lee College Board of Directors, 29 September 1980, Box 26, Folder 12, PRC, LCA.
10. Letter, Kenneth Rayborn to Charles Conn, 26 September 1980, Box 60, Folder 10, PRC, LCA.

11. Letter, Ray Hughes to Kenneth Rayborn, 6 November 1980, Box 60, Folder 10, PRC, LCA.
12. Jonathan Greenberg, "The April Fool's Day Massacre," 20 July 1981, *Forbes*, 35-37.
13. Letter, Paul Barker to Charles Conn, 20 April 1980, Box 61, Folder 2, PRC, LCA.
14. Letter, Charles Conn to R. L. Byrne, 5 May 1981, Box 61, Folder 2, PRC, LCA.
15. Letter, Charles Conn to Church of God Pastors, 30 April 1981, Box 61, Folder 6, PRC, LCA. For a detailed narrative of how the investment went forward and how the investment scam worked, see Memorandum, John B. White to Charles Conn, 27 April 1981, Minutes of the Executive Council, 16 May 1981, PRC.
16. Memorandum, Charles Conn to Ray Hughes, 5 August 1981, Box 61, Folder 8, PRC, LCA.
17. Letter, David Painter to Elton Chalk, 9 March 1982, Box 62, Folder 9, PRC, LCA.
18. Attachment, Memorandum, David Painter to Jerry Howell, 25 February 1982, Box 62, Folder 11, PRC, LCA.
19. Letter, Paul Walker and Bill Higginbotham to Charles Conn, 10 September 1981, Box 62, Folder 6, PRC, LCA.
20. Letter, Charles Conn to Paul Walker, 10 September 1981, Box, 25, Folder 11, PRC, LCA.
21. Letter and attachment, Sabord Wood to Charles Conn, 29 September 1981, Box, 25, Folder 11, PRC, LCA; Minutes of the Lee College Board of Directors Budget Task Force Committee, 2 December 1982, Box, 26, Folder 15, PRC, LCA.
22. Minutes of the Lee College Board of Directors, 27-29 April 1982, Box 27, Folder 1, PRC, LCA; Memorandum, Charles Conn to Students, 29 April 1982; Ray Hughes to Charles Conn, 30 April 1982, Box 103g, Folder: Board Correspondence, 1980, PRC, LCA, LTS; Report on Vote by Mail regarding Name of the Athletic Team, June 1982, Box 27, Folder 2, PRC, LCA. The final decision to change the name to the Flames was made in September 1982, Minutes of the Board of Directors, 3 September 1982, Box 36g Folder: Pending Board Recommendations, 1981, PRC, LCA, LTS.
23. Letter, Charles Lovelace to Paul Walker, 28 July 1982, Box 62, Folder 20, PRC, LCA.
24. Letter, Paul Walker to Administration, Faculty and Staff, undated (c. April 1982), Box 62, Folder 20, PRC, LCA.
25. Ray Hughes, Address to the Faculty, 1 January 1983, Box 43g, Folder: Faculty Meetings, Fall 1983, PRC, LCA, LTS.

26. Ray Hughes, Address to the Faculty, 12 January 1984, Box 43g, Folder: Faculty Meetings, Fall 1983, PRC, LCA, LTS.
27. Lee College, *Self-Study*, 1984, 84.
28. Letter, Ray Hughes to Joe Edwards, 6 September 1983, Box 65, Folder 12, PRC, LCA.
29. Lee College, *Self-Study*, 1984, 387-388.
30. Letter, Ray Hughes to Ron Wood, 11 April 1983, Box 69, Folder 4, PRC, LCA.
31. Letter, Mrs. H. Holman to Ray Hughes, 30 September 1982, Box 64, Folder 5, PRC, LCA; Susan Ashcraft, interview, *Hundred Year Journey* centennial project, 2018; *Vindagua*, 1983, 10.
32. Letter, Ray Hughes to Dewey Smith, 27 September 1982, Box 64, Folder 15, PRC, LCA.
33. Letter, Ray Hughes to Danny May, 5 October 1982, Box 64, Folder 10, PRC, LCA; Letter, Ray Hughes to Bill Hamon, 17 November 1982, Box 64, Folder 5, PRC, LCA.
34. Letter, Ray Hughes to E. C. Thomas, 23 March 1984, Box 68, Folder 9, PRC, LCA; Letter, Ray Hughes to B. Kelly, 30 November 1982, Box 64, Folder 7, PRC, LCA; Letter, Robert White to Ray Hughes, 26 January 1984, Box 69, Folder 3, PRC, LCA; Ray Hughes to William Walter, 21 February 1983, Box 65, Folder 3, PRC, LCA.
35. Lee College, *Self-Study*, 1984, 30, 433.
36. Ollie Lee, interview by Eric Moyen, 5 June 2014.
37. Letter, Ray Hughes to Beecher Hunter, 9 May 1983, Box 66, Folder 9, PRC, LCA.
38. Hunter Beecher, "A slap at our community," Cleveland *Daily Banner*, 8 May 1983, 32; Ray Hughes, "Dr. Ray Hughes presents an answer to the editor," Cleveland *Daily Banner*, 9 May 1983, 1, 5.
39. Report of the Visiting Committee for the Southern Association of Colleges and Schools, 8-11 April 1984, p. 2, Box: In Process, PRC, LCA.
40. Report of the Visiting Committee, 1984, Box: In Process, PRC, LCA.
41. Minutes, Lee College Administrative Council, 31 July 1984, Box 38g, Folder: Administrative Council, PRC, LCA, LTS.
42. *Alumnus*, Fall 1989, 3.
43. Minutes of Meeting of the Lee College Board of Directors, 15 April 1984, Box 27, Folder 7, PRC, LCA.
44. Paul Conn, interview by author, 10 October 2020.
45. Paul Conn, interview by author, 2 October 2020.
46. In all, Paul Conn wrote or coauthored twenty-three books, including *The New Johnny Cash* (Old Tappan, NJ: Revell, 1973), *No Easy Game* (Old Tappan, NJ: Revell, 1973), *Believe!* (Old Tappan, NJ: Revell, 1973),

Julian Carroll of Kentucky (Old Tappan, NJ: Revell, 1973), and *Eckerd: Finding the Right Prescription* (Old Tappan, NJ: Revell, 1987).
47. Paul Conn, interview by author, 2 October 2020, 19 October 2020, Paul Conn, interview by Eric Moyen, 22 December 2014.
48. Paul Conn, interview by author, 2 October 2020, 19 October 2020.
49. Minutes of Meeting of the Lee College Board of Directors, 8 May 1984, Box 27, Folder 7, PRC, LCA; Paul Conn, interview by author, 2 October 2020, 19 October 2020.
50. Letter, Paul Walker to E. C. Thomas, 9 May 1984, PRC, Box 69, Folder 1, PRC, LCA; Letter, E. C. Thomas to Paul Walker, 9 May 1984, Box 68, Folder 9, PRC, LCA.
51. Minutes of Meeting of the Lee College Board of Directors, 9 May 1984, Box 27, Folder 7, PRC, LCA.
52. Paul Conn, interview by author, 19 October 2020.
53. Lamar Vest, *Reflections of the Journey* (Cleveland, TN: PTS Press, 2018), 67-68.
54. Paul Conn, interview by author, 19 October 2020.
55. Paul Conn, interview by author, 19 October 2020.
56. *Vindagua*, 1985, 17.
57. Lamar Vest, Report to the Executive Council, 22 January 1986, Box 30, Folder 11, PRC, LCA.
58. Laud Vaught, Report to the President and Board of Directors, June 1984, Box 73, Folder 16, PRC, LCA; Minutes, Lee College Board of Directors, 7-8 May 1986, Box 28, Folder 8, PRC, LCA.
59. Report of the Task Force on Athletics, 7 May 1986, Box 26g, Folder: Athletic Task Force, PRC, LCA, LTS.
60. *Torch*, Fall 1989, 3.
61. Carolyn Dirksen, interview by author, 17 December 2020.
62. Report from Lamar Vest to the Executive Council, 22 January 1986, Box 30, Folder 11, PRC, LCA; Minutes Lee College Board of Directors, 3-4 December 1985, Box 28, Folder 4, PRC, LCA.
63. Philip and Mary Morris, *Uncharted Waters: The Life and Ministry of Raymond E. Crowley* (Cleveland, TN: Pathway Press, 2014), 242-43.

Chapter 8

1. Paul Conn, interview by author, 26 October 2020; Paul Conn, interview for the *Hundred Year Journey* centennial project, 2018. Readers who venture into the endnotes will notice a marked change in the types of sources referenced in the last three chapters. The Pentecostal Resource Center, which holds most of Lee's archives, does not hold the files of the

Paul Conn administration. Those files were not open. Therefore, these last chapters, which are built on interviews, publicly available sources, and a handful of internal documents, must be considered a first draft of Lee's history. When three decades of internal documents come to the archives, the broad strokes of my narrative will need to be reconsidered.

2. Paul Conn, interview by author, 26 October 2020.
3. Paul Conn, interview by author, 26 October 2020.
4. Laura Bridgestock, "World University Ranking Methodologies Compared," QS TopUniversities, accessed 26 September 2024, https://www.topuniversities.com/university-rankings-articles/world-university-rankings/world-university-ranking-methodologies-compared.
5. The Council, or CCCU, was founded in 1976 to advance the cause of Christian higher education. In 2024 it had 185 members, with 150 in the United States and Canada.
6. Mark Noll, *The Scandal of the Evangelical Mind* (Grand Rapids: Eerdmans, 1994), 16, 18.
7. Paul Conn, Inaugural Speech, *Vindagua*, 1987, 126-127.
8. Paul Conn, Inaugural Speech, *Vindagua*, 1987, 126-127.
9. Handwritten Notes of the Administrative Retreat, 4 January 1987, Box, 47g, Folder: Admin. Retreat at Big Canoe, PRC, LCA, LTS; Handwritten Notes, Faculty Seminar, 20 August 1987, Box, 47g, Folder: Faculty Seminar, PRC, LCA, LTS.
10. Handwritten Notes of the Administrative Retreat, 4 January 1987, Box 47g, Folder: Admin. Retreat at Big Canoe, PRC, LCA, LTS; Handwritten Notes, Faculty Seminar, 20 August 1987, Box, 47g, Folder: Faculty Seminar, PRC, LCA, LTS; Paul Conn, interview by author, 12 January 2022.
11. Paul Conn, interview for the *Hundred Year Journey* centennial project, 2018; Paul Conn, interview by author, 19 October 2020; Paul Conn, interview by author, 15 March 2021.
12. Paul Conn, interview by author, 26 October 2020.
13. Paul Conn, interview, *Hundred Year Journey* centennial project, 2018.
14. These numbers represent headcount, not the full-time equivalency (FTE). Headcount includes all students, including part-time, while FTE is a unit of measurement that represents the number of full-time students. *Torch*, Fall 1989, 3; "Enrollment," *Torch*, Fall 1991, 3.
15. Attachment to Executive Council Minutes, September 1989, PRC, Executive and General Council Minutes.
16. For example, see the *Lee College Catalog*, 1988, 27.
17. "A Growing Level of Academic Excellence," *Torch*, Fall 1991, 8.
18. "A Growing Level of Academic Excellence," *Torch*, Fall 1991, 9.
19. Paul Conn, "Dedicatory Address," 16 September 1988, *Vindagua*, 1989, 15.

20. Church of God, *Minutes of the Forty-second General Assembly*, 1948, 31; *Minutes of the Fifty-fifth General Assembly*, 1974, 39; Church of God, *Supplement to the Minutes of the Sixty-second General Assembly of the Church of God* (Cleveland, TN: Church of God Publishing House, 1988), 12-22; Conn, *Mighty Army*, 336-337, 442-443, 512-214.
21. *Supplement to the Minutes of the Sixty-second General Assembly*, 1988, 19, 21.
22. For more on the Religious Right, see Daniel K. Williams, *God's Own Party: The Making of the Christian Right* (New York: Oxford University Press, 2010); William Martin, *With God on Our Side: The Rise of the Religious Right in America* (New York: Broadway Books, 1996); Kenneth J. Heineman, *God is a Conservative: Religion, Politis, and Morality in America* (New York: New York University Press, 1998); and, Clyde Wilcox's *God's Warriors: The Christian Right in Twentieth Century America* (Baltimore: Johns Hopkins University Press, 1992) and *Onward Christian Soldiers? The Religious Right in American Politics* (Boulder, CO: Westview Press, 1996); Susan Friend Harding, *The Book of Jerry Falwell: Fundamentalist Language and Politics* (Princeton: Princeton University Press, 2000).
23. Susan Ashcraft and Suzanne Hamid, interviews, *Hundred Year Journey* centennial project, 2018.
24. Senior Exit Survey, 1992, Box 49w, Folder: Senior Exit Survey Results, Spring 1992, PRC, LCA, LTS; United States Bureau of the Census, Current Population Reports, Series P60-184. *Money Income of Households, Families, and Persons in the United States, 1992* (Washington, D.C.: U.S. Government Printing Office, 1993), x.
25. Paul Conn, "Celebration 1992," *Vindagua*, 1993, 6.
26. Paul Conn, "Celebration 1992," *Vindagua*, 1993, 6.
27. Paul Conn, *Believe!* (Old Tappan, NJ: Revell, 1973).
28. "Another Busy Summer," *Torch*, Fall 1992, 5; Paul Conn, "Ellis Hall Fire Anniversary," Lee University Chapel, 9 October 2018, accessed 30 May 2021, https://www.facebook.com/LeeUniversity/videos/chapel-paul-conn-ellis-hall-fire-anniversary/2143525642567287/.
29. "Fire Destroys Lee College Dorm," Cleveland *Daily Banner*, 3 November 1993, 1, 6; "Lee Students try to Rebuild Live after Fire," Cleveland *Daily Banner*, 7 November 1993, 1, 12; Memo, Paul Conn to Friends of Lee College, 11 November 1993, Box 66w, Folder: Ellis Hall Fire, Public Information, PRC, LCA, LTS; "Saved by the Hand of God," *Torch*, Winter 1994, 2-5.
30. Paul Conn, Lee College Chapel, 9 October 2018.

31. "Saved by the Hand of God," *Torch*, Winter 1994, 5.
32. Paul Conn, Lee College Chapel, 9 October 2018.
33. Henry and Iris Atkins gave the lead gift for the new hall, but sentiment caused the college to retain the Ellis name as well. "An Event Worthy of the Name," *Torch*, Fall 1994, 3-5.
34. "An Open Door of Opportunity," *Torch*, Summer 1995, 6-7.
35. Olympics: "A Once in a Lifetime Shot," *Torch*, Fall 1996, 10-14; "The Torch Stops Here," *Torch*, Spring 1995, 3-5; Paul Conn, interview by Will Reeves, author's personal file, 2 April 2016.
36. "Lee University to Be?" *Torch*, Fall 1996, 15.
37. "First Graduate Programs," *Torch*, Fall 1995, 11.
38. "College of Education Receives NCATE Accreditation," *Torch*, Winter 2011, 21.
39. "Lee's New General Education Core," *Torch*, Spring 1998, 10.
40. "Major Academic Administration Changes Announced," *Torch*, Spring 1999, 8; Ollie Lee, interview for the *Hundred Year Journey* centennial project, 2018.
41. Carolyn Dirksen, interview by author, 17 December 2020; Carolyn Dirksen, interview for the *Hundred Year Journey* centennial project, 2018.
42. Paul Conn, interview by author, 22 February 2021.
43. Paul Conn, interview by author, 19 October 2020, 26 October 2020.
44. "Enrollment on a Roll," *Torch*, Fall 1991, 3; "A Decade of Phenomenal Growth," *Torch*, Fall 1995, 8; "How Many is Too Many?" *Torch*, Fall 1996, 6.
45. "Decade of Distinction," *Torch*, Winter 1996, 6.
46. Paul Conn, interview, *Hundred Year Journey* centennial project, 2018.
47. Paul Conn, "Celebration 1992," *Vindagua*, 1993, 7.
48. "A Dozen Years of Celebrations," *Torch*, Winter 2001, 4.

Chapter 9

1. Lee University Institutional Research, "Fall 2010 Census Enrollment Report," 31 August 2010 (hereafter all such reports as Fall [Year] Census); *Lee University Catalog*, 2005, np.
2. Lee University Press Release, 5 April 2019, accessed 10 December 2020, https://visitclevelandtn.com/event/lee-day-2019/.
3. Lee produced a number of videos about the Pack and Stack event, many of which are available online. See, for example, Samaritan's Purse, "Operation Christmas Child-Lee University Shoe Box Packing Party," 20 August 2010, accessed 3 January 2024, https://youtu.be/DrKT_uTlO_s.

4. For example: "Lee Alum Takes Sixth on American Idol," *Torch*, Summer 2007, 8-9; "A Lee University American Idol," *Torch*, Summer 2015, 4-7.
5. Jayson VanHook, Lee University Institutional Research, "Census Trending Report," December 2020.
6. *Lee University Catalog, 2000-2001*, 24-27; *Lee University Catalog, 2015-2016*, accessed 29 May 2021, http://catalog.leeuniversity.edu/content.php?catoid=8&navoid=2855.
7. "Lee Named to US News Top Colleges List," *Torch*, Fall 2001, 10-11; "Lee Receives New and Continuing Honors in America's Best Colleges," *Torch*, Fall 2009, 8-9; "Lee Gets USN&WR Top-Tier Rating Again," *Torch*, Fall 2014, 12.
8. Susan Ashcraft, "My Vocation and My DNA," in Carolyn Dirksen and Rickie D. Moore, eds., *High Callings: Vocational Narratives of Lee University Faculty at the Century Mark* (Cleveland, TN: Lee University Press, 2018), 98-99.
9. Ben Christmann, interview by author, 16 December 2021.
10. Here, the author writes from personal experience, having accompanied Barnett on several of his trips to the United Kingdom.
11. "Lee Receives $2 Million for Poiema Project," *Torch*, Spring 2003, 4-5; Terry Cross, *Answering the Call in the Spirit: Pentecostal Reflections on a Theology of Vocation, Work, and Life* (Cleveland, TN: Lee University Press, 2007).
12. "Benevolence and Brains," *Torch*, Spring 2003, 8; "A Cup of Cold Water," *Torch*, Winter 2003, 4-5.
13. For camps, see "Summer Camps," *Torch*, Fall 2015, 10; for an overview of LUDIC, see "Lee Program Marks Decade of Leading Autism Awareness," *Torch*, Summer 2007, 20; for the start of Encore, see "Lee Launches 'Encore' Program," *Torch*, Fall 2007, 13.
14. Crossover, accessed 1 January 2020, https://leeuniversitycrossover.wordpress.com/; Cleveland *Daily Banner*, 4 October 2017.
15. *Lee University Catalog, 1998-1999*, 26-27; *Lee University Catalog, 2004-2005*, 37; *Lee University Catalog, 2014-2015*, accessed 2 June 2021, all available at https://www.leeuniversity.edu/publications/catalog-archives/.
16. "Northern Exposure: A Significant Gift Pushes Lee's Northern Border Northward," *Torch*, Winter 2000, 12-15.
17. Federal Reserve History, "The Great Recession," https://www.federalreservehistory.org/essays/great-recession-of-200709, accessed 26 December 2020; Renae Merle, "A Guide to the Financial Crisis—10 years Later," Washington *Post*, 10 September 2018, https://www.washington

post.com/business/economy/a-guide-to-the-financial-crisis--10-years-later/2018/09/10/114b76ba-af10-11e8-a20b-5f4f84429666_story.html, accessed 26 December 2020; Clifton B. Parker, "The Great Recession Spurred Student Interest in Higher Education, Stanford Expert Says," Stanford News, 6 March 2015, https://news.stanford.edu/2015/03/06/higher-ed-hoxby-030615/, accessed 26 December 2020; "When Money is Tight," *Torch*, Winter 2008, 3. Tuition data from the *Lee University Catalog, 2007-2008* and *Lee University Catalog, 2014-2015*.
18. For a full accounting of the campaign's success, see "Press Toward the Mark," *Torch*, Fall 2010, 4-22.
19. Paul Conn, "Celebration Address," *Torch*, Winter 2010, 14-17.
20. Lee University, *Student Handbook, 2020-2021*, 22-23.
21. On the topic of student conduct, the author's own observations and those of his two children, both graduates of Lee, enter the narrative.
22. Gallup, "Gay and Lesbian Rights," https://news.gallup.com/poll/1651/gay-lesbian-rights.aspx., accessed 26 May 2021.
23. For more on Soulforce, see their website at https://www.soulforce.org/.
24. Editorial, "The Power of Hospitality," *Christianity Today*, 1 June 2006, accessed 26 May 2021, https://www.christianitytoday.com/ct/2006/june/14.23.html.
25. "Equality Riders Visit Lee Campus," Cleveland *Daily Banner*, 17 March 2006, 1, 5; "Equality riders have little impact at Lee University," Cleveland *Daily Banner*, 19 March 1, 14; Paul Conn, Remarks at Lee University Faculty Meeting, 16 September 2015, author's notes.
26. Editorial, "The Power of Hospitality," *Christianity Today*, 1 June 2006, accessed 26 May 2021, https://www.christianitytoday.com/ct/2006/june/14.23.html.
27. See Alec MacGillis, "How Liberty University Built a Billion-Dollar Empire Online," *New York Times Magazine Online*, accessed 26 December 2020, https://www.nytimes.com/2018/04/17/magazine/how-liberty-university-built-a-billion-dollar-empire-online.html; Hope Kentnor, "Distance Education and the Evolution of Online Learning in the United States," *Curriculum and Teaching Dialogue*, vol. 17, Nos. 1 & 2, 2015. https://digitalcommons.du.edu/cgi/viewcontent.cgi?article=1026&context=law_facpub.
28. "Lee Launches Into Next Era of Online Degrees," *Torch*, Summer 2012, 19.
29. Paul Conn, interview by author, 3 March 2021.
30. Fall 2010 Census; Lee University Institutional Research, "Fall 2015 Census Enrollment Report," 1 September 2015; "Fall 2020 Census

Enrollment Report," 1 September 2020; Lee University Institutional Research, "Priority Survey Online Learners," April 2019.
31. Fall 2010 Census, Fall 2015 Census, Fall 2020 Census.
32. "School of Nursing Receives Accreditation," *Torch*, Summer 2016, 17; "Lee Gets Green Light for Nursing Program," *Torch*, Summer 2017, 17; VanHook, Census Trending Report.
33. NCAA, "History of Division II," accessed 26 December 2020, http://www.ncaa.org/about/history-division-ii; "Lee Gets Invitation to Join Gulf South Conference," *Torch*, Summer 2012, 23; Conn quoted in "Lee Begins Moves to NCAA," *Torch*, Fall 2012, 19.
34. See Lee University, "Flame Features: Making the Jump to the NCAA," Part 1 and 2, accessed 30 June 2021, https://leeuflames.com/news/2020/5/4/general-flame-features-making-the-jump-to-the-ncaa-part-1.aspx and https://leeuflames.com/news/2020/5/8/general-flame-features-making-the-jump-to-the-ncaa-part-2.aspx.
35. Paul Conn, interview by author, 26 October 2020; Larry Carpenter, interview, *Hundred Year Journey* Centennial Project, 2018; Larry Carpenter, interview by author, 28 April 2020.
36. Jay Sheridan, ed. *Lift High the Flame: Visions of Lee University* (Franklin, TN: Grandin Hood, 2018).

Chapter 10

1. Paul Conn, interview by author, 18 January 2021, 15 March 2021.
2. Carolyn Dirksen, "An Academic Revolution," *Torch*, Fall 2020, 17.
3. Sam Houston State University, "Chancellor McCall names Dr. Alisa White Sole Finalist for Sam Houston State University Presidency," Today@Sam, 18 June 2020, accessed 6 February 2021, https://www.shsu.edu/today@sam/T@S/article/2020/sole-finalist-president.
4. Centers for Disease Control and Prevention, National Center for Health Statistics, Provisional Death Counts for Coronavirus, accessed 20 March 2020, https://www.cdc.gov/nchs/nvss/vsrr/covid19/index.htm; "A Timeline of the Coronavirus Pandemic," New York *Times*, accessed 20 March 2020, https://www.nytimes.com/article/coronavirus-timeline.html.
5. Email, Paul Conn to the Lee faculty and staff, 30 March 2020, author's personal collection.
6. Email, Paul Conn to the Lee faculty and staff, 30 March 2020; Email, Paul Conn to the Lee faculty and staff, 6 April 2020, author's personal collection; Email, Paul Conn to the Lee faculty and staff, 9 April 2020, author's personal collection.

7. Email, Paul Conn to the Class of 2020, 14 July 2020, author's personal collection.
8. Lee University Institutional Research, "Common Data Set," 2019-2021.
9. Mark Walker, "Lee University Chapel," 9 March 2021, accessed 30 June 2021, https://livestream.com/leeu/events/9566550/videos/218627074.
10. The act had died in committee in 2015 and 2017 and passed the house in the 116th Congress in 2019.
11. Pew Research Center, "Views about Homosexuality," accessed 2 July 2021, https://www.pewforum.org/religious-landscape-study/views-about-homosexuality/; Pew Research Center, "Attitudes on Same Sex Marriage," accessed 2 July 2021, https://www.pewforum.org/fact-sheet/changing-attitudes-on-gay-marriage/.
12. Pew Research Center, "In U.S., Decline of Christianity Continues at a Rapid Pace," accessed 2 July 2021, https://www.pewforum.org/2019/10/17/in-u-s-decline-of-christianity-continues-at-rapid-pace/; definitions drawn from Mark Labberton, ed., *Still Evangelical: Insiders Reconsider Political, Social, and Theological Meaning* (Downers Grove, IL: InterVarsity Press, 2018), 3.
13. Burtchaell, *Dying of the Light*, 837.
14. Letter, Ray Hughes to Danny Drake, 7 January 1964, PRC, LCA, Box 34, Folder 10.
15. Burtchaell, *Dying of the Light*, 827.
16. "Common Data Set," 2019-2020.
17. Burtchaell, *Dying of the Light*, 829.
18. Burtchaell, *Dying of the Light*, 833.
19. "Lee University Mission Statement," *Lee University Catalog, 2021-2022*, accessed 5 February 2022, http://catalog.leeuniversity.edu/content.php?catoid=14&navoid=13829.
20. Mark Walker, "Presidential Welcome and Introduction," *Lee University Catalog, 2021-2022*, accessed 5 February 2022, http://catalog.leeuniversity.edu/content.php?catoid=14&navoid=13829.
21. While this manuscript was in the hands of the press, Lee underwent another transition. A budget crisis caused the university to declare financial exigency, make extensive cuts to faculty and staff, and temporarily suspend tenure. Furthermore, vocal traditionalists elements in the Church of God forced the university to alter faculty contracts in a way that ensured that faculty would not challenge the denomination's stance on LGBTQ+ issues. Mark Walker resigned, and Paul Conn returned as interim president during the presidential search process.

Appendixes

1. Church of God, Minutes 2018: Church of God Book of Discpline, Church Order, and Governance (Cleveland, TN: Church of God Publishing House, 2018), 17.
2. Lee University, *Student Handbook*, 2024-2025, 17-18.
3. The Executive Committee, now the top five executives in the church, was called the Executive Council from 1922-1926, then the State Overseer Appointing Board, 1926-1952. The Council of Eighteen, now the top eighteen leaders, was called the Council of Elders until 1929, the Supreme Council from 1929-1964, and the Executive Council until 1993. Conn, *Mighty Army*, 547-555. On two occasions the church chose new leaders for the school who accepted the position, then quickly resigned. I have chosen to follow the university's lead in not counting these brief interludes. R. R. Walker held the position briefly in 1942 and John Jernigan in 1948.
4. 1930-1931, 1934-1935: Simmons, *History*, 94; 1942-1943: *Evangel*, 10 October 1942; 1943-1944: *Supreme Council Minutes*, Minutes of the Church of God Supreme Council, 8 August 1944; 1944-1945, PRC: *Evangel*, 28 December 1944; 1945-1946: *Evangel*, 17 November 1945; 1946-1947: *Evangel*, 19 October 1946; 1947-1960: Enrollment Files, Box 91, Folder 5; Box 92, Folder 4; Box 92, Folder 10; Box 92, Folder 16; Box 92, Folder 22, PRC, LCA; 1961-1966: Letter, Hughes to Heagy, 17 November 1966, Box 38, Folder 7, PRC, LCA; 1966-1988: *Torch*, Fall 1989, 3; 1989-2003, *Torch*, Fall 2003, 20; 2004: *Torch*, Fall 2004, 18; 2005-2009: Census Report, 2009; 2010-2014: Census Report, 2014; 2015-2020: Census Report, 2020.

Bibliography

Archives, Newspapers, and Serials

Alumnus, 1989
Church of God Evangel, 1912-2020
Cleveland *Daily Banner*, 1947-2017
Echoes of the General Assembly of the Church of God, 1912-1914
Hal Bernard Dixon, Jr. Pentecostal Research Center, Cleveland, TN.
Lee College Catalog, 1947-1997
Lee *Torch*, 1989-2021
Lee University Catalog, 1998-2021
Lee University Student Handbook, 2020-2021
Minutes of the General Assembly of the Church of God, 1911-1988
New York *Times*, 2020
Southern Missionary College Catalog, 1957-1958
The Church of God Bible Training School Catalog, 1929-1946
The Evening Light and Evangel, 1910-1912
The Lighted Pathway, 1938-1967
The Vindagua, 1942-1980
University of Chattanooga Catalog, 1957-1958.
Washington *Post*, 2018

Sources Cited

ABC World News Tonight. "16 April 1981." Internet Archive. Accessed 19 May 2020. https://archive.org. stream/ ABCNews19781979/ABC%20News-1981-1982-A-b.txt.

Aultman, Donald S. *You Can Go Home Again: Journey of a Pentecostal*. Cleveland, TN: DSA Publications, 2010.

Beaty, James M. "How We Came to Have a Seminary, 2014." TMs (photocopy), PRC. Photocopy.

Bebbington, David. *The Dominance of Evangelicalism: The Age of Spurgeon and Moody*. Downers Grove, IL: Intervarsity Press, 2005.

Benne, Robert. *Quality with Soul: How Six Premier Colleges and Universities Keep Faith with Their Religious Traditions*. Grand Rapids: Will B. Eerdmans, 2001.

Blackwelder, Julia. "Southern White Fundamentalists and the Civil Rights Movement." *Phylon* 40 (1979): 334-341.
Bridgestock, Laura. "World University Ranking Methodologies Compared," QS TopUniversities. Accessed 26 September 2024, https://www.topuniversities.com/university-rankings-articles/world-university-rankings/world-university-ranking-methodologies-compared.
Brinkley, Alan. *The Unfinished Nation: A Concise History of the American People*, vol. 2. New York: McGraw-Hill, 1997.
Burtchaell, James. *The Dying of the Light: The Disengagement of Colleges and Universities from their Christian Churches*. Grand Rapids: W. B. Eerdmans, 1998.
Carpenter, Joel A. *Revive us Again: The Reawakening of American Fundamentalism*. Cambridge: Oxford University Press, 1997.
Centers for Disease Control and Prevention, "1918 Pandemic (HINI Virus)." Accessed 22 January 2020. https://www.cdc.gov/flu/pandemic-resources/1918-pandemic-h1n1.html
Centers for Disease Control and Prevention, National Center for Health Statistics, "Provisional Death Counts for Coronavirus." Accessed 20 March 2020, https://www.cdc.gov/nchs/nvss/vsrr/covid19/index.htm.
Christianity Today "The Power of Hospitality." 1 June 2006. Accessed 26 May 2021, https://www.christianitytoday.com/ct/2006/june/14.23.html.
Coggins, Allen R. "Influenza Epidemic of 1918-1919." *Tennessee Encyclopedia*. March 2018. https://tennesseeencyclopedia.net/
Conn, Charles Paul. *Believe!* Old Tappan, NJ: Revell, 1973.
———. *Julian Carroll of Kentucky*. Old Tappan, NJ: Revell, 1973.
———. *The New Johnny Cash*. Old Tappan, NJ: Revell, 1973.
———. *No Easy Game*. Old Tappan, NJ: Revell, 1973.
———. *Eckerd: Finding the Right Prescription*. Old Tappan, NJ: Revell, 1987.
Conn, Charles W. *Like A Mighty Army: A History of the Church of God*. Definitive edition. Cleveland, TN: Pathway Press, 1994.
———. Address at the Symposium on the Church of God Declaration of Faith Article VII: Holiness, November 1975. Accessed 3 January 2024. https://www.youtube.com/watch?v=X8_Fnb7FiiE
Conn, Paul. "Ellis Hall Fire Anniversary." 9 October 2018. Accessed 30 May 2021. https://www.facebook.com/LeeUniversity/videos/chapel-paul-conn-ellis-hall-fire-anniversary/2143525642567287/.
Cross, Terry. *Answering the Call in the Spirit: Pentecostal Reflections on a Theology of Vocation, Work, and Life*. Cleveland, TN: Lee University Press, 2007.
Crossover. Accessed 1 January 2020. https://leeuniversitycrossover.wordpress.com/.

Cuninggim, Merrimon. *Uneasy Partners: The College and the Church.* Nashville: Abingdon Press, 1994.

DeBenedetti, Charles and Charles Chatfield. *An American Ordeal: The Antiwar Movement of the Vietnam Era.* Syracuse: Syracuse University Press, 1990.

Dirksen, Carolyn, and Rickie D. Moore, eds. *Higher Callings: Vocational Narratives of Lee University Faculty at the Century Mark.* Cleveland, TN: Lee University Press, 2018.

Edwards, Mark U., Jr. "Christian Colleges: A Dying Light or a New Refraction?" *Christian Century* (April 1999): 459-463.

Federal Reserve History, "The Great Recession." Accessed 26 December 2020. https://www.federalreservehistory.org/essays/great-recession-of-200709.

Fry, Joseph F. *The American South and the Vietnam War.* Lexington: University of Kentucky Press, 2015.

Gallup. "Gay and Lesbian Rights." https://news.gallup.com/poll/1651/gay-lesbian-rights.aspx. Accessed 26 May 2021.

Glanzer, Perry, Joel Carpenter, and Nick Lantinga. "Look for God in the University: Examining Trends in Christian Higher Education" 61 (June 2011): 721-755.

Gleason, Philip. *Contending with Modernity: Catholic Higher Education in the Twentieth Century.* New York: Oxford University Press, 1996.

Gorbacheva, Tatiana. "Nora Chambers—Education Pioneer." *Church of God History and Heritage*, Fall 1997: 3-5.

Hankins, Barry. *American Evangelicals: A Contemporary History of a Mainstream Religious Movement.* New York: Rowman and Littlefield, 2009.

Harding, Susan Friend. *The Book of Jerry Falwell: Fundamentalist Language and Politics.* Princeton: Princeton University Press, 2000.

Heineman, Kenneth J. *God is a Conservative: Religion, Politis, and Morality in America.* New York: New York University Press, 1998.

Hughes, Ray. "The Transition of Church-Related Junior Colleges to Senior Colleges with Implications for Lee College." Ed.D. dissertation. University of Tennessee, 1966.

———. "The Power of His Name." Accessed 3 January 2024. https://youtube/DKlnoj21lqY.

Hurlbut, Jesse Lyman. *Hurlbut's Teacher-training Lessons for the Sunday School.* New York: Eaton and Mains, 1908.

Kean, Melissa. *Desegregating Private Higher Education in the South: Duke, Emory, Rice, Tulane, and Vanderbilt.* Baton Rouge: LSU Press, 2008.

Kennedy, David. *Freedom From Fear: The American People in Depression and War, 1929-1945.* New York: Oxford University Press, 1999.

Kentnor, Hope. "Distance Education and the Evolution of Online Learning in the United States." *Curriculum and Teaching Dialogue*, vol. 17, Nos. 1 & 2, 2015.

Labberton, Mark, ed. *Still Evangelicals: Insiders Reconsider Political, Social, and Theological Meaning.* Downer's Grove, IL: InterVarsity Press, 2018.

Lee College. *Institutional Self-Study Report of Lee College, 1973.* Cleveland, TN: Lee College, 1973.

———. *Lee College Institutional Self-Study Report, 1984.* Cleveland, TN: Lee College, 1984.

Lee University Institutional Research, "Fall Census Enrollment Report," 2010-2020.

Lee University Institutional Research, "Common Data Set," 2019-2021.

Lee University. Press Release, 5 April 2019. Accessed 10 December 2020, https://visitclevelandtn.com/event/lee-day-2019/.

———. "Flame Features: Making the Jump to the NCAA," Part 1 and 2. Accessed 30 June 2021. https://leeuflames.com/news/2020/5/4/general-flame-features-making-the-jump-to-the-ncaa-part-1.aspx and https://leeuflames.com/news/2020/5/8/general-flame-features-making-the-jump-to-the-ncaa-part-2.aspx.

Levy, Daniel. "Behind the Anti-War Protests that Swept America in 1968." *Time*. Accessed 4 May 2020. Time.com/5106608/protest-1968/.

Lloyd, Ralph Waldo. *Maryville College: A History of 150 years, 1819-1969.* Maryville, TN: Maryville College Press, 1969.

Lovett, Bobby. *The Civil Rights Movement in Tennessee: A Narrative History.* Knoxville: The University of Tennessee Press, 2005.

MacGillis, Alec. "How Liberty University Built a Billion-Dollar Empire Online." *New York Times Magazine Online*. Accessed 26 December 2020. https://www.nytimes.com/2018/04/17/magazine/how-liberty-university-built-a-billion-dollar-empire-online.html.

Marsden, George. *The Soul of the American University: From Protestant Establishment to Established Nonbelief.* New York: Oxford University Press, 1994.

Marsden George and Bradley Longfield, eds. *The Secularization of the Academy.* New York: Oxford University Press, 1992.

Martin, Robert F. "Tomlinson, Ambrose Jessup." Last modified January 2020. https://ncpedia.org/

Martin, William. *With God on Our Side: The Rise of the Religious Right in America.* New York: Broadway Books, 1996.

Mauldin, Ray A. *A Study of the History of Lee College, Cleveland, TN.* Ed. D. diss. University of Houston, 1964.

McBrayer Terrell. *Lee College: Pioneer in Pentecostal Education.* Cleveland, TN: Pathway Press, 1968.

MGM Ministries. "A Biography of Ray Hughes." Accessed 24 February 2022. gmministries.org/ray-hughes.

Morgan, Louis F., ed. Encyclopedia of Lee History. leehistory.com.

Morris, Philip, and Mary Morris. *Unchartered Waters: The Life and Ministry of Raymond E. Crowley.* Cleveland, TN: Pathway Press, 2014.

National Center for Education Statistics. *120 Years of American Education: A Statistical Portrait.* Washington: National Center for Educational Statistics, 1993.

National College Athletics Association. "History of Division II." Accessed 26 December 2020. http://www.ncaa.org/about/history-division-ii.

Noll, Mark. *The Scandal of the Evangelical Mind.* Grand Rapids: Eerdmans, 1994.

Padgett, Charles. "'Without Hysteria or Unnecessary Disturbance': Desegregation at Spring Hill College, Mobile, Alabama, 1948-1954." 41 (Summer 2001): 167-188.

Parker, Clifton B. "The Great Recession Spurred Student Interest in Higher Education." Accessed 26 December 2020. https://news.stanford.edu/2015/03/06/higher-ed-hoxby-030615/.

Pew Research Center. "Views about Homosexuality." Accessed 2 July 2021. https://www.pewforum.org/religious-landscape-study/views-about-homosexuality/.

———. "Attitudes on Same Sex Marriage." Accessed 2 July 2021. https://www.pewforum.org/fact-sheet/changing-attitudes-on-gay-marriage/.

———. "In U.S., Decline of Christianity Continues at a Rapid Pace." Accessed 2 July 2021. https://www.pewforum.org/2019/10/17/in-u-s-decline-of-christianity-continues-at-rapid-pace/.

Phillips, Wade H. *Quest to Restore God's House.* Volume 1 of *A Theological History of the Church of God.* Cleveland, TN: CPT Press, 2014.

Public Broadcasting System, "The American Experience." Accessed 4 May 2020. pbs.org/wgbh/americanexperience/features/two-days-in-october-student-antiwar-protests-and-backlash.

Purcell, Jr., Edward A. *The Crisis of Democratic Theory: Scientific Naturalism and the Problem of Value.* Lexington: University Press of Kentucky, 1973.

Pyle, Hugh F. *Skimpy Skirts and Hippie Hair.* Murfreesboro, TN: Sword of the Lord Publishing, 1972.

Ray, Mauldin A. *A Study of the History of Lee College, Cleveland, TN.* EdD Diss., University of Houston, 1964.

Reuben, Julie A. *The Making of the Modern University: Intellectual*

Transformation and the Marginalization of Morality. Chicago: Chicago University Press, 1996.

Ringenberg, William C. *The Christian College: A History of Protestant Higher Education in America*, 2nd ed. Grand Rapids: Baker Academic, 2006.

Robins, Roger. *A. J. Tomlinson: Plainfolk Modernist.* New York: Oxford University Press, 2004.

Roebuck, David. "Restorationism and a Vision for World Harvest: A Brief History of the Church of God." https://www.dixonprc.org/histories-of-the-church-of-god.html#/. Accessed 30 November 2024.

———. "Unraveling the Cords that Divide: Cultural Challenges and Race Relations in the Church of God." Paper presented at the *40th Meeting of the Society for Pentecostal Studies*, 2011.

———. "Declaration Prevents Church Division." *Church of God History and Heritage* (Summer 1998): 1-2, 5-6.

Salyer, Jeff, Rob Reid, and Chad Guyton, dir. *Hundred Year Journey.* Cleveland, TN: Lee University Films, 2018. DVD.

Sam Houston State University. "Chancellor McCall names Dr. Alisa White Sole Finalist for Sam Houston State University Presidency." Today@Sam, 18 June 2020. Accessed 6 February 2021. https://www.shsu.edu/today@sam/T@S/article/2020/sole-finalist-president.

Samaritan's Purse, "Operation Christmas Child-Lee University Shoe Box Packing Party," 20 August 2010. Accessed 3 January 2024. https://youtu.be/DrKT_uTlO_s.

Sánchez-Walsh, Arlene M. *Pentecostals in America.* New York: Columbia University Press, 2018.

Scarborough, Peggy. *Power to Witness: The Story of Charles Beach.* Cleveland, TN: Pathway Press, 2002.

Schrieber, E. M. "Opposition to the Vietnam War among American University Students and Faculty." *The British Journal of Sociology* 24 (September 1973): 288-302.

Sheridan, Jay, ed. *Lift High the Flame: Visions of Lee University.* Franklin, Tn: Grandin Hood, 2018.

Simmons, E. L. *History of the Church of God.* Cleveland, TN: Church of God Publishing House, 1938.

Simon, Kenneth A. and W. Vance Grant. *Digest of Educations Statistics.* Washington, D.C.: U.S. Government Printing Office, 1965.

Sloan, Douglas. *Faith and Knowledge: Mainline Protestantism and American Higher Education.* Louisville: Westminster John Knox Press, 1996.

Stephens, Randall J. *The Fire Spreads: Holiness and Pentecostalism in the American South.* Cambridge: Harvard University Press, 2010.

Stephens, Raphael. "A History of Governance at Lee College." EdD diss. College of William and Mary, 1981.
Tapley, Earl M. *The Way it Was: A Family History and Personal Memoirs*. St. Petersburg, FL: Southern Heritage Press, 2000.
Trammel, Joel. "Publishing the Gospel," *Church of God History and Heritage* Winter 1998, 1-5.
United States Bureau of the Census, Current Population Reports, Series P60-184. *Money Income of Households, Families, and Persons in the United States, 1992*. Washington, D.C.: U.S. Government Printing Office, 1993.
United States Department of Education, Office of Civil Rights. "Education and Title IX." Accessed 5 October 2016. http://www2.ed.gov/about/offices/list/ocr/docs/hq43e4.
United States Department of Veteran Affairs. "Education and Training: History and Timeline." Accessed 24 March 2020. https://benefits.va.gov/gibill/history.asp.
US Inflation Calculator. Accessed 6 May 2020. https://www.usinflationcalculator.com.
VanHook, Jayson. Lee University Institutional Research, "Census Trending Report," December 2020.
Vaughan, Stephen Benson. "The Influence of Music on the Development of the Church of God (Cleveland, Tennessee).: Phd Diss. University of Birmingham, 2015.
Vest, Lamar. *Reflections of the Journey*. Cleveland, TN: PTS Press, 2018.
Walker, Mark. "Lee University Chapel," 9 March 2021. Accessed 30 June 2021. https://livestream.com/leeu/events/9566550/videos/218627074.
Walsh, Arlene M. *Pentecostals in America*. New York: Columbia University Press, 2018.
Wilcox, Clyde. *God's Warriors: The Christian Right in Twentieth Century America*. Baltimore: Johns Hopkins University Press, 1922.
———. *Onward Christian Soldiers? The Religious Right in American Politics*. Boulder, CO: Westview Press, 1996.
Williams, Daniel K. *God's Own Party: The Making of the Christian Right*. New York: Oxford University Press, 2010.

Index

Accrediting Association of Bible Colleges, 70, 73, 87, 102–3
Admissions standards, 31, 126, 148, 158, 171–72
Alford, Delton, 91–92, 105–6, 183
Alumnus, 147
American College Test (ACT) scores, 126, 158, 172, 199
Appalachian Colleges Association, 131
Arrington, Frances Treadway, 131
Ashcraft, Susan, 183
Aultman, Don, 98, 105–6
Azusa Street (Apostolic Faith Mission), 12, 21

Bacon, Deborah, 113–14
Baptism of the Holy Spirit, 11–13, 29, 36, 59, 82, 87, 104, 213
Barnes, D. C., 1–2
Barnett, Alfred, 114
Barnett, Bob, 185
Barr, Edmond, 22
Beach, Charles, 65
Beach, Lois, 147
Bebbington, David, 10
Beckham, Clark, 179
Bible Training School: accelerated growth, 47–50; accreditation, 46–47, 51; administration, 40, 46, 50; alma mater, 43; and African Americans, 22–23; athletics, 44; board of directors, 34, 40, 51; Christian worker's course/department, 47, 55–56, 75; correspondence course, 26, 34, 74, 131, 193; curriculum, 17–19, 30–32, 46–47; enrollment, 24, 37, 47–49; faculty, 19–20, 24, 27, 30–31, 33–34, 37, 40, 43, 47, 49, 51, 209; finances, 24–26, 37, 39, 51; first class of students, 20–21; first graduates, 24; founding, 16–19; high school/academy, 16, 34, 36–37, 46–47, 52; liberal arts junior college, 46–47, 50, 52, 55–56; move to Sevierville, 37–38; music, 17–18, 31–32, 34–36, 45–47, 50; 1920s enrollment crisis, 24, 26–27; presidency created, 40; purchase of Bob Jones College Campus, 52; relocation to Cleveland, 55–57; student life, 24–25, 30–33, 43–45, 49–50, 65–66; World War II, 47–49
Bilbo, Jim, 202
Black, Josh, 193
Blackwell, Mildred, 34, 36
Brinkley, Alan, 118
Brinsfield, J. Stewart, 63–64, 67–69, 76, 189, 218
Burtchaell, James, 6, 206–10

Campbell, Sarah, 195
Card, Paul, 188
Carpenter, Joel, 63
Carpenter, Larry, 97, 164, 196
Carroll, Julian, 144
Carroll, R. Leonard, 66, 69–70, 78, 84, 218

263

Cashwell, G. B., 13
Centenary College and Music School, 89
Chambers, Nora, 19–20, 22, 24, 26, 34, 57, 60, 207
Chesser, H. L., 61, 64, 72
Christian Right, 161
Christian Union, 9, 14
Christmann, Ben, 183
Church of God: abortion, 161; African Americans, 22–23, 78, 107–13, 116; anti-creedal stance, 1, 5, 11, 58–59, 188; Appalachia(n), 9, 14–15, 42, 58, 131; board of education, 33, 129; Church of God of Colored Work, 78; Declaration of Faith, 59–60, 120, 213–14; early governance, 15–16; executive committee, 33–34, 84, 96, 171, 209, 217–18; financial support, 26–27, 30, 37–39, 49–50, 57, 76–77, 82, 102, 126–29, 131, 138, 142, 166, 208–9; founding, 9–10, 62–63; growth during the Great Depression, 40–42; other colleges, 38, 129; progressives, 2–3, 5, 61, 60–62, 64, 67–70, 72, 84–86, 101, 117, 118, 120–22, 126, 130, 135, 138–39, 143–46, 149–50, 151, 154, 160–61, 169, 171, 173, 191; practical commitments, 12, 160–61; Publishing House, 16, 18, 19, 25, 30, 34, 37, 76, 77, 128, 159; rising socioeconomic status, 41–42, 60; Supreme Council, 1, 68, 107–8, 110–11, 129, 138, 140, 144–46, 149, 155–56; traditionalists, 2–5, 57, 60–61, 64, 68–70, 72, 85–86, 101, 118–26, 130, 135, 139–40, 144–45, 149, 152, 155, 159–60, 171, 201, 204, 253
Church of God Hour, 45
Church of God of Prophecy, 25
Church of God School of Theology (Seminary), 81, 84, 87, 130, 142
Civil Rights Act of 1964, 110
Cleveland, Tennessee, 9, 14, 16, 17, 30, 52, 55–57, 113, 142, 147, 154, 167, 181, 187–89, 200
Conine, Chris, 194
Conn, Charles, 218; academic structures, 131–32; appointed president, 117, 218; background, 117–18; Bible Training School student, 43; church historian, 63, 70, 87, 90, 130; church service, 84; cultural challenges, 118–20; cutbacks, 138; endowment, 128, 136–38; enrollment, 126, 136; *Evangel* editor, 63; finances, 126–29; general overseer, 84, 102, 125, 130; grants, 126–28, 136–38; holiness standards, 86, 119–26, 132–33; *Lighted Pathway* editor, 64; moderate leader, 84, 117–18, 119–20, 122, 125–26, 132–33; 1970s challenges, 135–36, 149–50; resignation, 139
Conn, Darlia McLuhan, 144, 189, 199
Conn, Paul: background, 143–44; capital campaigns, 157, 163–64, 166–67, 172, 190; chancellor, 201, 204; Church of God, 151–52, 155–56, 159, 171; community relations, 147, 154; COVID-19, 203–4; endowment, 172, 190, 200; enrollment, 148, 157–59, 165, 171–72, 175, 194; goals, 151–55; inaugural address, 154; legacy, 173, 199–201, 208–10; New Right, 162; president, 149, 218; presidential nomination, 145–46; Ray Hughes, 152, 155, 171; resignation,

199; student life, 93, 155, 159, 162;
vice president, 146–47; writing
career, 144, 146–47
Cook, Phil, 194
Council for Christian Colleges and
Universities, 131, 153
COVID-19, 203–4
Cox, Larry, 113–14
Crews, Mickey, 60
Cross, James: 84–85, 87, 98, 118, 218;
accreditation, 101–3; integration,
115
Cross, Terry, 186
Crossover, 187
Crowley, Raymond, 146
Culpepper, Raymond, 193

Deke Day, 186
DeVos, Helen, 164
DeVos, Richard, 144, 146, 164
Dirksen, Carolyn, 170–71, 181,
194, 201
Dirksen, Murl, 170
Dixon, Bernard, 164
Dobson, James, 161
Dorm Wars, 177

Echols, Evaline, 83, 121–22
Eckerd, Jack, 144
Edmond, Mollye, 115
Edward, Hazel, 113–15
Ellis, J. B., 18, 23, 26, 57, 217
Ellis Hall Fire, 165–66
Encore/Elder Hostel, 165, 186
Endowment, 128, 136–38, 172
Entrepreneurial spirit, 5, 34, 47, 52,
73, 100, 158, 175, 195
Evangel, 14, 16, 25–26, 30, 37, 61,
63–64, 92–93, 102
Evangelical, 5–6, 8, 10–11, 13, 17, 56,
60, 62–63, 103, 106, 120, 151, 153,

155, 159, 161–62, 171, 191, 199,
204–206, 208–11
Evangelistic Singers, 93, 169, 179

Falwell, Jerry, 161–62, 191
First Baptist Church property, 189
Forward in Faith, 90–91
Fry, Joseph, 97
Fundamentalism, 11, 62–63

Gause, R. Hollis, 102, 130
GI Bill of Rights, 52, 55, 75
Global Perspectives Program, 93, 169,
182, 184–85, 204
Goff, Dale, 170
Green, Henrietta Ayre, 34, 36
Green, Mary Elizabeth (Harrison),
51, 71–72, 76, 170

Hammond, Jerome, 194
Hart, Robert, 146
Hayes, Mike, 177, 194
Higginbotham, Bill, 137–38, 144
Hilbun, Bertha, 19–20
Holiness, 2, 4–5, 9, 11–14, 17, 29,
32–33, 42, 45–46, 57–59, 61–62,
65–67, 69, 84–87, 95, 96, 119–26,
132–33, 138–41, 144–45, 148–50,
159–61, 175, 207, 213
Horton, Wade, 84, 86, 124–25,
129–30, 152
Hudson, Andrea and Kevin, 164
Huges, Dale, 96
Hughes, Ray: 171, 207; accreditation, 89, 100–101; career, 81–82;
church-college relationship,
139–40; community relations,
142; enrollment, 82–83, 85,
87–88; first presidency, 81, 218;
first resignation, 90; first term
accomplishments, 83, 89–90;

Hughes, Ray (*cont.*)
  general overseer, 137; holiness, 85–87, 139–41, 159; innovations, 88; Paul Conn, 152, 155, 171; race and integration, 107–12, 115; SACS review, 141–42; second presidency, 139–43, 149–50, 218; second resignation, 142–43
Hughes, Ray, Jr., 193
Humphries, A. T., 91
Hurlbut's Teacher-training Lessons for the Sunday School, 18, 31, 45

Influenza Epidemic, 23

Jernigan, John C., 41–42, 61, 63, 66–67, 69, 217–18
Johnson, Heidi, 180

Kean, Melissa, 107
Knight, Cecil, 84, 146

Ladies of Lee, 93, 169, 179
Lamb, William, 186
Lee, F. J., 24, 25–26, 217
Lee, Ollie, 170
Lee Centennial, 197
Lee College: academic freedom, 102, 104–5, 132, 142; accreditation, 68, 70–76, 83, 85, 87, 89–90, 99–106, 129, 131, 142, 150, 207; administration and organization, 70, 73–76, 83, 87, 90, 99–102, 105, 129, 132, 138, 141, 146, 169–70; admission of first African American students, 112–13; athletics, 95–97, 123–24, 164; Bible College, 73, 77, 102–3, 105; board of directors, 68–70, 74, 96, 104–5, 107–8, 110, 129–30, 132, 137–39, 142–46, 149, 151, 168; closing of the junior college, 101; creation of a liberal arts college, 100–101; curriculum, 56, 61, 72–74, 104; enrollment, 55, 70, 74–77, 82–83, 85, 87–88, 90, 98, 117, 126, 135–36, 141, 143, 148, 149, 154–58, 167, 165, 219; faculty, 55, 60, 62, 70–71, 73, 87, 90–91, 98, 100–106, 131–32, 138, 140–43, 149, 151, 153, 156–58, 168, 209; first bachelor's degree, 72–73; first liberal arts college, 73; first varsity sport, 95; fraternities and sororities, first, 93–94; high school and academy, 71, 73–76, 82–83; mascot, 95, 139; music, 74, 90–94, 101, 165; naming, 55, 57; 1950s enrollment crisis, 55, 70, 74–77, 82–83; nursing, 147–48; racial segregation, 77–78, 99; religious education department/division, 56, 73–76, 78, 82–83, 95, 100; SACS accreditation, 106; segregation, 77–78, 99, 106–11; student life, 64–66, 70, 89, 92–97, 113–16, 122–26, 140–41, 155, 159, 162–63; third financial crisis, 135–36
Lee Community Covenant, 191, 215–16
Lee Day, 89, 156, 176–78, 203
Lee Experience, 175–81
Lee Singers, 88, 91–93, 144, 169, 179
Lee University: accreditation, 169, 187, 195; administration, 169–70, 177, 193–95, 201–2; athletics, 195–96; board of directors, 168, 193, 201–2, 208–9; Celebration events, 163, 166, 168–69, 171, 189–90, 200; chapel, 180–81,

188, 190, 192, 204, 215; Church of God, 171, 191, 194, 207–8; COVID-19, 203–4; curriculum, 169, 184–88, 195; Developmental Inclusion Classroom (LUDIC), 186; distance learning, 192–94; enrollment, 171–72, 175, 194, 219–20; faculty, 182–85, 193–94, 198, 207, 209–11; fraternities and sororities, 177–78; graduate degrees, 168, 181, 183, 194; LGBTQ+, 191–92, 204–5, 214; music, 168–69, 178–80, 186; nursing, 195; online programs, 192–94; student life, 175–81, 191; transition from Lee College, 168
LeFevre, Mylon, 155
Lemons, M. S., 17, 24
Leonard Center, 186, 189
LGBTQ+, 4, 122, 124–25, 161, 180, 191–92, 204–5.
Liberty University, 162
Lighted Pathway, 63
Linley, Mike, 114

Mauldin, Walt, 177, 194
Mayfield Elementary School, 188
McCoy, Otis, 34–35, 90
Miller, Roosevelt, 93
Modernism, 11, 17, 63
Morris, Mary Smith, 93
Murray, Danny, 148, 169
Murray, Debbie, 194, 202

National Association of Evangelicals, 50, 63, 81, 118
National Association of Independent Colleges and Universities, 131
National Association of Intercollegiate Athletics, 195

National Association of Schools of Music, 139
National Christian Colleges Athletic Association, 96, 164
National College Athletic Association, 195
National Council for the Accreditation of Teacher Education, 131, 169
New Deal, 29, 41
New Right, 161
Noll, Mark, 153

Olympic Games, 167–68
Operation Christmas Child, 177

Padgett, Charles, 107
Painter, David, 170
Parham, Charles Fox, 12
Payne, T. S., 33, 57, 217
Perry, Sam, 14
Pioneers for Christ, 65
Platt, Rufus, 70, 73, 218
Presidential Concert Series, 186

Ray, Gary, 169, 175
Regent College, 162
Revival, 10–13, 16, 26, 43, 64, 81–82, 180, 209
Richardson, Thomas, 22
Robertson, Pat, 161–62, 191
Robinson, B. C., 35
Roebuck, David, xii, 58, 131
Rowan, Earl, 139

Sanctification (doctrine), 1, 11–12, 58
Seymour, William J., 12
Sharp, Jim, 157
Simmons, E. L., 50, 52, 56, 66, 217
Simmons, Philip B. and Marjorie, 78

Simpson, Brooke, 179
Sinclair, Andy, 185
Smith, Henry, 170
Smith, Jordan, 179
Soulforce, 192
Southern Association of Colleges and Schools (SACS), 47, 70–72,
Southern Association of Colleges and Schools (SACS) (*cont.*) 74, 76, 83, 85, 87, 89–90, 99–106, 128–29, 131–32, 141–42, 146, 169, 187, 207
Southern Christian Athletic Conference, 96
Speaking in tongues, 12–13, 21, 31–32, 59, 64, 104, 213
Springer, Vernon, 78
Spurling, Richard, 9, 14
Stacey, Phil, 179
Stagflation, 135–36
Steele, Randy, 164
Stephens, Raphael, 50
Summer Honors, 175–76
Swiger, Avis, 34, 226

Tapley, Earl M., 51–52, 57, 67, 69–72, 76
Tennessee Temple College, 96–97
Tharp, Zeno C., 39–40, 49, 57, 61, 64, 68–69, 217
Thomas, E. C., 146
Tilley, David, 166, 169
Title IX, 124, 205
Tomlinson, A. J., 9, 13–17, 19–26, 34, 58, 217
Touring Choir, 88, 91
2008 economic recession, 189–90

U.S. News and World Report rankings, 181–82, 200

VanHook, Jayson, 194
Vest, Lamar, 143–49, 218; general overseer, 171
Vietnam War, 97–98
Vindagua, 44–45, 115, 122, 148
Voices of Lee, 169, 179

Walker, J. H., 34, 36–39, 42, 50, 100, 102, 217
Walker, Mark: and Church of God, 205, 211; background, 202; board member, 196; COVID-19, 203–4; enrollment, 204; president, 202–5, 218
Walker, Paul L., 139, 145, 169–71, 202
Walker, R. R., 34, 36–37, 40, 64
Walker, Udella, 203
Washington, Pauline, 115
Wesley, John, 11
White, Alyssa, 202
White, Robert, 145–46
Women, 21–22, 30, 34, 44–45, 48–49, 61, 119–20, 122–24, 148, 161
World War I, 21
World War II, 47–49

www.ingramcontent.com/pod-product-compliance
Lightning Source LLC
Chambersburg PA
CBHW030248010526
44107CB00031B/1363/J